Divided by the Wall

The publisher and the University of California Press Foundation gratefully acknowledge the generous support of the Anne G. Lipow Endowment Fund in Social Justice and Human Rights.

Divided by the Wall

PROGRESSIVE AND CONSERVATIVE
IMMIGRATION POLITICS
AT THE U.S.-MEXICO BORDER

Emine Fidan Elcioglu

UNIVERSITY OF CALIFORNIA PRESS

University of California Press
Oakland, California

© 2020 by Emine Fidan Elcioglu

Library of Congress Cataloging-in-Publication Data

Names: Elcioglu, Emine Fidan, 1984– author.
Title: Divided by the wall : progressive and conservative immigration
    politics at the U.S.-Mexico border / Emine Fidan Elcioglu.
Description: Oakland, California : University of California Press,
    [2019] | Includes bibliographical references and index.
Identifiers: LCCN 2020010040 | ISBN 9780520340350 (cloth) |
    ISBN 9780520340367 (paperback) | ISBN 9780520974500 (epub)
Subjects: LCSH: Borderlands—United States. | Borderlands—Mexico. |
    United States—Emigration and immigration—Government policy. |
    Mexican-American border region—Emigration and immigration. |
    United States—Foreign relations—Mexico. | Mexico—Foreign
    relations—United States.
Classification: LCC JV6483 .E525 2019 | DDC 325.73—dc23
LC record available at https://lccn.loc.gov/2020010040

Manufactured in the United States of America

28 27 26 25 24 23 22 21 20
10 9 8 7 6 5 4 3 2 1

To Alev Rosa

Contents

Acknowledgments

Although it is solo-authored, this book is built on the ideas, wisdom, and support of numerous people and organizations.

My greatest debt is to the people who let me into their busy lives and showed me how they were waging political struggle in Arizona. Thank you for sharing your insights and your observations, your hopes and your fears.

At the University of California, Berkeley, my faculty advisers provided me with encouragement and guidance. My deepest gratitude goes to Michael Burawoy, who championed my work every step of the way, instilling in me the confidence to pursue my vocation. Michael taught me how to use theory to do ethnography and ethnography to build theory. It was in Kim Voss's seminar, as a first-year graduate student, that I fell in love with sociology. Over the years, Kim has gently, but firmly, pushed me to make my arguments rigorous and relevant. I had the good luck to learn political sociology from Cihan Tuğal, who responded to my ideas with enthusiasm. In later years, I greatly benefited from his feedback on the manuscript. Kathy Abrams generously first met with me during her sabbatical, in the midst of her own Arizona-based research. With the sharpness of a logician, Kathy challenged me to think about state strength in intriguing ways, and for this, I thank her. I also benefited from conversations with Irene Bloemraad, Cybelle Fox, Raka Ray, and Cristina Mora.

The best part of this journey has been the lifelong friendships and intellectual camaraderie that emerged from Berkeley Sociology. Above all, I am grateful to my comrade, confidante, and role model, Abigail Andrews. My dear friends Mike Levien, Jenny Carlson, Ryan Calder, and Marcel Paret were a constant source of joy, inspiration, and intellectual engagement. I am also indebted to Chris Chambers-Ju, Elif Kale-Lostuvali, Suchi Pande, Jonathan Smucker, Alice Sverdlik, Becky Tarlau, and Kara Young for their unparalleled friendship. The generous feedback I received from the Burawoy dissertation group helped push my work forward; I give thanks to Laleh Behbehanian, Andy Chang, Julia Chuang, Siri Colom, Herbert Docena, Elise Herrala, Gabe Hetland, Zach Levenson, Marcel Paret, Josh Seim, and Ben Shestakofsky. When I returned from fieldwork, I had the good fortune of receiving support from the Center for Research on Social Change at UC Berkeley. Christine Trost, David Minkus, and Deborah Lustig were excellent mentors. Many thanks also go to my colleagues at CRSC: Roi, Veena, Mimi, Lisa, Alex, and Pam.

My support system in Arizona was invaluable. Noelle and Jeff Sallaz welcomed me to the Southwest, making Tucson feel like a second home. My friends Kaylee Farnolli, Lindsey Gaydos, Noam Dorr, Amber Thomas, and Sophie von Hagen brought much-needed levity into my life, sustaining me through some of the more trying moments of fieldwork. Lindsey, thank you also for laboriously transcribing hours of interviews. My old friend, Joe Rosenberg, visited me in Tucson, and I was happy that he eventually wound up in the Bay Area after I returned from fieldwork. I am also grateful to Oscar Medina, with whom I explored Nogales, Sonora, for the first time and who let me try out my ideas on his junior high social studies class. Many thanks also to Orencio and Paulina Medina for their hospitality in Phoenix.

The University of Toronto was a wonderful setting to write this book. There, I had the good fortune of meeting Neda Maghbouleh, Kim Pernell, and Rania Salem, colleagues who instantly became close friends. For their mentorship and gentle support, I thank Clayton Childress, Hae Yeon Choo, Jennifer Chun, Ping-Chun Hsiung, Anna Korteweg, Patricia Landolt, Ann Mullen, Dan Silver, and Judy Taylor. Warm thanks also to

Ellen Berrey, Irene Boeckman, Soma Chatterjee, Jerry Flores, Angelina Grigoryeva, Sida Liu, Ashley Rubin, and Luisa Farah Schwartzman. In particular, I thank Ellen, Soma, Jerry, Sida, Neda, Kim, Ashley, and Luisa for their valuable feedback on early drafts of chapters. My brilliant student Tamera Campbell also deserves much praise for transcribing and helping code follow-up interviews from 2017. Thank you also to my dear friend of many years, Lucas Wiesendanger, for helping me think through the book's argument and title.

Research is costly, and I was helped along the way by several institutions. At UC Berkeley, I received funding from the Department of Sociology, the Center for Research on Social Change at the Institute for the Study of Societal Issues, the Center for Latino Policy Research, and the Center for Race and Gender. Later, the University of Toronto Research Startup Fund and SSHRCC Institutional Grant were instrumental in helping me complete my fieldwork and write this book. I also thank the University of Toronto Scarborough Vice Principal Academic and Dean office for supporting my enrollment in the National Center for Faculty Development and Diversity's Faculty Success Program. It was through this program that I met my writing accountability group, Mirjam Furth, Alexis Karteron, and Ava Purkiss. With their gentle and unwavering support, Mirjam, Alexis, and Ava helped me get through the daily frustrations of writing, and for this, I am very grateful.

I thank Naomi Schneider and the team at UC Press for helping this manuscript see the light of day. I am also indebted to Sergio Chavez and the three anonymous reviewers whose feedback sharpened the book's argument and organization. Letta Page's meticulous editing improved the manuscript's readability.

Lastly, I would like to thank my family, which has grown in size over the years. Above all, my deep gratitude and immense love go to my parents, Funda and Mehmet Elcioglu, and my sister, Zeynep Elcioglu. My mother and father, each in their own way, made countless sacrifices so that I could always have the best opportunities in life. My sister was a fountain of love and laughter throughout this journey. I owe my parents and my sister everything. On this side of the pond, the Elci family infused my life with affection and encouragement. Thank you to my uncle, Ahmet; my aunt, Marni; my cousin, Süreyya; and especially to my two little cousins, Tristan and

Ethan. Thank you also to Tamara Jackson, Marguerite Richmond, Rob McCord, and Jamie McCord for welcoming me into your family. The moment I met him, Ben McCord became a pillar in my life. He has inspired, nurtured, and loved me in a way that only a lifelong partner can. Ben, thank you for making me feel at home whenever I'm with you. As I was completing this book, Ben and I joyfully welcomed our daughter, Alev Rosa, to our family. It is to her that I dedicate this book, with the hope that she and her cohort will grow up in a more humane world.

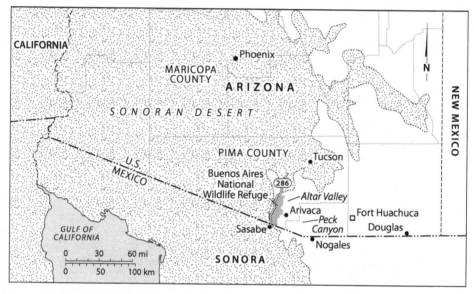

Map 1. Arizona-Sonora borderlands.

Introduction

STATE EFFECTS AND THE POLITICS
OF IMMIGRATION IN ARIZONA

Renee fantasized about crashing her truck right into the U.S.-Mexico border fence. The proud thirty-five-year-old Tejana had first laid eyes on the international boundary in 2000, shortly after she moved to Southern Arizona. Before that, she had completed a college degree in California and, much to her father's disapproval, had organized migrant farmworkers in Florida. Once in Arizona, Renee joined the Advocates, a local pro-immigrant nonprofit group. By the time we met, Renee had been a member of the Advocates for just over a decade; during that time, she had worked long hours as the organization's director. She had also recently earned her master's degree in public administration. As I watched her run meetings and coordinate events, I could not imagine the Advocates surviving without her.

When Renee confessed her recurring fence-crashing fantasy, we had just arrived in Douglas, a city of seventeen thousand residents in southeastern Arizona. Renee parked her truck close to the tall, rusted metal fence that separated Douglas from the sprawling Mexican city of Agua Prieta. A handmade memorial along the barrier signaled that we were in the right spot. We had come here for a silent vigil organized by the family of Carlos, a nineteen-year-old Latino who had been shot three times in the back by a U.S. Border Patrol agent. Carlos, a Douglas resident and

1

American citizen, was killed fleeing into Mexico, reportedly transporting marijuana. He bled to death right there at the border.

Shortly after Carlos's family fashioned their memorial, the Border Patrol delivered a letter demanding it be taken down. Agents claimed their makeshift shrine was obstructing their view across the fencing. The Advocates and other pro-immigrant groups encouraged the family to resist the Border Patrol's demands, and they organized a caravan to bring activists to the Douglas–Agua Prieta border for a silent vigil. Everyone gathered there knew that the agents were scheduled to remove Carlos's memorial the following day; his family and community activists planned to videotape the agents destroying it.

I had an eerie sense that I was being watched. Renee pointed at two white-and-green vans parked about a quarter mile away, waiting for the vigil to begin. Next to one of the vehicles stood three uniformed Border Patrol agents. They gazed in our direction. Renee shook her head grimly and expressed doubt that even if they figured out which agent pulled the trigger, they would ever find him guilty of murder. That the Border Patrol could kill an American without fear of consequence and then stop his family from memorializing the young man showed how strong, punitive, even vindictive the state had become.

Renee's group, the Advocates, counseled Carlos's family to grieve publicly as a way to challenge their formidable foes. They would call a series of press conferences and bring a lawsuit against the agency, yet Renee was convinced none of it would mean the agent responsible for this young man's death would face justice. The whole process, she surmised, could drag out for years. Ultimately, it would offer little comfort to the bereaved family. Nonetheless, Renee believed these actions were crucial. Even if the campaign to publicize the family's grief failed to elicit sufficient public outrage, even if the lawsuit failed to exact retribution, any effort to weaken the state was valuable, she explained.

The border fence, a painful symbol of state power for Renee, looked different to Dale. On a ranch forty miles west of the silent vigil's site, I stood with Dale in front of a vehicle barrier marking the U.S.-Mexico boundary. Dale, a thirty-six-year-old white man, had spent his early childhood in Europe before his father was re-stationed to Arizona. He was an "Army brat" who always wanted to be a cop, but a childhood injury had left him unable to pass the physical exam. Now, Dale worked as a jack of all trades—at least, whenever he could find work.

Manual labor was actually what brought him to the Engineers, a small nonprofit focused on immigration restriction. Phil, their leader, had hired Dale to do some work on the sprawling ranch the group used as its base. The pay was good, and the work was interesting. Dale manned infrared cameras and flew, with other Engineers, in a small airplane to assess the condition of the border fence. Dale was frustrated with how often the group encountered technological bottlenecks and unexpected setbacks, but he stuck around for the camaraderie. Eventually, he became a core member of the six-person group.

When he was a kid, Dale remembered, he thought a "border" meant a tall, sturdy wall, guarded around the clock by armed government agents. Especially when he thought about the U.S.-Mexico border, he had pictured the Berlin Wall. "I was sure that nobody could come across and hurt America." Working with the Engineers on border issues had taught him otherwise.

"I couldn't believe it," he said, shaking his head incredulously. Because the Engineers' ranch abutted the international boundary, the Border Patrol would sometimes call Dale's colleague Malcolm for "intel." "Malcolm's phone would ring. . . . 'Can you look over at the wash [river] and see if anyone is there?'" Climbing up onto the barrier, Dale straddled it and touched one foot down on the Mexican side as if to demonstrate its ineffectiveness for me. The Border Patrol was nowhere to be seen, and, for Dale, the flimsy barrier only proved the state's weakness. The Border Patrol, Dale confided, had needed the Engineers' help on more than one occasion.

A few weeks later, I watched a livestream image of Dale walking across a field. The image was being projected onto a screen set up in the Arizona State Legislature. At the invitation of a state senator, the Engineers were broadcasting a real-time demonstration of their newest surveillance equipment for a State Senate committee. The Engineers were developing a system of ground sensors; they were not yet ready, but the glitches were being worked out, Malcolm explained to the committee. Up on the screen, Dale began walking. He tripped a sensor. The screen lit up with a map showing Dale's location. Another Engineer remarked that if their sensor-based system was installed, it could detect people walking northward long before they even crossed the border. The sensor system would be a vital addition to the Border Patrol's toolkit, the Engineers explained. As it stood, the Border Patrol dispatched agents haphazardly and belatedly. The sensors' early detection promised ample time for agents to be directed to the precise areas where crossers were trying to make illegal entry. The Engineers urged the legislators to focus on creating a comprehensive surveillance system. Dale hoped the Engineers could help the state improve this flawed enforcement strategy.

Dale and Renee had stood a mere forty miles apart. They had gazed at the very same border. But where Renee had felt the state's dominating presence, Dale only observed its impotence and disorganization. When juxtaposed, their experiences indicate how ambiguous the state of the border was. This book explains how activists like Renee and Dale arrived at such wildly different conclusions about the state's coercive power and how they mobilized to change it.

THE PUZZLE

Despite their clearly divergent worldviews, Renee, Dale, and all the other activists I spoke to—whether left-wing, pro-immigrant or right-wing, immigration-restrictionist—shared two characteristics that puzzled me. First, none had any direct connection with the issue around which they mobilized. That is, none of these committed activists struggling for change were *personally* impacted by U.S. immigration and border policies.

Second, perhaps stranger still, none of my respondents really believed that their organizations' work would be successful. Renee, for instance, harbored serious doubts that activists could actually do anything to help Carlos's family or hold someone responsible for his death. Likewise, Dale was hopeful, but in no way certain that the sensor system the Engineers had spent years developing would work, let alone gain a government contract. Many of their previous projects had failed. It was very likely this one would too.[1]

Why, then, were these primarily white American citizens flocking to the Arizona-Sonora borderlands? Why were they getting involved in strenuous, frustrating, and, by their own admission, ineffective kinds of activism? Why did they commit to this mobilization *even though* they thought radical change—building a wall or tearing it down—was wholly unlikely?

To answer these questions, I draw on data collected from participant observation with five grassroots organizations in Arizona. Two of these groups (the Advocates and the Humanitarians) were left-wing and pro-immigrant. The remaining three organizations (the Engineers, the Soldiers, and the Arpaiositos) subscribed to a right-wing and immigration-restrictionist worldview.

My research is bookended by three interconnected events that were the backdrop to the groups' mobilization. When I started this project in early 2011, my respondents were absorbed by the political buildup of Arizona Senate Bill 1070. The previous year, the governor of Arizona, defying the federal government, had signed the bill into law. Its most controversial provision required police to investigate the immigration status of anyone they detained, while also allowing local law enforcement to stop and arrest anyone they thought it "reasonable" to suspect was undocumented.[2] I continued fieldwork until the summer of 2012, when the U.S. Supreme Court affirmed the constitutionality of this provision.

In January 2017, shortly before the inauguration of the forty-fifth president of the United States, I revisited Arizona. I re-interviewed veteran participants and spoke with newcomers to the activist groups. On my revisit, the elected federal government had shifted sharply to the right, thanks in large part to how Republican candidates leveraged the politics that SB1070 had generated years earlier. For my interlocutors, important political events—like Supreme Court deliberations or presidential electioneering—unfolded in faraway places. I observed how they made sense of these events. What remained unchanged throughout the period of my study was activists' intense frustration with the state of the U.S.-Mexico border.

This book is about why the activists in these organizations were so frustrated and how they acted on this frustration.[3] Although it is about the politics of immigration, this book is not actually about im/migrants themselves.[4] In fact, it has little to say about the experiences of racialized non-citizens living in or crossing through Arizona's borderlands. With the exception of two activists who were naturalized American citizens, none of my interlocutors had immigrated to the United States and experienced the deportability that accompanies noncitizen status. The pro-immigrant activists I studied were what sociologists call "conscience constituents," or individuals who participate in a social movement but do not stand to gain personally from the movement's successes.[5] Indeed, as conscience constituents they could "easily eschew their activist identity when it [was] inconvenient or dangerous."[6] Like their restrictionist opponents, most were white American citizens. And, also like their opponents, few were even originally from Arizona.[7]

This book does not document the experiences of immigrants, but rather the ways citizens *talk* about immigrants. To make this explicit, I often refer to the imagined, composite figure of the "third-world migrant." In this, I am inspired by a critique about how feminists in the West imagined the experiences of women elsewhere, and how the heterogeneities across such an expansive group of human beings were discursively collapsed into the singular "third-world woman."[8] In addition to its homogenizing tendency, this representation was problematic, critics argued, because it essentialized the "third-world woman" as a victim of forces outside of her control. In contrast to this "object status," Western feminists saw themselves as subjects with agency and the capacity (and moral obligation) to save the third-world woman from her misery.[9]

Similarly, what this book recounts is not the complex ways in which migrants fared. Rather, it is about how an *imagined* third-world migrant fared—in the minds of my interlocutors. As a container, this figure held different meanings for the two sides. On the left, the third-world migrant was reminiscent of the third-world woman: a racialized, powerless, often feminized victim. Americans had the agency and moral duty to provide "her" with relief. On the right, the third-world migrant was a racialized, highly agentic, often (over-)masculinized subject, who wreaked havoc. "His" victims were ordinary Americans and even frontline state actors. However, when committed activists collectively mobilized, they could provide fellow Americans with a modicum of protection from this dangerous Other.

Simplistic and problematic, these discursive, racializing representations are nonetheless powerful. They merit our attention. As this book illustrates, these representations reveal how left-wing and right-wing activists make sense of themselves and their actions. Importantly, understanding the work that the construct of the "third-world migrant" does for activists also exposes the contrasting ways that the left and the right perceive state power in Arizona's borderlands.

STUDYING THE LEFT AND THE RIGHT TOGETHER

Even if the activists on both sides were American citizens and even if most identified as white, it may still seem odd to compare a politically conservative group of restrictionists with a progressive organization that pushes for a pro-immigrant agenda. Indeed, amid rising hostility toward immigrants, is it even fair to put these two movements on the same plane, let alone compare them to each other?

Comparison does not mean drawing a moral equivalence across the two sides. Indeed, as a noncitizen and a woman of color, my own political sympathies lie with pro-immigrant mobilizations.[10] Assuming that they would be more receptive to my presence, I even considered *just* studying pro-immigrant activists. However, as a mentor quickly pointed out, examining one side of a political conflict was like watching only one team play in a soccer game: I would end up with a very partial picture of what was happening on the field.

Sociologist Pierre Bourdieu relied on a similar analogy in discussing politics. He made the point that politics, like many other domains of life, constitute a *field* of relations, wherein participants engage in high-stakes competition.[11] Any position in any field assumes meaning only *in relation to* other positions. For this reason, without understanding the underlying conflict or opposition, the significance of a position is hard to determine.[12] In fact, Bourdieu argued, beliefs and practices once associated with one political orientation, can, over time, be associated with its opposite.[13] By this logic, to understand the content of a pro-immigrant position at a given historical moment, one must also examine the content of restrictionism. The unique nature of a movement is most evident in relation to its opposition.[14] Understanding the contours of pro-immigrant politics requires an analysis of the countermovement against which it wages a struggle.

I was also frustrated with the stalemate that discussions of immigration reform had reached. When political discourse has calcified into familiar rhetoric and each side preaches to the choir but not beyond it, sociologists have shown how comparison of oppositional movements can offer fresh insights. This kind of analysis can get at the unspoken, but core issue in a debate.[15] It can expose unexpected similarities and overlooked differences.[16] It can explain a group's mobilization strategy.[17] And it can illuminate the nature of the broader context from which these political struggles spring.[18] Inspired by such possibilities, I set out to replicate this research design.

Observing Renee and Dale's respective organizations drew my attention to the fact that these were not only two separate political groups, but also two distinct social groups. Although most of the respondents in this study were white (77%), and all were American citizens, women dominated the pro-immigrant organizations, while men dominated the restrictionist groups that I studied. Perhaps more striking than the gendered composition of the two sides, was that it was also accompanied by differences in social class—something that I would have missed without a comparative approach.

The pro-immigrant activists I met tended to be highly educated, well-traveled, and on a trajectory of upward mobility. Meanwhile, restrictionists were largely blue-collar white men with far less education, far less income, and far less day-to-day certainty than the leftists. Almost all had experienced downward mobility.

Among participants on the left, the decision to volunteer one's time in causes like immigrant rights advocacy carried a personal cost. Civic engagement meant forfeiting professional opportunities and giving up lucrative career prospects. That activism was often a personal sacrifice and was reflected in the disapproving reactions of activists' loved ones—such as Renee's parents. By contrast, on the right, activism offered restrictionists camaraderie and respite from social alienation. Sometimes, activism even offered right-wing participants a modicum of economic certainty, as it did for Dale. As we will see, these distinct social positions structured activists' politics and participation.

BRINGING POLITICS BACK IN

Divided by the Wall thus advances research on U.S. immigration politics, which has largely focused on one, rather than both sides of the struggle simultaneously.[19] Past scholarship is overwhelmingly about left-wing, pro-immigrant mobilization.[20] It either overlooks right-wing, restrictionist activism altogether or paints this activism as a direct reflection of anti-immigrant government policies.[21] Moreover, this body of research under-examines the class backgrounds, racial identities, and motivations of those who mobilize.

Studies about pro-immigrant politics in the United States tend to focus on enumerating the factors that facilitate mobilization.[22] For instance, some scholars have focused on how religion, conventionally the hand-maiden of *right-wing* politics in the United States, has become a resource for leftist groups that wish to change immigration policy.[23] Albeit meticulous in its level of empirical detail, such scholarship leaves out a discussion of "variation in the political orientation of movements: their ideologies, aim, [and] motivations."[24] In other words, researchers' focus on movements' *means* overshadows consideration of movements' political *ends*.

Research about right-wing restrictionist activism also tends to ignore the actual ideas and goals of these mobilizations. Studies about restrictionist activists are fewer in number. They are also less empirical in nature, often relying on media reports.[25] To the extent that they discuss ideology, researchers tend to portray restrictionist groups as taken in by the symbolic power of anti-immigrant laws, uncritically accepting of the state's ideas.[26] This approach *presumes* what grassroots restrictionism is like, employing labels like "vigilantism," which misleadingly suggest that these are fringe groups with no relationship to the state.[27] How activists on the ground actually interpret state practices, let alone how they understand the world, escapes empirical study. Even the lone ethnographic account of restrictionism at the U.S.-Mexico border refuses to engage with activists' ideologies and political goals.[28]

The discounting of a movement's political ends is not unique to studies about immigration struggles, but part of a paradigmatic shift across sociology. Political sociology traditionally asked questions about the *content* of struggles, including why participants adopted certain political orientations and goals. Many such classic works tried to understand these political orientations in relation to social structures.[29] In recent decades, however, a new paradigm emerged in which the dominant approach to studying struggles came to focus more on mobilization strategies than political character.[30]

Today, this proclivity to dismiss the relevance of ideology is motivated by a concern that focusing on the "ends" of a mobilization can undermine the sociological depth of a study,[31] ultimately "reduc[ing] [research subjects] to stereotypes."[32] According to this view, what merits attention, then, are the *means* of mobilization—the "during" of a movement rather than its "before" (i.e., participants' ideologies) and "after" (i.e., outcome)[33] or "political process" rather than "specific policy preferences."[34]

The impulse to ignore activists' ostensibly subjective worldviews and to focus on their practices is understandable. However, without delving into their social backgrounds and ideological motivations, let alone their organizations' political programs, it would be hard to explain why activists participated and *kept* participating, especially when their preferred endeavors were not necessarily the most effective choices available.[35]

In my research, political orientation was very important to sustaining grassroots struggles around immigration. And, I found that political ideology (namely, ideas about state power) and the strategic collective action that this ideology shaped, was profoundly meaningful at a *personal* level. This was because their state-directed ideas and practices gave activists the tools to manage their own complex, intersectional identities.[36]

As mentioned earlier, pro-immigrant activists were socioeconomically better off than their restrictionist opponents. Despite this difference, however, members of both sides shared an important attribute: all grappled with a tension or conflict in their identity. These *conflictual identities* were, in part, what rendered particular forms of state-directed collective mobilization attractive.[37] I detected two kinds of conflictual identities among my respondents: pro-immigrant activists struggled with being *progressive, but privileged.*[38] Their restrictionist counterparts grappled with being *white, but working-class.*[39] Hints of both of these conflictual identities are scattered across studies about whiteness.[40] They can also be found in research on conscience constituents.[41] Each conflictual identity sheds light on why people who otherwise had little to gain personally from changes in immigration policy nonetheless felt compelled to join organizations dedicated to changing immigration policy.

Restrictionists struggled with the disparity between their in-group status as white men and the diminishing sense of control that accompanied their experience of downward mobility. The tension of being white but working class was a key element in the narratives that emerged when I asked about who they were and why they mobilized on the border. This tension reflects the idea that "real" white people (particularly men), by definition, cannot be economically precarious.[42] Joining a restrictionist organization and mobilizing to strengthen the state in the borderlands was a way to resolve, or at least manage, this mismatch. It restored restrictionists' sense of mastery and control in the world. Empowering the state was also about empowering the white-but-working-class self.[43]

Meanwhile, the main preoccupation among pro-immigrant activists was the tension between their progressive worldview and their privileged backgrounds. Leftist activists grappled with the incongruence between their desire for more equality and the inequality from which they had personally benefited. In most cases, a respondent's sudden realization of their own privilege in relation to a global "other" initially prompted their awareness of this tension. As one scholar has observed, "Acknowledging one's racialized privilege is difficult and fraught with contradiction" and can easily lead to "ambivalence, doubt, and ethical struggle."[44] There can also be "confusion, [. . .] anger and backlash."[45] Together, these feelings reflect another feature of hegemonic whiteness: that white middle-class people (especially women) have an obligation to "do what's right."[46]

Among my left-wing respondents, recognition of their privilege spawned the desire to perform what they thought of as moral virtue by volunteering. But it was only by joining a pro-immigrant organization and mobilizing on the border that my leftist interlocutors finally felt at peace with themselves. Their efforts to weaken the state mitigated the dilemma of being progressive but privileged in a way that other forms of civic engagement did not.

Thus, rather than taking activists' motivations and goals as self-evident—something that previous research has tended to do—this book empirically examines participants' life histories and the content of their organizations' political projects. Certainly, the mobilization I observed was "about" immigration and the radically different policies each side wanted to see implemented. However, what initially attracted participants, what sustained their commitment over time, and what made their mobilization profoundly meaningful was the fact that their activism was part of a project of remaking the self.[47] That is, the borderland served as a place for American self-actualization as class differences grew starker. Why this was so requires us to attend to how the people in this study perceived the state.

THE STATE EFFECTS AND THE POLITICS OF IMMIGRATION

This book takes insights from whiteness studies and puts them in conversation with a critical variant of political sociology to understand why and how people mobilize even when they harbor serious doubts about the efficacy of such collective action. I contend that scholars must fight the tendency to take the motivations of participants or the goals of their organizations as self-evident, even when considering contentious struggles that seem to have obvious sides.

To suture together participants' subjectivities and their mobilization practices with their organizations' political orientations, this book draws on the concept of the "state effect," first introduced by Timothy Mitchell. Mitchell, responding to earlier work, claimed that the state was not a bounded, structure-like thing that floated above society.[48] In fact, the apparent boundary between state and society was an illusion, helping legitimate the illegitimate. In the banking sector, for example, one would be hard-pressed to distinguish between public and private, because private banks, central banks, and international institutions like the World Bank together "represent interlocking networks of financial power and regulation."[49] Nonetheless, the economic order is reproduced when banks assume the appearance of being private institutions, separate from the state.

Mitchell thus urged his colleagues to shift their inquiry from "what does the state do?"' to "what practices fostered the *appearance* of 'the state' as a coherent and separate entity?" Social science, he contended, should investigate how the organization of space, time, and bodies created the "state effect" or the "metaphysical" appearance of the state as an autonomous, structure-like thing.[50]

This framework, however, did not account for instances when state institutions *failed* to give the impression that there was a coherent state.

Nor was it clear how the presence or absence of a state effect shaped collective action. Other scholars have begun exploring these questions.[51] In particular, Brissette attends to the ways that "implicit assumptions" about the state can shape political subjectivities.[52]

Relatedly, this book examines how activists' perceptions of state institutions—and particularly, their experiences of the state's coercive capacity—are key to understanding what makes mobilization so compelling to participants and the array of specific tactics movements come to rely on. In doing so, this book makes three interrelated contributions.

Perceptions of State Power Can Vary—Even at the Border

First, this study empirically illustrates that the state does not always appear as a "structure-like" thing and that there can be significant variation across social groups' perceptions of state power. Mitchell predicted that the state effect would always be the strongest at an international border because that was where "the mundane arrangements" of policing "help manufacture an almost transcendental entity, the nation state."[53] Others have also posited that the border is where the state engages in its most visible kind of policing, communicating its resolve and its sovereignty.[54] But the state's intended self-presentation is not the same as its actual effect. Differently positioned groups can and do have disparate understandings of the state's policing capacity, as I witnessed at Arizona's border.

To theorize this variation in perceptions of power, I distinguish between the *strong-state effect* and the *weak-state effect*, and I theorize each as a cohesive *worldview*.[55] As worldviews, these two state effects simplify and render intelligible the complexities of the social world. They give their bearers a way to evaluate what is and is not significant. The strong-state and weak-state effects share an important element, though: both sides saw the state's central function in terms of its capacity to wield coercive power and believed that this coercive capacity shaped immigration trends. They diverged when it came to assessments of how competent the state was in this function.

Thus, with Renee, we see the experience of a strong-state effect. Everyday immigration enforcement practices were a reminder to pro-immigrant activists like her that a coherent, domineering structure had a redoubtable hold over society, and particularly, noncitizens. Within the strong-state effect framework, the U.S. Border Patrol agent figured as a highly competent and dangerous figure. The restrictionist countermovement, on the other hand, experienced the weak-state effect. Restrictionists like Dale came to believe that the state was internally incoherent and incapable of policing its jurisdiction. In this view, the Border Patrol agent was an emasculated state actor, unable to carry out his basic enforcement tasks.

Arizona can therefore be analytically described as an *ambiguous* border, a place where radically different conceptualizations of state power coexisted. These state effects functioned as more than mere impressions of the state. They constituted worldviews, or interpretive schema, helping activists make sense of how power was organized in American society, and guiding their political strategy.

Ideology Shapes Tactics

Second, I found that state effects, as worldviews, shaped *how* activists mobilized. Attending to activists' assessments of state power allows us to develop an analytical typology to understand a political movement's strategic choices. In this manner, we move away from merely listing and describing tactics.

That is, the state-effect lens allows us to see the common thread that links together an extensive repertoire of practices among politically like-minded organizations; it also sheds light on how any given tactic confronts an opposing movement. In this study, I found that pro-immigrant tactics intended to *weaken the state*. Undermining the state, pro-immigrant activists believed, would restore agency to the otherwise oppressed, third-world migrant. Meanwhile, right-wing activists mobilized to *strengthen the state*. For restrictionists, the third-world migrant was dangerously agentic, and the lax border made unauthorized entry attractive.

Thus, the state-effect framework illuminates how behind their very different activities, the Humanitarians and the Advocates, as pro-immigrant organizations, both pursued the same strategy of undermining state power. While the Humanitarians made it a core task to put out gallon-sized jugs of water along migrant trails in the desert, close to the Arizona-

Sonora border, the Advocates rarely ventured into the wilderness. Instead, they organized know-your-rights trainings for noncitizen residents in the city. I realized that in order to understand the relationship between these otherwise dissimilar activities—water drops in the desert, know-your-rights workshops in the city—I had to consider how they reflected a shared analysis of enforcement. Both groups' favored strategy undercut state power, but by different means.

The state-effects framework also sheds light on how each organization's tactics challenged those of its opponents. For instance, the Humanitarians distributed water in the very same regions where a Minutemen-type restrictionist group I refer to as the Soldiers assembled for their "reconnaissance operations." On the same trails where the Humanitarians left water, the Soldiers installed cameras, hoping to capture footage of border crossers. When either the Humanitarians or the Soldiers stumbled upon their opponent's objects—water or cameras—they resentfully cleared them.

What distinguished their strategies was the underlying analysis of the state. For the Humanitarians, water drops were as much about critiquing state power as quenching thirst. By distributing water and framing the practice as a form of humanitarianism, these activists contended that the U.S. Border Patrol had created a humanitarian crisis. The borderlands needed to be relieved of state presence, they argued. Meanwhile, by installing cameras, the Soldiers tried to extend the Border Patrol's reach in the desert. The Soldiers relayed any footage of migrants and other "intel" they gathered to the Border Patrol in hopes of shoring up what they believed was an overwhelmed state institution.

Oppositional state-effects and state-directed strategies also shed light on the tactics of the Advocates and the Arpaiositos. In addition to know-your-rights workshops for noncitizens, the Advocates strove to prevent institutions—like local police departments and hospitals—from working with immigration authorities. The philosophy behind both actions aimed to empower different sectors to resist what the Advocates saw as the colonizing pressures of the immigration state apparatus. Meanwhile, the Arpaiositos publicly supported Joe Arpaio, the controversial Maricopa County sheriff who was vocal about his restrictionism, in an attempt to do the opposite: to defend collaboration between immigration authorities and local institutions as laudable law enforcement.

The state-effect framework, therefore, allows us to do more than document a social movement organization's tactics. It forces us to consider how participants analyze state power and act on that assessment. This approach also calls our attention to how mobilization is embedded in struggle. That is, it illuminates the *political* nature of tactics—the ways each aimed to reconfigure the distribution of power. It shows how any tactic, like water drops in the desert, fit into a field of complementary and rivaling strategies. Table 1 broadly summarizes the characteristics of the five organizations in this study, while figure 1 maps out how variations in state effect shaped their strategies.

Immigration Activism Is a Way to Do Whiteness and Cope with Inequality

Finally, this book shows how contemporary immigration politics is driven, at least in part, by a *gendered politics of whiteness* amid widespread inequality. The people who experienced the conflictual identities that drove them to Arizona's border, who were capable—both materially and psychically—of engaging in state-directed mobilization, and who used this mobilization as a way to manage conflictual identities, were mostly white. *That is, even though activism was ostensibly about resisting extant immigration policy, it was also about figuring out how to manage the anxieties of being an upwardly mobile or downwardly-mobile white person in contemporary America.* Immigration politics was not *just* about immigration. For both those on the left and the right, immigration activism was also a terrain on which to placate racial and class anxieties, to "do (gendered) whiteness."

Scholars Candace West and Sarah Fenstermaker (1995) argue that "race is not simply an individual characteristic or trait but something that is accomplished in interaction with others."[56] Society assesses and holds an individual "accountable" for whether or not they act like a member of the racial category to which they have been assigned.[57] Failing to "act like" a white man or a white woman, for instance, causes others to "become disconcerted."[58] "Accomplishing" one's racial identity, however, does not mean that one fully or even partly achieves the ascribed norms of the race category to which one is assigned. Rather, it means routinely, often

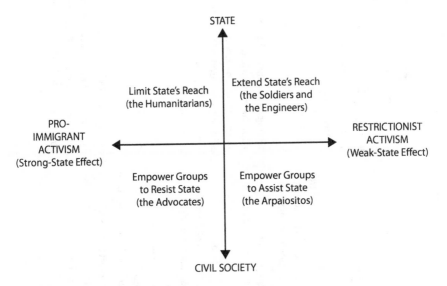

STATE

Limit State's Reach
(the Humanitarians)

Extend State's Reach
(the Soldiers and
the Engineers)

PRO-
IMMIGRANT
ACTIVISM
(Strong-State Effect)

RESTRICTIONIST
ACTIVISM
(Weak-State Effect)

Empower Groups
to Resist State
(the Advocates)

Empower Groups
to Assist State
(the Arpaiositos)

CIVIL SOCIETY

Figure 1. State effects and opposing movement strategies.

unthinkingly, managing one's behavior, in a given situation, to suit what is considered appropriate for one's racial category, because it is how one can be a competent member of society.

That the activism I observed was gendered—and indeed, also a way to "do gender"—is also noteworthy.[59] Scholars have discussed how political projects that are not directly related to gender, nonetheless, give participants opportunities to make claims on being "good (white) men" or "good (white) women." For instance, politically conservative mobilization, such as gun rights activism, can be an attractive domain for performing white masculinity, especially amid foreclosed alternative domains (such as being the family breadwinner).[60] Similarly, helping the unfortunate Other has been a particularly attractive calling to Western white women in the postcolonial era. Development work, for instance, allows white women to "perform goodness."[61]

In this study, women outnumbered men among pro-immigrant activists, while the reverse was true among restrictionists. This is not surprising. The fraught subjectivities I observed are just as much *gendered* dilemmas as they are racial ones. These dilemmas reflect hegemonic conceptions of white masculinity and white femininity. That is, what made

Table 1 Organizations at a Glance

Types	Orientation	Year(s) Active[a]	Size[b]	Main Activities	What Winning Means[c]
Humanitarians	Pro-immigrant	Mid-2000s–2017	40–50	Distributing water and other humanitarian aid in the desert to migrants Writing critical reports about Border Patrol Searching for migrants lost in the desert Organizing anti-deportation campaigns	Eliminating all migrant injury and death in the Arizona borderlands
Advocates	Pro-immigrant	Early 1990s–2017	15	Conducting know-your-rights and *prepárate* (prepare yourself) trainings with noncitizens Organizing citizenship fairs Coordinating searches for lost migrants Helping medical examiner identify migrant remains Pressuring police to cut ties with immigration control Organizing pro-immigrant religious rituals	Ensuring all local noncitizen denizens know their rights and are plugged into protection networks Ending all local-level collaboration between police and immigration authorities
Soldiers	Restrictionist	2008–2017[d]	20 core & 20–30 occasional participants	Conducting armed desert patrols in search of migrants Installing cameras in the desert	Helping Border Patrol "secure" the border so that all undocumented migration and drug trafficking in Arizona's borderlands is deterred

Organization	Orientation	Years active	Members	Activities	Goals
Engineers	Restrictionist	2000–2017	6	Developing surveillance technologies Attending border security conferences Cultivating ties with politicians and DHS personnel Sharing "intel" with Border Patrol Uploading videos of migrants to social media	Securing a DHS contract to help government prevent all attempts at unlawful entry into the United States
Arpaiositos	Restrictionist	2008–2017	15–20	Participating in Maricopa County Sheriff's Office volunteer posse Supporting Sheriff Arpaio at public events Disrupting recall campaign against Arpaio	Keeping Arpaio in office Expanding local police collaboration with immigration authorities so that undocumented people are deterred from residing in Maricopa County

a. At the time of this writing (2019), some of these organizations are still active. However, I have only indicated their tenure until the end of my fieldwork, April 2017.

b. The number of members listed for the Humanitarians, Advocates, and Soldiers are approximations; membership fluctuated over the course of study.

c. See note 1 about the difficulty of defining success for these organizations.

d. The Soldiers started out as a chapter of the Minutemen, which was founded three years earlier, in 2005. In 2008, they officially became their own organization.

"white but working class" a troubled identity was the idea that in order to be a good (read: competent) white man, one could not be or feel precarious. Similarly, to be "progressive but privileged" was to be plagued by the sense that that privilege came with a moral obligation and that a truly good (competent) white woman carried the burden of helping the less fortunate Other.

Activists were certainly motivated by their desire to see a change in the world. But what initially attracted people's involvement and sustained their mobilization over time was the fact that participation fulfilled their desire to see a change *in themselves*.[62] Immigration activism provided opportunities for (white) Americans to wrestle with their own structural location in society and to find their footing amid the insecurity of an increasingly stratified world.

This is not to say that activism was merely a meditative, self-oriented endeavor. It was certainly a purposeful, state-directed activity, a *political struggle* aimed at changing power dynamics in the borderlands. But the meaningfulness of this political struggle was tied up with participants' own identities. Empowering an emasculated state bolstered restrictionists' claims on white masculinity. Weakening the state to help the third-world migrant, meanwhile, offered pro-immigrant activists an opportunity to "do" white middle-class femininity. Thus, I show how immigration politics has become as an arena in which white people can carry out projects of self-affirmation as they cope with the effects of inequality.

METHODS AND DATA

This study draws on almost twenty months of participant observation, eighty-six formal interviews, and extensive content analysis of organizational ephemera. I was initially in the field from January 2011 to June 2012, studying two pro-immigrant and three restrictionist activist groups. Five years later, I revisited my fieldsites from January to April 2017. Participant observation is particularly well suited for studying social movements, allowing researchers to get at the "proximate, implicit meanings" that activism holds for activists.[63] Moreover, it offered a "close-up and real-time observation of actors involved in politics."[64] Thus, I found that ethnography illuminated how activists made sense of and acted on the "official rhetoric" around immigration policy.[65]

To triangulate this ethnographic data, I conducted semi-structured interviews with forty pro-immigrant activists, thirty-four restrictionist activists, and twelve other interested parties. Pro-immigrant interviewees ranged from age eighteen to seventy-eight, 58 percent were women, and 71 percent identified as white. Restrictionist interviewees ranged from age thirty to seventy-three, 89 percent were men, and 85 percent identified as white. I also had hundreds of informal conversations during participant observation. I supplemented this data with content analysis of groups' ephemera: websites, blogs, reports, short films, newsletters, and the like. A detailed discussion of methodology and the challenges I faced can be found in appendix 1. Appendix 2 summarizes basic demographic information about interviewees.

The organizations I eventually decided to study had relationships of conflict and cooperation. Together, they constituted an immediately evident field of relations. My ethnographic foray into Arizonan immigration politics began in Mexico, where I met Lori in a Spanish-language immersion course. Lori was a member of an organization that I refer to as the Humanitarians. This group first gained notoriety in the mid-2000s for placing jugs of water along migrant paths in Arizona's Sonoran Desert. As we became friendly, Lori invited me to come out to Arizona and meet other Humanitarians. At the time, the encounter seemed serendipitous. Much later, I realized that going abroad to learn a language, particularly Spanish, was actually common among this group of pro-immigrant activists.

When I took Lori up on her invitation to visit Arizona, several Humanitarians told me that I could not understand pro-immigrant activism without also talking to the Advocates. This was a fifteen-person operation that strove to equip noncitizen residents with tools to resist the state in daily life. For years, the Advocates also tried to undermine relationships of cooperation between local law enforcement and immigration authorities. While their memberships did not overlap, many Humanitarians believed that their work in the desert complemented what the Advocates were doing in the urban context. Indeed, this synergy spawned several inter-organizational collaborations between 2013 and 2017.

The three restrictionist organizations that I studied were also well aware of each other, as well as their pro-immigrant counterparts. Dale, as we have seen, was one of six core members of the Engineers. Funded by 150 donor-members nationwide, the Engineers used a ranch in Southern Arizona as a laboratory for researching and developing border surveillance methods that they hoped to contract out to the Department of Homeland Security (DHS). As the Engineers publicized disparaging stories about the Advocates' founders, they also tried repeatedly to collaborate with the Soldiers.

Like the Engineers, the Soldiers worked out of a ranch near the U.S.-Mexico border. However, in their outward appearance and actions, the Soldiers more closely resembled the Minutemen. The Soldiers originally started out patrolling a fifty-five-thousand-acre ranch as part of a self-directed reconnaissance program to be of assistance to the Border Patrol. By 2017, their patrol regions had begun to include areas where the Humanitarians were making water drops. The groups interacted in the field and on several occasions, the two groups had run into each other. Meanwhile, in Phoenix, the Arpaiositos opposed the Advocates' activism by publicly supporting a restrictionist local official, Sheriff Joe Arpaio, and the Maricopa County Sheriff's Office (MCSO). By working to tighten the relationship between the MCSO and immigration authorities, this twenty-person group hoped to strengthen the state.

THE STRUCTURE OF THE ARGUMENT

We begin by examining the setting of this study: How did Arizona become such an important site of immigration politics? Chapter 1 discusses how a 1990s shift in policy—from regulating immigration to criminalizing it—transformed Arizona into an *ambiguous* border, or a place where opposite experiences of state power could coexist. In particular, the chapter homes in on the paradoxical consequences of two federal government initiatives: a program called prevention through deterrence, aimed at deterring unauthorized border crossings, and 287(g), an effort to partner immigration enforcement agencies with police departments throughout the country.

We then turn to unpacking the puzzle of why activists mobilized at the ambiguous border in spite of a belief—shared by both left-wing and right-wing respondents—that their organizations would *not* actually bring about the social change they envisioned. Chapters 2 and 3 examine patterns in activists' lives and demonstrate that, contrary to what we might expect, their *conflictual identities* compelled respondents to seek out the ambiguous borderlands as a site of personal reconciliation.

The significance of the two opposing state-effect frameworks, as well as the conflictual identities they helped pacify, were on display as activists grappled with the topics for which their respective movements were most criticized. Chapter 4 shows how the anxious politics of privilege made pro-immigrant activists reticent to comment publicly on the growing connections they observed between undocumented migration and drug smuggling. In particular, I show how the collective narrative that activists developed about drug smuggling derived from their strong-state-effect framework.

Chapter 5 illustrates how restrictionists relied on the idea that they were strengthening the state to deny that racism motivated their mobilization. Borrowing from conventional understandings about the extremism of racist ideology, restrictionist activists distinguished themselves from "real racists," who, they claimed, were fringe actors operating on society's margins. By contrast, restrictionists pointed to their own groups' efforts to work with frontline state actors, as if to underscore that theirs was a *legitimate* form of mobilization. The weak-state paradigm thus served as a powerful boundary-making tool.

Chapters 6 and 7 further explore how the organizations' tactical repertoires gain analytical meaning only when considered in relation to people's perceptions of the state. The hyper-focus on religion in studies about pro-immigrant activism and scholars' tendencies to dismiss restrictionist activism as "hysteria" have been misleading. This book presents a corrective framework and shows the importance of examining immigration-related activism not merely as collective mobilizations, but as a *field of struggle*.

I conclude by placing this study's key contributions into conversation with today's vitriolic debates over "The Wall." I argue that the public discourse is part and parcel of the same puzzle that opened this book: why do people with no personal stake in border and immigration policy feel so strongly about the prospect of a wall? I argue that this debate may not entirely be about borders or immigration at all. Rather, as this book illustrates, inequality and insecurity has intensified the significance of immigration politics for many Americans across the socioeconomic spectrum.

PART I Using Immigration Politics
to Remake Oneself

The people in this study desperately wanted to change the rules of immigration. Immigration did not personally affect them, and they were uniformly uncertain that their collective action would bring about the social change they envisioned. So, what sustained their continued participation in immigration politics and these specific organizations? Why did they endure, despite hardship and setbacks? I came to learn that the relationship between participants' personal identity conflicts and organizations' state-directed mobilization held the keys to unpacking these puzzles.

Here on the southern border of the United States, immigration politics was not just a political struggle about immigration. It was a highly symbolic struggle, wherein the integrity of participants' core identities were at stake. The very act of mobilizing was saturated with a constellation of meanings that went far beyond changing immigration policy.

Among the activists I studied, left and right, conflictual identities were just below the surface. Pro-immigrant activists wrestled with being "progressive, but privileged," while restrictionists contended with their "white-but-working-class" selves. Informed by particular intersections of class, race, and gender, these identities presented dilemmas. Mobilization in the ambiguous borderlands felt compelling precisely because they presented

courses of action through which participants might *cope* with their conflictual identities.

To understand how mobilization helped resolve these conflictual identities, we must pay attention to the *site* of mobilization and the dual "state
effects" it produced. New federal approaches to immigration policing in
the mid-1990s transformed Arizona into an ambiguous borderland, a
place where divergent perceptions of state power—or multiple state
effects—were possible. Consequently, leftist activists believed the state
was far too powerful, bullying vulnerable people and necessitating the
kind of help a privileged and progressive citizen might provide. Meanwhile,
right-wing activists believed the state was too weak and required vigilant
citizens' help if it was to stand up to a tide of lawlessness. Each side acted
on its diagnosis, working to weaken or strengthen the state in ways that
helped attenuate participants' particular identity dilemmas.

Pro-immigrant activists were usually from middle-class backgrounds,
and all were upwardly mobile. Those statuses made them deeply uncomfortable, as they also desired a more equitable world. The dilemma between
their progressive worldview and their personal privilege animated many of
their life decisions. Their willingness to forgo professional career opportunities and their long histories of civic engagement stood testament to the
restlessness that a conflictual identity can foster. Unlike other settings, the
borderlands of Arizona seemed to offer a productive outlet for this
unwanted status. Armed with the analysis that the state's oppressive power
made the borderlands a hostile place to the third-world migrant, but not to
(white) Americans like themselves, participants found that they could use
their privilege to work within spaces that were off-limits to immigrant and
racialized groups. They could take actions on behalf of and for noncitizens.
Weakening the state was not simply an instrumental strategy. It was also
profoundly meaningful for participants' self-understandings. Mobilization
offered a way to be progressive *and* privileged.

On the right, activists struggled with being white but working-class.
Empowering the state felt like a chance to empower oneself. The restrictionists were mostly downwardly-mobile white men, many hailing from
working-class backgrounds. Unlike pro-immigrant activists, they rarely
had any prior experience with civic engagement. For the average restrictionist, life felt like a solitary struggle against an endless array of hurdles.

Using a mix of explicit and coded racial language, right-wing activists described a painful disconnect between their in-group status as white men and the various forms of marginalization they experienced.

The borderlands presented an opportunity for white-but-working-class restrictionists to feel relevant and agentic. Believing that the problem of unauthorized border crossing was linked to the weakness of the state, restrictionists mobilized to help law enforcement become a more coordinated and powerful entity. They aided rank-and-file Border Patrol agents in the field. They developed technologies to boost the agency's capacity. They encouraged active cooperation between sheriff's departments and immigration authorities. All of these efforts were part of a state-strengthening project, but they were also ways a group of white-but-working-class Americans rejected marginalization.

The chapters in part 1 contribute to a critical strand of scholarship[1] that posits the importance of *both* state-focused mobilization *and* participants' identity management in analyzing social movements. Participation in the struggle around immigration, in this case, was certainly an effort to change the distribution of power in society. In this sense, participation was deeply *political*. However, mobilization was also about a group of Americans' self-transformation in a context of deepening precarity and escalating privilege. Activists managed their identities by taking actions vis-à-vis the state. This insight helps shed light on why the people I studied cared so much about a topic that did not seem to affect them.

1 Arizona and the Making of an Ambiguous Border

In 2010, when I first began my research, Arizona seemed to have become a barometer that Americans used to gauge the degree to which "their" border with Mexico was "secure." Depending on the interpreter, the barometer seemed to give wildly different readings.

For some, the Grand Canyon State was becoming a lawless and dangerous place. An article in the *Wall Street Journal*, "Our Lawless Mexican Border," described how residents of small Southern Arizona towns lived in constant fear for their personal security amid a growing number of smugglers. "Americans shouldn't have to live like this," a resident of Portal, Arizona, was quoted as saying. Her brother, a Douglas cattle rancher, was killed on his property, allegedly by Mexican drug smugglers.[1]

Other reports painted the scene very differently. *Time* magazine argued that the rate of violent crime was down across Arizona's cities. This included Nogales, a municipality abutting the Arizona-Sonora border that was otherwise "rife with illegal immigration and drug trafficking."[2] "The murderous mayhem raging across the border in Mexico" notwithstanding, the U.S. side, "from San Diego to Brownsville, Texas," the author wrote confidently, was "one of the nation's safest corridors."

How did Arizona come to be understood in such divergent ways? Why did the same region incite fear in some, and insistent avowals about the area's safety from others? In this chapter, I argue that underneath words like *dangerous*, *lawless*, and *safe* are assessments about the state apparatus. For this reason, it is useful to think about Arizona as an *ambiguous border*, a space that lends itself, simultaneously, to perceptions of heavy state presence *and* diminished state control.

Southern Arizona was not always an ambiguous border. Rather, decades of border and immigration policing culminated in a pair of mismatched effects. First, over time, the U.S.-Mexico border has simultaneously become more fortified *and* more porous. That is, even though the U.S.-Mexico border has experienced unprecedented buildup since the 1990s,[3] undocumented immigration across this border has persisted.[4]

Second, the more that immigration enforcement has been upheld as a federal prerogative, the more it has turned into a local affair. Put differently, the federal government maintains that it is has sole power to enact immigration policy, yet day-to-day immigration enforcement increasingly requires the involvement of local actors such as police.[5]

These two facts—that there is a large undocumented population despite border buildup and that there is localized enforcement despite federal preemption—have been instrumental in rendering Southern Arizona a space of ambiguous borderlands. Opposite assessments of state power are possible here.

PREVENTION THROUGH DETERRENCE: BORDER BUILDUP AND UNABATED MIGRATION

Arizona has not always been a bellwether border state. To the extent that public commentators talked about the country's southern frontier before 2010, the topic was generally associated with California. In the mid-1990s, approximately two-thirds of all migrants coming from south of the international border crossed through California.[6] Migrants entered the country at populous, urban points of entry like those along Imperial Beach in San Diego.

This crossing pattern changed when the federal government embraced a new approach to managing migration. In 1993, the Immigration and Naturalization Services (INS) developed a program called "prevention through deterrence." Conceived of as a way to deter extra-legal migration, this initiative called for the deployment of border enforcement resources in well-populated, urban points of entry. Meanwhile, the isolated, rougher, and more rural terrain surrounding these urban areas—the Rio Grande River and Arizona's Sonoran Desert, for instance—was left to act as a natural barrier to unauthorized migration.[7] By increasing the strenuousness and physical risks associated with migration, the INS claimed the new program would discourage prospective border crossers from even attempting to journey northward.

The INS's confidence that this initiative could work was rather odd. Earlier that year, the Border Patrol's deterrence experiment in El Paso, Texas, had yielded mixed results. Operation Blockade involved posting hundreds of Border Patrol agents and dozens of vehicles along a twenty-mile stretch of the El Paso–Ciudad Juarez boundary.[8] A retrospective report conceded that the maneuver did not deter but shifted migration to other points of entry. Yet officials and politicians considered the initiative a success.[9] Scholars suggest that the program's popularity owed to its having moved undocumented migration—and concomitantly, immigration enforcement—out of sight.[10]

A year later, Operation Gatekeeper was launched in San Diego. From 1994 onward, the prevention-through-deterrence model would be central to U.S.-Mexico border policing.[11] Its effects were immediate: Migrants began avoiding traditional urban crossing points, such as Imperial Beach, as they became more fortified. Rather than deterring them from crossing altogether, however, the prevention-through-deterrence program funneled these migrants toward Arizona.[12]

Meanwhile, in Arizona, the 1995 launch of Operation Safeguard further built up this "infrastructural funnel,"[13] by investing more border enforcement resources into the state's urban crossing points. Border fences were erected in Douglas, Nogales, and Naco, Arizona. A hundred more Border Patrol agents were deployed to the region, aided by new surveillance and apprehension technology. And the Tucson Sector, the division of the agency that covered most of Arizona, received a mandate to prosecute and deport immigrants on criminal grounds. As a result of these initiatives, border crossers wishing to evade capture, incarceration, and deportation were pushed into the arid terrain of Arizona's Sonoran Desert.[14]

U.S. Border Patrol data bear out this new pattern of crossing. In 1994, the Tucson Sector of the agency apprehended 139,473 people. Meanwhile, the San Diego Sector reported 450,152 apprehensions. By 2000, the rates had flipped: the Tucson Sector reported 616,346 apprehensions, and San Diego reported 151,681.[15]

That crossings had become riskier was also evident in the migrant death toll. By one government estimate, 171 people died while trying to cross the border in 1994. That number jumped to 250 in 1999 and averaged 431 per year between 2005 and 2009.[16] The Tucson Sector became a particularly fatal area: from 11 in 1994, the death toll reached 225 in 2010.[17] Migrants began paying steep fees to professional smugglers who could guide them through the rugged, lonely terrain of Southern Arizona.[18] Drug-trafficking organizations worked their way into this growing market.[19]

Soon, the U.S.-Mexico border was among the most heavily fortified land-crossings in the world.[20] Between 1993 and 2012, 651 miles of additional fencing were built along the border. The same period also saw an unprecedented investment in the U.S. Border Patrol, as the agency's annual budget mushroomed from $363 million in 1993 to $3.5 billion twenty years later.[21] By 2012, the Border Patrol's umbrella agency, the U.S. Customs and Border Protection, had become the largest federal law enforcement agency, with a budget of $18 billion.[22] This investment swelled the ranks of the agency: From 1994 to 2017, the number of Border Patrol agents grew from four thousand to nearly twenty thousand.[23] Approximately seventeen thousand, or 85 percent of the field agents were stationed on the country's southwestern border. In sum, the government's "prevention" policy fortified border protections at an unprecedented rate.

Yet migration continued unabated. In 1990, prior to the policy's implementation, the population of undocumented people living in the United States numbered 3.5 million. In 2007, fourteen years after the prevention-through-deterrence initiative was first conceived, the undocumented immigrant total more than tripled to 12.2 million, eventually stabilizing at 10.5 million in recent years.[24] Immigrants had not been deterred.

Arizona became the focal point—the spot along the U.S.-Mexico border where this paradoxical development was most acutely experienced. As the vignettes about Renee and Dale in the introduction illustrate, opposing groups were soon reading the very same stretch of the Arizona-Mexico border in vastly different ways.

To pro-immigrant activists like Renee, the combination of border buildup and a mushrooming undocumented population were signs of the state's *strength*. The state instigated migration, then illegalized it, and eventually, made cyclical migration so dangerous that a large undocumented population formed in the United States. Moreover, when people were forced to put down roots in American cities, it meant that, in the event of deportation, immigrants were more desperate to *return* to the United States. The fact that people traveled through Arizona's rugged Sonoran Desert, then, was evidence of the alarming amount of power that the immigration policing apparatus had accumulated.

Restrictionist activists, like Dale, vehemently disagreed with this narrative. From their vantage point, the growth of an undocumented population within the country demonstrated that the state was feeble rather than competent and coercive. Border enforcement's weakness had turned Arizona into a popular border-crossing point—a vast terrain that was challenging to police. No matter how many resources the federal government had channeled into border enforcement, the state simply could not keep up with migrants and smugglers. The evidence was in the desert.

THE 287(G) PROGRAM: DEVOLVING CONTROL
DESPITE FEDERAL PREEMPTION

Arizona also became a site for a second paradoxical effect of enforcement. The 1990s and 2000s were a period in which the federal government and state legislatures fought vigorously over the power to enact immigration policies.

The roots of this disagreement lay with the Immigration and Nationality Act of 1965. While the act gave enforcement powers to local authority on immigration crimes, including smuggling, transporting, and harboring, it left vague whether that authority extended to the violation of civil provisions of immigration law, such as unauthorized presence.[25] This jurisdictional issue was never firmly resolved. Instead, it led to a tag-team effort of experimenting with localized approaches to immigration enforcements. That would culminate in Arizona's infamous passage of SB1070 in 2010, but to understand how we got there, we have to head back to California in the early 1990s.

A year after the federal government implemented the prevention-through-deterrence initiative, voters in California overwhelmingly passed a ballot measure called Proposition 187. Street-level government bureaucrats—from police officers to public school teachers and health care providers—were required to collude with immigration authorities. These public institutions had to verify the legal status of the people they serviced and report anyone with an irregular status to the INS.[26] Eventually ruled unconstitutional, Prop 187 nonetheless helped shape federal immigration reform.

In 1996, President Bill Clinton signed the Illegal Immigration Reform and Immigrant Responsibility Act (IIRIRA) into law. One component directly echoed the California initiative: Section 287(g) of IIRIRA allowed the federal government to train and authorize state and local authorities to enforce *both* civil and criminal immigration laws.[27] By deputizing local law enforcement officers to check immigration status during routine police work, the program served as a "force multiplier" for the INS.[28] The provision marked a clear departure from the long-standing "legal and practical consensus" among government officials and others that immigration policing was strictly a federal power.[29] The 287(g) program paved the way for a dozen similar federal government initiatives—including the more far-reaching Secure Communities program, or "287(g) lite"—under the umbrella of Agreements of Cooperation in Communities to Enhance Safety and Security or ICE ACCESS programs.[30] Together, ICE ACCESS constituted a systematic effort to partner immigration enforcement agencies with police departments throughout the country.

This context of devolving immigration enforcement set the stage for Arizona legislators, in 2004, to pass a measure resembling Prop 187. Arizona Proposition 200 mandated social service providers to look into the immigration status of applicants and required proof of U.S. citizenship for voter registration. Worried that the successful passage of Prop 200 would encourage more state-level restrictionist bills, Janet

Napolitano, Arizona's Democratic governor at the time (and later Homeland Security Secretary in the Obama administration), decided to take action. Napolitano brokered an agreement between ICE and an Arizona Sheriff—Joe Arpaio of Maricopa County—to bring the 287(g) program to her state and prioritize the removal of "criminal aliens."[31] Certainly, Arizona was not entirely new to this kind of local-federal cooperation. Less than a decade earlier, the police department of Chandler, Arizona, had participated in a five-day joint immigration sweep with the Border Patrol, which had resulted in the deportation of more than four hundred people.[32] While such interagency collaboration was on the rise throughout the nation, it was still relatively infrequent.[33] But 287(g) codified this kind of cooperation.

Like Clinton and IIRIRA, Napolitano's decision to introduce 287(g) to Arizona was motivated by the desire to reinscribe the federal government's monopoly over immigration enforcement. Ironically, neither tried to do so by getting rid of localized immigration enforcement. Instead, each spread the practice *further*. In 2006, 414 people were identified for removal through the 287(g) program in Arizona. In 2008, 16,373 were identified. Of these, 82 percent were so designated by 287(g)-deputized officers in the Maricopa County Sheriff's Office.[34]

Indeed, it was federal initiatives like 287(g) that Arizona state legislators had in mind when they introduced subsequent restrictionist legislation including SB1070.[35] Signed into law in 2010, SB1070's key provision required immigration status checks during law enforcement stops. In conservative circles, the measure became the gold standard for immigration reform. It generated enormous pushback as well as a flurry of copycat bills in other states. From the get-go, the federal government expressed disapproval of SB1070: two months after it was signed into law, the U.S. Department of Justice even filed a lawsuit against Arizona.[36]

In 2012, however, the Supreme Court upheld the measure's central provision, in part, because it remained unclear how different SB1070 was from the federal government's existing enforcement practices.[37] The ruling seemed to reflect and reinforce the very ambiguity that had prompted both SB1070 and ensuing lawsuits: although immigration enforcement was the domain of the federal government, in practice, federal authorities needed local help to meet stricter enforcement mandates.

This ambiguity has continued to incite a powerful politics at the federal level: less than a week after his inauguration in January 2017, President Trump signed two executive orders that expanded the 287(g) program and restored another ICE ACCESS program, Secure Communities, which had been reluctantly phased out in 2014.[38] In doing so, the new administration signaled its commitment to a conservative agenda of "securing the border." Ironically, however, the executive orders reinvigorated the ambiguities and jockeying for legitimacy initiated by IIRIRA more than twenty years earlier and so diligently maintained under the Bush and Obama administrations.

The devolution of immigration enforcement localized immigration politics. It made the state's reach something that local groups believed they could—and should—either extend or curtail. In Arizona, for instance, Renee's group, the Advocates worried that local institutions were in danger of being caught up in immigration control. From 2011 to 2017, the Advocates' efforts were dedicated, in part, to preventing local entities from cooperating with federal immigration agencies. Meanwhile, restrictionist groups strived to *keep* immigration control localized. A Phoenix-based restrictionist organization I call the Arpaiositos spent most of their time defending Sheriff Arpaio's ability to continue using his 287(g) powers. When analyzed in tandem, these grassroots organizations' goals and tactics reflect the ongoing ambiguity around who has the power to police immigrants.

Just as they had with prevention through deterrence, activists perceived the devolution of immigration enforcement in divergent ways. To pro-immigrant activists, the localization of immigration policing revealed how a dominant state was spreading its punitive logic across all spheres of life. To restrictionists, however, this very same devolution suggested that the state needed the help of local institutions precisely because it was too weak to enforce immigration laws on its own.

THE AMBIGUOUS BORDER AS A FRONTIER

Together, these two paradoxes—the persistence of unauthorized entry and the growth of the undocumented population *despite* border buildup and the localization of enforcement *despite* federal preemption—transformed

Arizona into an ambiguous border.[39] There, the border became a place where citizens disputed to what extent the state maintained a monopoly over the legitimate use of force.[40]

To be clear, "ambiguous border" is my analytic imposition. If I suggested to my respondents, whether on the left or the right, that there was anything ambiguous or uncertain about the nature of the state in the borderlands, they probably would have been bewildered. For my pro-immigrant respondents, the fact that people risked life and limb to cross Arizona's Sonoran Desert was evidence of the state's coercive power. To suggest otherwise would be to deny the calculatingly lethal nature of the government's ongoing prevention-through-deterrence program. For restrictionist respondents, these circumstances proved that the state was anemic and overwhelmed. Whatever border enforcement authorities had hoped to do with the prevention-through-deterrence program, it was not working. In this manner, the ambiguities of the borderlands have created the conditions for controversy and mobilization.

And, as the rest of the book shows, specific social groups were attracted to this political struggle. We might thus theorize the ambiguous border as a productive outlet—or a "frontier"[41]—for the tensions arising from particular intersectional identities. In the United States, frontiers have historically served as a "gendered safety valve" where an unsuccessful "boy" could disappear and return a "self-made man."[42] The frontier has also been theorized as a place to channel "the 'fury' of class resentment . . . thereby render[ing] class struggle unnecessary."[43] The traditional frontiers of the past have largely disappeared: there is no longer an American Wild West, nor are there colonies that need to be subjugated. Yet unresolved spaces like the ambiguous borderlands reveal that frontiers have not disappeared altogether.

The next two chapters show how immigration and border enforcement created a new frontier—and not just for conservative "angry white men,"[44] but also for progressive groups of American citizens. The ambiguous border of Arizona can be understood as a frontier for self-actualizing—but also deeply *political*—activism. It is a place where gendered and racialized class anxieties—ranging from the guilt of the privileged to the frustration of the downwardly mobile—can be channeled into action with respect to the state.

2 Being Progressive, but Privileged

THE MORAL MANDATE

When I asked Gary, a charismatic, white, seventy-year-old, why he was an avid volunteer with the Humanitarians, his face was placid. "I don't think there's a choice," he said. The former pastor had helped found the Humanitarians shortly after retiring from the ministry. The group's main task was to put out water for migrants crossing the border through Arizona's Sonoran Desert without authorization. Gary's organization also provided basic services to people who had been deported from the United States to Mexican border towns.

Gary would go on to describe what felt like a *moral* obligation: "I don't think there's a choice for progressive Americans, for privileged Americans. I mean, we have to live for what we really think is the best, and that's to be on the side of the poor, the migrants, when we can and to use our privileged position to fight for that. We're not going to *be* the poor. [...] We can't take the *place* of the poor. But we can use the influence we have, with privilege, to work for that and bring change." This theme would emerge, time and time again, as I spoke with pro-immigrant activists. Progressive and privileged citizens should not try to renounce their privilege but use it to improve the circumstances of those less fortunate.

Camila, a Latina woman in her late sixties, was a former social worker who helped establish another pro-immigrant organization, the Advocates. They tried to help noncitizens avoid deportation. Additionally, the organization coordinated searches to find and rescue migrants believed to have gotten lost in the desert. The Advocates, like the Humanitarians, largely ran on *volunteer* labor. To Camila's mind, however, none of the group's endeavors was truly *voluntary*: their work "came out of the sense that . . . we live in the belly of the beast. Therefore, we had, and we [as Americans] continue to have, a moral responsibility."

This moral mandate was unsurprising, given the fact that religion and moral frameworks have been integral to pro-immigrant mobilization in the United States, particularly at the U.S.-Mexico border.[1] What scholars have not discussed, however, is the *relationship* between this sense of moral duty and the unique social backgrounds of pro-immigrant participants like Gary and Camila, who, as American citizens without noncitizen kin, were not personally impacted by immigration policy.

This chapter shows how the salience of "moral responsibility" was firmly tied to a common attribute among my left-wing respondents: being what even they called "privileged." *Privilege* referred to *class* privilege, and it sharply distinguished my leftist respondents from their right-wing counterparts, who were predominantly lower-middle class and working class.[2] Often, it also referred to *racial* privilege, something they shared with their right-wing counterparts. Pro-immigrant activists frequently reflected on how their privilege was at odds with their worldviews. The *combination* of progressivism and privilege presented an uncomfortable dilemma: How can someone who has personally benefitted from inequality legitimately act on their desire for more equality?

If one constructed an ideal type out of pro-immigrant activists' life histories, based on the characteristics that they shared, this dilemma would appear at the climax of the narrative arc, and its resolution would emerge after the subjects joined groups in Southern Arizona. This ideal typical narrative goes as follows. Having grown up in middle-class households in the United States, and, in some cases, all-white neighborhoods, respondents were poised for professional careers, material comforts, and high-status roles in society. They showed tremendous promise. Some had already accrued achievements ranging from impressive postsecondary degrees and travel experience to coveted jobs and settled family lives. Then everything changed.

Respondents described discrete, identifiable turning points in their lives, when they became aware of their privilege, particularly in relation to racialized noncitizens. They were overcome by urgency. They needed to *do* something. Often to the consternation of their family members, respondents showed a willingness to forfeit the certainty and success that their social status promised them. They enlisted in progressive organizations. They participated in leftist projects. They tried to fashion themselves into morally responsible allies. For various reasons, all these efforts fell short of their expectations. Their privilege seemed incongruent with their political desires. Finally, they arrived in Arizona to volunteer with the Humanitarians or the Advocates. At the border, their involvement felt rewarding. They reported feeling "transformed."[3]

In listening to this satisfying story, I sometimes caught myself feeling a pang of envy. As they narrated their versions of the ideal-typical narrative, my interlocutors seemed to have figured out how to engage in one of the defining political conflicts of our times. They had worked out how to effect change, to "be on the side of the poor" from a position of privilege. As Humanitarians and Advocates, they were enacting their moral mandate. Soon, however, I realized that it would be difficult to attribute any long-term social change to their efforts. In fact, the more I examined it, the more I realized that the pro-immigrant activism I studied was not very effective at all.

Even the activists knew their work at the border was basically a long-running effort in futility. Gary, for instance, acknowledged that despite the Humanitarians' best efforts, border crossers would continue to die from dehydration in the wilderness of Southern Arizona. Camila knew that no matter how much the Advocates tried to protect them, immigrants would continue to be detained and deported. Many would return to the desert, risking life and limb to enter the United States. If the Humanitarians and the Advocates were not achieving their goals, I wondered, *why* did Gary and Camila refer to American citizens' participation as morally mandatory?

More baffling still, some of my respondents had participated in far more impactful efforts and organizations *before* arriving in Arizona. So why was *Arizona* the site of their transformation?

The key came in realizing that the exigencies of political transformation and social change did not power these activists' social-movement participation. Rather, their devotion (oftentimes, in the face of severe burnout) was sustained by a need for *personal* transformation. That is, the border provided a place for activists on the left and the right to manage *conflictual identities*.

This chapter explores how the border worked to help progressive and privileged Americans make sense of their seemingly paradoxical identities. For the Advocates and the Humanitarians, their groups' attractiveness was not based on their concrete accomplishments, but on the ways their actions felt *personally transformative to activists*. Specifically, we will see how the strong-state effect served as a baseline understanding onto which pro-immigrant activists built their analysis of the social world. In this schema, the variations in immigrants' backgrounds and the specifics of their lived experiences were secondary, even insignificant. In the pro-immigrant worldview, the third-world migrant was a victim of the state, forced to cross the border, and endure all the hardship that undocumented migration entailed, because of *American* policies.[4]

Within this interpretive schema, weakening the state was a meaningful endeavor. Privileged Americans had the agentic capacity and moral duty to do that work. The Humanitarians and the Advocates discovered that their power and status, which in other settings had felt like a hindrance and a source of guilt, was, at the border, a welcome and necessary tool for diminishing the state. According to Gary and other like-minded activists, the very places where migrants were most vulnerable to the state's power were the places where privileged Americans could and *should* "use the influence [they] had."

The vast desert that the third-world migrant crossed, the rural and urban spaces where they encountered the U.S. Border Patrol, the cartel-controlled Mexican border towns they were deported to, and the desolate regions where they died in transit—in short, the entirety of the Arizona-Sonora borderlands—became sites in which activists managed the dilemma of being progressive, but privileged. In a manner that my respondents claimed was rare, they could finally be progressive *and* privileged. This chapter showcases five activists, each of whom recounts a variation of this journey.

"I WANT TO BE ABLE TO ACTUALLY AFFECT THIS HUMAN IN SOME WAY": GAIL'S AND LUCAS'S STORIES

As she sat down at my kitchen table, I reflected on my luck: I had caught Gail long enough to interview her. A twenty-eight-year old white woman, Gail, like a lot of the other young people who participated with the Humanitarians, spent almost all of her free time out in the desert. Indeed, she had recently returned from a weeklong stay in Southern Arizona's border wilderness, among the long-term volunteers running the Humanitarians' medical camp for migrants. Prolonged exposure to the desert sun had left Gail's face lightly sunburned. It had been a physically exhausting week, walking miles of rugged trails in order to find migrants who might need water or medical aid. Yet Gail seemed extraordinarily energetic. She told me how she looked forward to going back out to the desert.

"My family is very rustbelt," Gail began when I asked her about her background. I learned that she grew up in an all-white community half an hour outside of Akron, Ohio. The region's once booming steel and rubber industries had, for a long time, attracted immigrants, Gail's great grandparents among them. They left their Eastern European homelands and crossed the Atlantic to settle in the United States. Within two generations, the family had managed to secure a middle-class life. Gail's mother, one of the first in her family to attend college, earned her keep as a cartographer before she quit her job to start a family. Although he hailed from a family of academics, Gail's father broke with family tradition after completing his bachelor's degree to go work in the sales department of a rubber packaging company. When Gail completed high school, college was the expected next step, and, wanting to "escape" Ohio, it was a welcome change. She won a scholarship to attend Boston University.

Gail would drop out of BU before her first year was up, but she "became more politically aware." Ending up closer to home, she took Spanish-language classes at the University of Pittsburgh, studied abroad in Spain for half a year, and enjoyed a summer of traveling through South America. Gail majored in political science and studied how the global political economy worked.[5] Perhaps more than any of these experiences, it was a friendship with a coworker that would be instrumental in shaping Gail's political consciousness. Through that friendship, Gail grew increasingly aware of and uncomfortable with social inequality. It taught Gail about her own race and class privilege.

The coworker, originally from Honduras, had lived in Texas since the time she was ten years old. Gail recounted how, as far as she was concerned, the two young women "were both just eighteen-year-old women working in a bakery." That illusion of equality vanished suddenly: Immigration and Customs Enforcement (ICE) raided the bakery and took away Gail's friend. In an instant, Gail realized the vastly different life opportunities she and her friend had in the United States: "I feel close to my friend, my bud. 'We're equals, right?' . . . Not even close. . . . [R]ealizing that she could be deported and dropped off in Honduras, and she's like, 'I guess I could call my second uncle and see if he'd pick me up from the airport.' I mean, what would happen if somebody picked me up and dropped me off in Guatemala? How would that go? That was one of the stories that got me interested in immigration."

Gail lost touch with her friend, but the experience of uniformed agents taking that friend away stuck with her. After graduation, Gail felt sure she had to move to Washington, D.C. It was the only place where she could imagine being "politically active": "I'm a middle-class white person who has been trained through college that if you want to be active, you work for nonprofits. [My friend's apprehension] made me think about, 'Okay, how do you prevent people like [her] from being deported? You get a job at a nonprofit and do broad-based litigation.'" And so she did. At twenty-three, she began working as a paralegal with a well-known D.C.-based nonprofit advocating for immigrant rights. Soon, however, she began grappling with her privilege again.

Her position of power became acutely visible to Gail when her organization started putting together a class-action lawsuit on behalf of asylum seekers. The lawsuit was "a big deal" because it intended to make asylum seekers eligible for work visas before a final decision was made on their cases. Using the organization's networks, Gail was charged with finding the "right" plaintiffs—those who would make the lawsuit as compelling as possible in the eyes of the court. What this entailed, she realized, was sorting the "good" asylum seekers from the "bad": "So I'm this middle-class white person. I know the courts are going to view the most or least vulnerable people. We want this Nigerian woman who's protecting her daughter from female genital mutilation. But the Honduran dude is escaping violence. 'Nah, he's fucking gang. Nope.'" She remembered, "To be in that position—I'm this young person in this room, deciding who are going to be the plaintiffs. It's a game! And we won. And by playing that game and winning, that affects a lot of people." Still, Gail noticed,

> It was the first time for me where I realized that I don't feel good in this position and I don't want to do this anymore. [. . .] Up until that point, I *had* *to* go to D.C. to meet my definition of success. [. . .] I was being so competitive, and wanted it [the job] so bad. [But] once I had it, I realized that this is the nonprofit complex. I think they do incredible work. But it just made me realize that I didn't want to work on things in this broad-based way.

It was ironic: On the one hand, this kind of litigation could "affect a lot of people." It brought economic relief in contexts of tremendous uncertainty. People anxiously waited on their asylum decisions, and they had to make ends meet in the meantime; now they would no longer risk their whole case just because they got caught working illegally. Moreover, the win had an important equalizing effect: it ensured a bare minimum to which *all* asylum seekers were entitled, no matter if they were a "Nigerian woman" or a "Honduran dude." Gail and her organization had won the game.

On the other hand, winning the game meant Gail had to play the game in the first place. It was always rigged against asylum seekers, and she felt she had reinforced the legitimacy of its rules by playing by them. More importantly, her work bolstered the very thing that made Gail uncomfortable: her own privilege and power. Despite her young age and relative inexperience, she had been tasked with making decisions about whose lives were supposedly good enough to be showcased in the court of law. Gail had the visceral realization that she did not "feel good in this position." Feeling jaded, she made plans to leave D.C. as soon as the case was over. Through her nonprofit's networks, she had met a few Humanitarians. She remembers asking them, of their direct activism, "'So you guys just do it?' . . . Just like that? You just go out there?' And they're like, 'Yup, that's how it works.'" Gail was accepted for a two-week internship with the Humanitarians and made her way to the Southwest.

A short-term internship turned into a long-term endeavor, in the way it would for many of my other pro-immigrant respondents. Gail kept extending her stay until finally moving to Arizona for good (in both senses) as a full-time volunteer. Being in the Sonoran Desert, rather than a D.C. court, was a far more satisfying way to be progressive but privileged. Certainly, the work did not do away with her privilege—it hinged on it. The combination of her U.S. citizenship, whiteness, and middle-class disposition gave her a protective shield every time she encountered the Border Patrol in the desert. Exploiting her privilege in this manner somehow *felt* different. When I asked Gail to explain how Arizona was different from Washington, D.C., she kept circling around the idea that had first intrigued her—that the Humanitarians engage in a more direct form of activism.

> Being out here [in the border wilderness] and being the first people at [the Humanitarians'] camp, *there's that direct human thing*. And it's not this big—if we can just change this one policy that will spread and affect all these people and I value that and that's really important. *But having an actual human in front of you* and being like, 'Okay, so what do we need to do to get you where you need to go?' [. . .] I remember the first week there was a group of Hondurans there, specifically, which I just related that back to [my friend from the bakery], even though they weren't anywhere near similar people. There's probably some secondary trauma in watching a workplace raid happen, being fine myself but watching my friends be targeted. And then years later, to be in this situation where this human being, *who is directly in front of me*, in this very small-scale way, *to be able to actually affect this human in some way*, this human, if we hadn't run into him, Border Patrol would have. That's meaningful. [emphasis mine]

In the desert, Gail did not have to sort individuals according to their moral worth. In fact, as a Humanitarian, she felt that she could forego the morality question altogether. She could simply help a person because that person was hurt. It was a raw and straightforward interaction, unencumbered by severe social hierarchies—"there's that direct human thing." For a brief instant, Gail felt like she lived in a world in which it was accepted, *expected*, for white, middle-class Americans to kneel down on the ground to tend to the bruised feet of racialized, undocumented migrants. In those moments, Gail felt like she could relinquish the power that came with her background—whether it was the power to decide someone's moral worth or the power to stand back, unharmed, during an immigration raid. She could step up and "actually affect this human in some way."

Gail's was a powerful story: upon becoming aware of a dilemma between her progressive worldview and her privilege at a young age, she spent a decade trying to resolve it, even forgoing opportunities for upward social mobility. In the span of one work shift, a stunned eighteen-year-old Gail swiftly learned how much she personally benefited from inequity every day. As I interviewed her ten years after the raid, I could hear the restlessness and urgency in her story. I sensed it in the narrated life histories of other pro-immigrant activists as well.[6] Gail, I realized, could not stay put until she resolved, or at least, could comfortably live with, this dilemma. In fact, her quest to become a responsible ally even remained strong, despite the steep opportunity costs it involved.

I learned, for example, that Gail had gotten into a prestigious graduate program; she declined in favor of her volunteer work at the border. In quitting her paralegal job, she had effectively quit another professional trajectory that could have led to a potentially high-status career in D.C.'s nonprofit complex. Indeed, when she landed that job, Gail initially felt like she had arrived. "I had to go to D.C. to meet my definition of success. [...] I was being so competitive, and wanted [the job] so bad." Soon, though, she decided to give up that kind of success and, with it, the opportunity to move up the rungs of the professional advocacy world. Steered by a restless pursuit for a moral life—as she understood it—Gail effectively relinquished the opportunity for upward social mobility.

As I mulled over her story, I was also struck that Gail had traded in a more efficacious endeavor—litigation work that could potentially improve the lives of hundreds of thousands, even millions of noncitizens—for a direct, but also very *individualistic* form of action. Repeatedly, she conceded that the D.C. group did "incredible work" but that she personally "didn't want to work on things in this broad-based way." This remarkable rationale centered on *her* and *not* the exigencies of social change. That is,

what mattered for Gail was, ultimately, how *she felt about herself*, her positionality. She assigned far more meaning to the singular act of giving
water to an undocumented border crosser in the desert than to a large-
scale legal effort aimed at improving the economic opportunities of three
million asylum seekers. That she did so is, in a word, noteworthy.

This was an activism driven not by its actual outcomes but by the pursuit to answer grating questions about morality and positionality. How
can one be progressive, but white and middle class? How can one be progressive, but poised for a successful career and a life of material comfort?
These questions, sometimes explicitly and sometimes implicitly, framed
activists' stories about themselves and the decisions they made.

What exactly was it about the border that helped Gail bear her conflictual identity?

Taking water out into the desert, at its most fundamental level, allowed
Gail to exploit her privilege in order to *weaken the state*. Drawing a distinction between desirable "direct action" and less desirable "charity
work," Gail explained how she thought about the Humanitarians:

> Is this direct action or weird Band-Aid, charity work? Kinda both, for sure.
> But aid [in the desert] is absolutely direct action because every time a[n
> undocumented] person makes it [to their destination in the United States]
> *in spite of all the state power that is ensuring that they don't make it*, that
> one person making it and anyone helping them along the way, that's direct
> action. [. . .] That feels like a privilege—to be able to wake up and put water
> in the desert and feel useful in some way. [emphasis mine]

That Gail could "directly" help someone make it "in spite of all the state
power" gave her unparalleled satisfaction. That outcome was, on a personal level, far better than anything she could achieve through broad-
based litigation. Both tending to individual migrants and working to
change policy were important, in Gail's conception, but she felt she needed
to perform direct actions to satisfy her personal discomfort.[7]

This satisfaction, I realized, stemmed from the particular way that Gail
and other pro-immigrant interlocutors came to understand the state. In
this pro-immigrant narrative, the U.S. state was a powerful antihero,
racialized migrants were its helpless victims, and Americans—especially
white Americans—were potentially significant allies enacting a particular

vision of a benevolent Western superpower against what they saw as the corrupted, distorted version symbolized in the Border Patrol agents' work. When migrants crossed the Arizona-Mexico border, activists told me, they were doing so against their will. The state *forced* migrants to cross without permission and then systematically abused them on their journey north. If agency was conceptualized as a spectrum, migrants were on one end, while Americans—particularly white, middle-class Americans—were on the opposite end.

As a group, white, middle-class Americans not only had the ability to withstand the state, they could potentially undermine state power to help less advantaged groups. This was no easy task, however. The life stories of activists revealed that privilege could often feel like an impediment in the pursuit of alliance with the oppressed. At the border, where the state appeared particularly strong and predatory, there was an *opportunity to exploit one's privilege* in order to *directly* weaken the state and help migrants. The framework of the strong-state effect resolved the dilemma of being progressive but privileged into a self-conception as progressive *and* privileged.

Opportunity was exactly the word Lucas, a thirty-six-year-old white activist friend of Gail's used. Originally from Texas, Lucas had first gone to Ecuador to learn Spanish as part of a college study-abroad program. After graduating with a degree in women's studies, he returned to Central America to work as an English teacher. Lucas told me he was shocked that nearly a tenth of Ecuador's population was "forced" to emigrate, with many ending up in major American cities. Meanwhile, he was in Ecuador voluntarily, working a job and living a life that he wanted. Lucas struggled with the fact that he was the beneficiary in this system of inequality. He wondered how to be a responsible ally to Ecuadorans, to any immigrants. "Part of me wanted to stay there [in Ecuador] and not return [to the United States. . . .] But I felt that being from the U.S., it was more effective to be doing some type of solidarity work." So, he returned to Texas, where for the better part of a decade, he worked at a shelter for refugees. He then moved to Southern Arizona to volunteer with the Humanitarians.

When we met, Lucas had been a Humanitarian for nearly a year, and he was making ends meet as a freelance cab driver. He said the Humanitarians provided "*a real opportunity*" to make a difference, "despite the fact that

[. . .] U.S. state policy is causing death and suffering." Pontificating on the double meaning of privilege in much the same way Gail had, Lucas added, *"the chance to actually to do something that directly [that] diminishes suffering and death, that's a privilege, in the sense that it's an honor"* [emphasis mine]. He paused.

> To me, being out [in the U.S.-Mexico borderlands], where many other people have fear related to being there—migrants fear law enforcement [. . .] Border Patrol fear cartels, or fear migrants themselves. So being the Humanitarians, [. . .] *being neutral, it provides this cloak of . . . being in a position of aid and helping people. It's a strategic role that allows us to move through that space without fear.* We have no reason to fear the cartel, or the migrants, or the Border Patrol, because we're there to give people water.
>
>   The more privileged—which is a lot of the volunteers—if you're a citizen and you know your rights and you're very well educated, then you know that you just have to say you're a U.S. citizen and you don't have to say anything else [to the Border Patrol]. You can totally ignore them. Knowing that right and being protected because you have an identity which won't be racially profiled, then you really can expect that they [the Border Patrol] won't be aggressive, and you can go help people. [emphasis mine]

Privilege, which so often functioned as a complicating factor, in this case *facilitated* progressive action. Normally, privilege had a distancing effect. At the U.S.-Mexico border, however, privilege closed the distance between the volunteer and those they wanted to help. It created the possibility for *directness*. Participants' middle-class dispositions ("you're very well educated") and whiteness ("you have an identity which won't be racially profiled") allowed them to be "neutral" and "move through the space without fear" to "go help people." Privilege allowed activists to bypass state actors in a manner that others could not—"you can totally ignore" the Border Patrol. Note that Lucas used the word *cloak*; his whiteness, his education, his middle-classness, were like an invisibility cloak when it came to the Border Patrol. He could use this "superpower" for good.

   Once they bypassed state agencies, activists could directly work to weaken the state. Aid in the desert was direct because it facilitated passage *"in spite of all the state power that is ensuring that they [border crossers] don't make it"* [emphasis mine]. Similarly, for Lucas, what made the provision of water a privilege for him was that it seemed to mitigate the state's intentional program of causing "death and suffering." For both Lucas and Gail, the border—where the state seemed to have a formidable presence—was a place where privilege was instrumental to progressive action.

"NOTHING ELSE IS AS FULFILLING; IT'S BIBLICAL": NINA'S STORY

When I asked Nina, a friendly, white woman in her early thirties, what attracted her to the Humanitarians, I was thinking about my most recent three-day camping trip in the desert. I had borrowed a friend's military-style sleeping system, because a regular sleeping bag could not withstand nighttime temperatures in the winter. Despite having put on every piece of clothing I had brought with me, the cold nights had left me miserable and eagerly anticipating the end of the trip. So I marveled at Nina when she shared that she had recently returned from the Humanitarians' desert camp and looked forward to going back.

Before Nina could even answer my question, "Why do you like to volunteer with the Humanitarians?" I added, unthinkingly, "after all, you could be *paid* to do other things." She laughed, "I could!"

"This is what my parents tell me all the time. *All* the time."

"So, what do you tell them?" I pushed.

"Nothing else is as fulfilling," she answered, matter-of-factly.

Nina, like Gail and Lucas, had experienced an almost magnetic pull to the Humanitarians, despite all the sacrifices that had entailed. Raised in the Midwest, the daughter of two tenured professors, Nina had been poised for a comfortable, upper-middle-class life. She had attended an elite private liberal arts college and majored in Latin American studies and anthropology. Nina then completed two years in AmeriCorps, gaining experience in public health. She worked at a nutrition education program that catered to impoverished families without papers and later served as a health educator at the county department of public health. Nina completed a master's in social work and was working on her second, in public affairs, when she learned about the weeklong internship program with the Humanitarians. "I came down here kind of on a whim and was totally transformed with my week," she reflected. "Then, I spent the rest of the many years trying to get back here."

It would take her two attempts to finally settle down in Arizona. The first came less than a year after her transformative introduction to the Humanitarians, when Nina and her boyfriend moved down to Arizona from the Northwest. Armed with her masters' degrees and work experience, Nina nonetheless found herself working at a pizza parlor while volunteering full-time with the Humanitarians. Within months, her boyfriend, a recent PhD, was offered a job at a university in the Midwest and the couple moved again. Three years later, when they broke up, Nina immediately moved back to Arizona. By the time we met, she was a program coordinator in a field study program attached to a private liberal arts college. She enjoyed the job and liked her colleagues—many were also volunteers with local pro-immigrant organizations. However, her paid position remained secondary to her volunteer work. Nina's friends joked that she spent more time in the desert than in the city.

For Nina, a happenstance border experience became a compass point in her life. It would take four years, a painful breakup, and three moves across the country before she could create a life for herself in Southern Arizona. As she spoke, Nina seemed to sense how surprised I was by her life decisions. "One other piece to my story that makes me feel like border work is so important," she finally said, "is that I've worked within the system." Like Gail, I learned, Nina had done other immigrant advocacy work, but it had ended in disillusionment and set the stage for the transformation both women would experience at the border.

Much like almost all the other pro-immigrant activists that I interviewed (and unlike most of my restrictionist respondents), Nina had a history of civic engagement related to immigration before volunteering in the borderlands. During the three years she was in the Midwest with her boyfriend, Nina had been at a nonprofit that worked closely with the Office of Refugee Resettlement. Her organization trained volunteers to become guardian ad litems for unaccompanied minors in immigration custody. The nonprofit had emerged to meet a gap in the immigration system: neither minors nor adults in immigration detention were appointed attorneys. They were forced to either find their own legal representation or file by themselves. Volunteers would support minors through the process as guardian ad litems—attending hearings, for instance.

Despite her organization's efforts, many minors remained in detention. Others were repatriated to their sending countries. The system did not seem to give unaccompanied minors any reprieve, and there was no "right way" available. A significant backlog of immigration cases meant extremely long wait times for visas. Nina reminded me that, among all the things refugees lack, time figures prominently: "If you're somebody who is fleeing unimaginable violence or [. . .] your mom is dying and you're trying to get money for her cancer medicine, you don't have ten years. You don't even have one year." There were many times, Nina recalled, when she wanted to urge children to try again to migrate into the United States, with the hope that they would avoid the "system" the next time they crossed without papers. "Crossing the border [illegally] becomes the better option, sadly, because of how bad our system is." Nina grew weary of working within the system.

While Gail conceded the efficacy of broad-based litigation, Nina had serious doubts about the usefulness of her work at the nonprofit—a conclusion that I found surprising for two reasons. First, a report released by the U.S. Government Accountability Office (GAO) indicated that 70 percent of the time, the program's recommendations about a child's care and custody were in fact adopted by the receiving institution.[8] This included, in some cases, the immigration judge who made the final adjudication about a child's asylum claim.[9] For this reason, the GAO report recommended the program's expansion, concluding that it gave "children—especially those who are unable to make an independent decision due to young age or trauma—a voice during the immigration process."[10] Against this glowing report, I thought about how unclear it was that the alternative form of pro-immigrant mobilization that attracted Nina—putting out water along a limited number of migrant trails in the desert—was necessarily helping unaccompanied children. There was no way to definitively conclude that working within the system (child advocacy work) was less effective than working outside of it (desert-based humanitarian work).

Once again, I realized that my interlocutors were making the distinction between "good" and "bad" endeavors on the basis of their *own* existential struggles as progressive but privileged people. When Nina assessed her volunteer work in Arizona, she weighed it against her experiences of working within the system. There was the time, for instance, when she counseled undocumented women on their children's nutritional intake, with a specific focus on obese children. "That was a miserable job. It was a totally miserable job," she said solemnly. Ineligible for government assistance, mothers without papers would turn to Nina's organization to feed their families. However, the program did not have the resources to give families low-fat foods that could address the problem of obesity. "There was honestly not a lot I could do for a lot of the families," Nina told me as she reflected on that time.

To illustrate her frustration, she explained how her organization's go-to plan for physical activity overlooked families' circumstances. Clients would tell her, "'We can't go outside because there are shootings all of the time.' It was like, how do we come up with physical activity in the house because you're afraid of going outside? It was a real eye-opener to environmental racism." Nina harbored similarly mixed feelings about another job in which she worked with incarcerated mothers and their daughters. "There's not much you can really do for them." Thus, Nina came to see working within the system as a "miserable" pursuit.

At the U.S.-Mexico border—outside "the system"—however, Nina did not feel miserable. In fact, she told me that "nothing else is as fulfilling." When I asked her to elaborate, she described the "magical" experience of "taking down borders" and weakening the state:

I feel like there's this thing that happens sometimes at camp [where volunteers attend to medically distressed migrants] where you really have time to get to know people and you sit with them for many days in the middle of a desert. It's like *biblical*. The shit out there is biblical. It's so bizarre. You sit with them [border crossers] and you hear their stories and there are sometimes these *magical* moments where everyone will be sitting around a fire at night just telling stories to each other and *it feels like we won, like the border isn't there anymore for a second* and . . . *because somebody like me, like white upper-middle class [with] many master's degrees should not necessarily be having a conversation with an undocumented person from El Salvador who will probably work in menial labor in the United States.* Otherwise our lives would never touch. *It's those moments of having your lives touch that are so profound that it just feels like we're actually taking down borders in those moments* and that feels really incredible. I've met people who said that they wouldn't have survived if they hadn't met us. [...] I have never found another activist project where *your mere presence in a physical space is radical and revolutionary.* [...] I love that about it. There's just nothing else like it. [emphasis mine]

Nina echoed many of the themes that had surfaced when I spoke with Gail and Lucas. Like her fellow participants, Nina explicitly broached the topic of her privilege and how it normally functioned as a frustrating obstacle— "somebody like me, like white upper-middle class [with] many master's degrees should not necessarily be having a conversation with an undocumented person."

What was striking about this statement, of course, was that up until that point, Nina had, in fact, had many encounters with undocumented people. By her own telling, she had counseled unaccompanied minors on their legal options and mothers on how to feed their families. Certainly, like most other people living in the United States, Nina may have had numerous "conversations" with undocumented people doing menial labor simply by participating in the consumer economy. Her life necessarily touched that of an undocumented person every time she employed or benefited from the services of a housekeeper, a waiter, or a gardener. Why had none of these interactions counted?

Nina's dismissal of her previous interactions with racialized Others is not unusual among white, middle-class women. In examining how white women describe the places that they grew up, Ruth Frankenburg notes that some middle-class respondents narrate an "apparently all-white childhood" although "there were in fact at least one or two people of color not too far away," including the "forgotten and suddenly remembered [Black] domestic worker."[11] Frankenburg suggests that these statements reflect the "conceptual" rather than the "physical distance"[12] that middle-class white women felt, particularly in the context of employer-employee relationships. In Nina's case, that sense of social distance was also contained in the service provider–client relationship, which was also imbalanced. Despite her progressive desires, therefore, Nina's privilege had inhibited "conversations" and meaningful encounters in these contexts.

In the deserts of the border, Nina experienced an enthralling kind of directness, tied up with the strong-state framework. She ascribed the meaningfulness of her activism to the direct, person-to-person interactions, finding them weighty even when it was just a matter of "telling stories to each other" or providing water. The "magical" and indeed, "biblical" quality of these interactions stemmed from the strong-state effect. Every encounter with the third-world migrant seemed to occur under the shadow of a forbidding state. Every encounter occurred *despite* the state.

According to pro-immigrant activists like Nina, the state had transformed Arizona's Sonoran Desert into a weapon against border crossers; for this weapon to be effective, however, the state had to maintain a particular spatial order wherein middle-class, white humanitarian aid workers were kept out of the desert. This meant, to Nina, that she could trouble the state's power simply by being in the places where migrants crossed ("your mere presence in a physical space is radical and revolutionary"). Here, her social biography could serve a purpose that it never had before. Instead of getting in the way of meaningful alliances with disadvantaged groups, her privilege could be a tool in helping lift them up. The strong-state effect actually gave her presence here meaning, and undermining it allowed her to touch the lives of others who strained under its weight—"I've met people who said that they wouldn't have survived if they hadn't met us."

"IT WAS—IS—TOTALLY WORTH IT": RENEE'S STORY

When Renee decided to go organize migrant farmworkers in the late 1990s shortly after she graduated college, her father was appalled. The subject of anxious parents was not an uncommon one among pro-immigrant interlocutors; I soon realized that it was an especially salient topic in interviews with activists of color like Renee, for whom the price of activism felt higher than it was for their white counterparts. Reflecting back on the experience in 2011, Renee, now thirty-five years old and an eleven-year veteran of the Advocates, understood her father's dismay. After all, she was her family's first college graduate. The thirteen-foot sculpture she carved as her final project for her art degree had won a national contest and was eventually acquired by the Smithsonian American Art Museum. The museum even sent a small crew to specially wrap the sculpture for shipping—"these are the same guys who wrap [Thomas] Jefferson's desk," Renee noted with pride.

So her father's assumption that Renee would embark on a more prestigious and professional career than farmworker organizing was not unreasonable. "I graduated magna cum laude. He was very proud," Renee commented. "Then when I started organizing, my dad was just like, '*Magna cum laude* for what?'" Although she did not come from the same kind of well-to-do background as Gail and Nina, like them, Renee was also poised for upward social mobility. Her father had been in the Air Force while her mother was a homemaker. Living on military bases and raising six kids meant household finances were always tight. Attending college had distinguished Renee: "Yeah, out of six kids, I'm the only one that has a college degree and I actually have a master's now [in public administration]," she explained. Renee was aware of the fact that activism disrupted her upward trajectory. "[U]ntil I got married [to a tenured professor], I was the poorest of the six."

All that her parents had done had been aimed at the kind of upward mobility Renee rejected after college. Long before she had acquired a college degree or gained recognition as a skilled artist or gone on to graduate school, Renee told me, her parents had tried to safeguard their children's future success. They urged the siblings to "imagine themselves as belonging to a greater 'American' community . . . that is often framed as racially white."[13] This practice, which might surprise some readers, has been documented by sociologists: racially stigmatized ethnic groups sometimes negotiate their racial self-identification in an effort to achieve inclusion into whiteness. For instance, naturalized immigrants of color may vote for the Republican Party and hold immigration-restrictionist views.[14] Renee continued, "It was like this conscious decision to 'Americanize' the family." Her parents had deliberately not picked traditional Hispanic names for their children. They only spoke English, not Spanish, with their children and tried hard not to sound foreign: "My father told me 'I don't want you to have an accent, because I saw how people with accents are treated.'"

Most importantly, perhaps, Renee's parents tried to cultivate a distinctly Tejano identity in their children, in hopes that deliberate disassociation from Mexican heritage would give them a leg up in American life. Her father chalked up many of his own achievements to his decidedly non-Mexican, Tejano identity, which he had paired with a long career in the Air Force, strong patriotic feelings, and "staunch Republican" ideology. He was firm in boundary making, proudly reminding his children that their grandparents were all from a part of Texas that, depending on the period, had belonged to Mexico, the Republic of Texas, and the United States. While the national borders shifted, the family had never experienced migration. Like other Tejanos, Renee's family thus drew boundaries that allowed them to distinguish themselves from Americans of Mexican origin and, particularly, from Mexican migrants.

Renee's activism was a firm rejection of this version of Americanization, and, in her father's eyes, a rejection of the safety and comfort that this self-identification promised. Renee learned Spanish fluently so that she could work with monolingual immigrant communities, like Mexican farmworkers. She also spent time in activist circles where she began to question her father's unwavering faith in the U.S. government and its military. For instance, Renee recalled how in her early twenties, she was confronted by a friend who talked about the School of the Americas.[15] "I had never heard of that. I was just like, no, somebody must be really confused. The government wouldn't do that. I was very defending the military." And, of course, activism also meant questioning her inherited Tejano identity. In Florida, Renee was dismayed by the sense of superiority that Tejano crew leaders harbored toward Mexican farmworkers. One Tejano worker, who ran a hardware store, had asked directly, "Why are you helping them [migrants]? You should be helping us. What are you doing?" His question felt abrupt and bizarre, "I said, 'What are you even talking about? What do you mean "us," and what do you mean "them"?' Yeah, so that was my awakening." Renee was becoming aware of the connection between being Americanized and being "racist against Mexicans," and soon the identity boundaries with which her parents had raised her seemed "bizarre," too.

Less dramatic than Gail's experience of the workplace raid, Renee's turning point was nonetheless memorable. For both, it was the moment they moved from lesser to greater awareness of the ways that race and citizenship made a difference in people's lives.[16] Experienced as an awakening, this moment was accompanied by a before-and-after narrative.[17] *Before* the turning point, they had believed that there was basic equality. *Before*, they had either not really thought about the role of the United States in the world (Gail) or had believed it to be benign (Renee). *After*,

Gail was shocked by the unforgiving nature of the color, class, and citizenship lines separating herself from her friend. *After*, Renee was stunned by how jealously Tejanos guarded their power over Mexican migrants.

For both women, what came after their turning point was anxiety about their location in the social hierarchy and the extent to which they were complicit in perpetuating inequality. Privilege began to feel like an embarrassing impediment. Indeed, in Renee's case, privilege was an *immediate* obstacle to the task at hand—organizing monolingual, Spanish-speaking workers. As the only Tejano volunteer her farmworker organization had ever had, Renee had no roadmap for how to be a responsible ally to the migrants. Her privilege surfaced in the form of her inability to speak Spanish, her instinctive defense of the U.S. state, and her decidedly, non-Mexican, Tejano identity.

Despite these uncomfortable revelations, Renee gave no indication that this experience—her first time advocating for migrants—was a disappointment of the sort Gail and Nina had experienced. Nor did Renee ever describe feeling the magnetic pull to Arizona. Still, she shared with Nina and Gail and other pro-immigrant activists a restlessness in her turning-point moment. Renee spent a year organizing among the Florida farmworkers before she moved to Arizona. Immediately, she was looking for a group to join and a way to remain politically active.

The costs of her activism included parental disapproval. Renee told me, "There was a lot of fighting with my father, and we finally . . . decided, okay, Thanksgiving, Christmas, we're not going to talk about politics or my activism . . . because it would just be a huge fight." They also included passing up career opportunities and accepting that she was the "poorest" of the six siblings. They required coming to terms with the fact that she had to depend on her husband's income to make ends meet.

Being an Advocate also meant being severely overworked. The Advocates survived on a shoestring budget, a small and underpaid staff, and a *lot* of volunteer labor. It wasn't long before Renee knew the organization would "take over [her] life." Shortly after she was hired as an organizer for the Advocates, the logistics coordinator quit. Renee assumed that position's workload, too. "I took on her job plus my job, and so I became the 'coordinating organizer,'" she said smiling and shaking her head at the blended job titles. "It was—*is*—totally worth it, though," she added quickly.

It was hard *and* she loved it. By the time that I interviewed her, Renee had been with the Advocates for eleven years and could not imagine doing anything else. Just as I had with Gail and Nina, I tried to understand Renee's seemingly bottomless devotion to her activism.

Even though she never used such a word, I realized that for Renee, too, activism at the borderlands took on a sort of magical quality. She perceived the Advocates' actions—and her personal involvement—through the strong-state framework, and that helped her satisfy the conundrum of being progressive, but privileged. Consider her description of the third-world migrant:

> Most of my [undocumented] friends [in Florida] and . . . here in the local communities [of Southern Arizona] have *told me they don't want to be here. They don't*. . . . There was woman once who'd lived here seventeen years. Her elderly mom got sick so she went back [to Mexico] to take care of her. Then, the woman's own daughter was getting married [in the United States], and so she [the bride-to-be's mother] was coming up [from Mexico] to get to [her daughter's] wedding. She never made it. It was really awful, because it was right around that time that I was planning my own wedding. . . . I cannot *imagine* my mother not being there. Imagining like, how do you grieve? . . . *We're creating like these victims of this—it is war.* And, I mean that's how Timothy Dunn defined what's happening on the border. *He calls it 'low-intensity conflict.' It's warfare [against migrants].* I mean *it's really messed up.* So yeah, I look at them [undocumented people] and I'm like, 'Wow, it's *like the same side effects with people that come back from war.' Some of these people live like war refugees.* They have to live in this underground system to get things, to live, to work, to get paid, to cash checks. You know, *it's really sad.* [emphasis mine]

Renee, like her fellow pro-immigrant activists, referred to the movement of Latin American people to the United States as an inherently forced form of migration. Many of her word choices, like *low-intensity conflict* and *warfare*, suggested not only that the U.S. state apparatus was responsible, but also that the harm was *intentional*.

In other words, the state was deliberately and systematically "creating victims" and "war refugees." It *coerced* third-world migrants into leaving their homelands, then engaged in "warfare" against them. As a result, those who crossed the border illegally came to assume the same "side effects" as combat veterans. I noticed a gradual shift in how Renee referred to the subjects in her narrative—"my friends," "a woman," "these victims," and finally, "these people." Discursively, a group of heterogeneous, migrant subjects were transformed into a composite Other object. This homogenizing shift subtly suggested the yawning distance that Renee felt between her own experiences as an agentic, privileged American and those of the third-world migrant (as an object of oppression).

If unauthorized migration was fundamentally an involuntary and oppressive phenomenon, and the state's formidable power was responsible for it, then weakening the state could presumably achieve desirable changes in immigrants' lives. Also, this worldview suggested that privileged Americans might be best positioned to do this kind of state-weakening work. It proposed a meaningful mobilization strategy, one that allowed people like Renee to *exploit* their privilege for good. By fashioning themselves into a protective buffer for migrants, Advocates took the "gift" of privilege and whittled it into a weapon.[18]

"EVERYONE SEEMED LIKE THEY HAD BEEN TRANSFORMED": CHLOE'S STORY

I first met Chloe, a friendly, white woman in her late twenties, in the spring of 2012. We had both signed up to participate in a weeklong pilgrimage that would begin just south of the U.S.-Mexico border and end in Tucson. This annual event was much anticipated among left-wing respondents. Organized by a coalition of faith-based groups and pro-immigrant organizations—including the Advocates and the Humanitarians—the pilgrimage was supposed to give the participants (almost all of whom were American citizens, many white) a limited, but experiential insight into the plight of unauthorized border crossers and to honor migrants who had died while crossing Arizona's Sonoran Desert.[19] Over the course of a week of walking, talking, sharing meals, and praying together, participants got to know each other well and, in my informal conversations, many reported feeling moved by the whole experience.

Two years before we met, Chloe had participated in just the last day of the walk. She remembered, "I felt really inspired by the camaraderie that I sensed. . . . Everyone seemed like they had been transformed." The following year, in 2011, Chloe completed the pilgrimage with two of her students from Michigan, where she was teaching Spanish at a research university as she worked on her PhD in Spanish. By the end of the week, she said, "I had so much to learn. . . . I thought I was so educated, [with] my master's. [But I realized,] 'Oh my God, but I have so much more to learn.'" Her "interest was piqued in terms of immigration."

In many respects, Chloe's narrative reminded me of Nina's. Both were living relatively comfortable middle-class lives when, fortuitously, they ended up in Arizona. There, at the border, they experienced an unexpectedly transformative moment. In its aftermath, neither could shake off the allure of activism in Southern Arizona. Both were willing to forfeit careers and relationships to return. Indeed, when I met her for the first time, Chloe confided she was reconsidering her marriage, her PhD, and her career—in a word, the entire life she had made for herself in the Midwest. After the pilgrimage, she stayed in Arizona for the rest of the summer to volunteer with the Advocates.

Ironically, Chloe's main task as a volunteer seldom yielded the desired results. In that memorable summer, she was assigned to answering a hotline for friends and family members of migrants who had gone missing while crossing the Arizona desert. The hotline came out of the strong-state framework: namely, the state was quietly disappearing people in the desert as part of its deterrence program. The relatives of missing migrants had little recourse, but the hotline might help. It dovetailed neatly the buffering work that the Advocates did to protect migrants from the reach of a formidable state.

Specifically, the Advocates' hotline created liaisons between the person reporting a missing migrant and various authorities, including the medical examiner's office, ICE detention facilities, local law enforcement, and the Border Patrol. In many cases, Chloe explained, the callers themselves might be living in the United States without papers. They were not comfortable calling law enforcement. So the Advocates would use *their* contacts to try and locate a missing border crosser. Chloe would call various detention centers, including the Border Patrol's short-term processing facility where migrants were taken if they were apprehended in the desert. She would try to determine if the individual in question was in custody. If not—as was often the case—the migrant was likely still in the desert, probably lost. This provided at least some information for loved ones without putting them at risk of state-inflicted harm.

Chloe recounted one of the first calls that she took on the hotline that summer. No one had been available to train her because the Advocate who normally answered these calls had had to take leave unexpectedly. More perplexing, however, was that, in this case, the caller was not a border-crosser's friend or family member. It was the missing person himself, who was lost in the desert. Along with the rest of the office staff, Chloe panicked.

"None of us knew what the fuck to do about it. It was awful. I talked to the person, the *actual* missing person," Chloe marveled. On a whim, she reached out to a volunteer with the Humanitarians. They barely knew each other, but Chloe didn't know who else to call: "I just knew that she had more knowledge than I did." Her Humanitarian contact coordinated a search with other volunteers, already in the field, and the makeshift effort was successful. The missing man was found, and he was okay. "It was like, 'Oh my God, this can make a difference! This hotline—this work feels super life-or-death! It has a direct effect!' That was when I knew I had to keep doing this work." This task's immediacy was almost addictive: One moment, Chloe was speaking with a man in distress. The next, her actions had saved him.

In actuality, successful outcomes like this one were extraordinarily rare. The people who were reported missing almost always *stayed* missing. After a decade of calls to the hotline, I learned, there were still over two thousand open cases. Trying to gather the resources needed to locate someone in the vast wilderness is a logistically difficult, if not hopeless, undertaking for anyone, and the only entity with the resources to carry out true search and rescue operations—the U.S. Border Patrol—was untrustworthy and usually uncooperative.

> In most conversations with Border Patrol, you get used to being dismissed pretty regularly. [They say] really heinous things. 'We don't want to waste that gas. We don't want to waste those resources.' I heard that all the time. 'Not enough information to ask our guys to go out. Call back when you have more information.' Sometimes they would say, 'We need coordinates. We're not going to search without point-last-seen.'

In fact, law enforcement seemed so reluctant to help that the Advocates started another project: documenting every instance that the Border

Patrol *refused* to help search for a missing border crosser. The missing migrant hotline thus evolved into one documenting its own *futility*. By the time that I returned to the field in 2017, the Advocates were trying to close down the hotline. Still, it was precisely this task—manning a hotline that seldom yielded successful rescues—that had been instrumental in convincing Chloe to quit her life in Michigan.

Just as with other respondents, I realized that the meaningfulness that Chloe attributed to certain practices over others had little to do with their actual outcomes. Instead, her desire to volunteer was motivated by personal, existential turmoil. After that first internship with the Advocates in 2012, Chloe had been deeply "conflicted" about resuming her life in the Midwest. She volunteered remotely, taking calls about missing migrants. Her body was in Michigan, she told me, but her mind was always at the border: "I kept thinking about these missing people on the border and I kept thinking, you know, 'I *need* to be there. This—my marriage, my PhD, teaching—just *doesn't feel right*. Being here [in Michigan], doing all this just *doesn't feel good*.'" A year later, she acted on her visceral sense: Chloe finalized her divorce, quit her job, withdrew from the PhD program, and moved to Arizona permanently. Her goal was to volunteer with the Advocates for the foreseeable future.

Although Chloe attributed her "political awakening" to the Advocates, it became clear that her worldview had begun to shift during college. This trend, which I observed with other pro-immigrant activists, is in line with previous scholarship about university campuses as sites of white respondents' awakenings to race and inequality.[20] Even though she was raised in predominantly white neighborhoods in Michigan and Arizona, Chloe's life resembled Renee's in important respects. Like Renee, for instance, Chloe was the first person in her politically conservative, working-class family to attend university and, later, graduate school. Chloe's stepfather had a high school education and worked mostly in manufacturing jobs. Her mother, who never finished middle school, worked in retail. The family managed to make a decent living, though, and so it was not surprising to Chloe that the ethics of personal responsibility and patriotism dominated their household.

Once she left for college, Chloe, like Renee, experienced surprise and confusion when she was exposed to a different narrative. Specifically, Chloe began to grow uncomfortably aware of her own privilege, especially what she referred to as the "privilege of my ignorance." In her Spanish classes, she began to learn an unfamiliar story about the United States:

> It felt like I was learning things that felt like truth that was denied to me, you know? I guess it's the liberalization process at college. 'What? Dirty Wars in Argentina? Oh my God. CIA-backed coups in Central America? What the fuck?' So, like, really finding this stuff out. After living in an all-white town of three thousand [in Michigan], thinking that America was somehow this force for good in the world, I felt very indignant and mad about the things that I was learning and mad that it was held from me.

Just like Renee, Chloe was dumbstruck that the United States was involved in unsavory operations abroad, particularly in Latin America.

Chloe's narrative also recalls Renee's discussion of her parents' deliberate efforts to Americanize (read: whiten) their children. Even though she never mentioned "Americanization," Chloe also linked her ignorance to a particular kind of racial identity and upbringing—specifically, the experience of "living in an all-white town of three thousand." This racially homogenous environment had allowed Chloe to unquestioningly accept that "America was somehow this force for good in the world." It had allowed for the privilege of ignorance. And as it had for Renee, learning Spanish became a path by which she might challenge her upbringing. In fact, Spanish was the subject of Chloe's college major, master's degree, and her aborted PhD.

Particularly through her "liberalization process at college," Chloe shared a lot with other pro-immigrant respondents. She majored in the social sciences, completing a degree in political science, like Nina and Gail. She used college as an opportunity to travel to Latin America, like Gail and Lucas. She became uncomfortably aware of inequality *as well as* her own advantages in life, like all of the activists we've met thus far. And she became restless.

Chloe was grappling with questions about how to be a responsible ally when she showed up to walk the last leg of the pilgrimage. In a sense, the dilemma of being progressive but privileged had primed her to feel transformed by the experience as my other respondents had. Later, she further internalized the organization's analysis about the formidable nature of state power. Weakening the state at the border gave Chloe a way to come to terms with who she was.

CONCLUSION

Although it may seem that social movements exist in order to bring about change in the world (or, in some cases, preserve the status quo), I found that pro-immigrant mobilization was sustained by something entirely different. In fact, if one were to put together a ledger with "participant input" on one side and "social movement output" on the other, the resulting accounting would be lopsided. When my left-wing respondents joined the Advocates and the Humanitarians, they *suffered* and *sacrificed* for their activism. The rate of return seemed negligible.

The "participant input" side of the ledger was replete with stories of pain, misery, and forfeited opportunities. Interlocutors like Nina, Chloe, and Renee, at various times, reported severe burnout. One person I came to know very well routinely experienced nervous breakdowns during which she could not leave her bedroom for a week at a time. Others mentioned secondary trauma accrued through their sustained contact with distressed migrants and their families.

Less immediately, respondents were relinquishing upward social mobility for the chance to be active on the border. Left-wing activists declined professional trajectories, economic stability, and, in some cases, relationships in favor of economic uncertainty and alienation from their loved ones. At the conclusion of an interview, one pro-immigrant activist half-laughingly remarked how her mother "really wishes I was in grad school right now." Her comment was an apt reminder of the middle-class expectations that left-wing respondents in this study grew up with (and which distinguished them from their right-wing counterparts). Pro-immigrant respondents were upwardly mobile. When they joined the Humanitarians and the Advocates, some measure of sacrifice, of opportunity cost, filled the "participant input" side of the ledger.

The "social movement output" side, meanwhile, was sparse. The first time that Chloe coordinated a search, the missing border crosser was ultimately rescued. Making this life-or-death difference was exactly why Chloe had signed up for activism at the border. But the serendipitous outcome she saw in her first call was exceedingly rare—so rare, in fact, that Chloe and other hotline volunteers had adopted a new project documenting the *ineffectiveness* of such searches. Similarly, Gail conceded the possibility that the Humanitarians' day-to-day practices were not a viable solution, but a haphazard, stopgap measure. Their work was barely a drop in the bucket, yet Chloe and Gail remained deeply devoted to their activism. The input/output analogy thus falls short of explaining what makes some types of mobilization attractive to prospective recruits.

This chapter has illustrated that what drove pro-immigrant activists to the border and what sustained them despite the difficulties that they encountered was a particular kind of conflictual identity. The tension with which left-wing participants grappled was the dilemma of being progressive but privileged. This dilemma was usually narrated around an event that served as a turning point. In their inner conflict, pro-immigrant respondents came to feel the kind of moral obligation that Camila and Gary touched upon in the chapter's opening. However, the harmonious coexistence of progressivism and privilege Camila and Gary cited eluded my respondents—until they arrived in Arizona's borderlands and learned their privilege could be a weapon against the state. At the border, activists posited that they had the power to intervene where others—particularly the third-world migrant—could not.

Among my left-wing respondents, therefore, the strong-state effect created a hopeful sense. It provided a progressive outlet for their status. The dispensation of humanitarian aid, for instance, was meaningful in that it was a *state-directed tactic*. The relevance, in individuals' risk-reward calculus, of both participants' backgrounds and their perceptions of the state suggests that we need to rethink conventional analyses of pro-immigrant mobilization in the United States.

Scholars have extensively documented the popularity of moral frames in pro-immigrant activism, but this chapter has anchored these frames within a particular intersectional identity. In this study, the idea of moral obligation did not resonate with everyone; it resonated with a *specific* social group (white middle-class people, particularly women) whose members shared clear patterns of life experiences. Being progressive but privileged made these participants receptive to the idea that they had a moral duty, and a certain way of seeing the state—the strong-state effect—resolved the tension that their identity posed. Thus, our analysis of pro-immigrant mobilization is incomplete without considering the *kinds* of selves that are attracted to this kind of activism. It is also incomplete without considering the odd ambiguity of the borderlands as a site that produces variegated conceptions of state power. This relationship between identity management and state-directed action is not unique to pro-immigrant activists. As the next chapter shows, it also emerges among right-wing, restrictionist activists.

3 Being White, but Working Class

When I asked Rick, a longtime restrictionist activist, why he was committed to his volunteer work in Arizona, he replied, "You know, I'm more at peace here, doing this, than I've ever been in my life." Rick was a fifty-seven-year-old white man from California and a U.S. Marines Corps veteran. We were in the middle of the vast wilderness of the Arizona-Sonora border, a few miles north of the U.S.-Mexico border. I thought his answer was both revealing and puzzling. It was revealing because I knew that Rick was not exaggerating. Indeed, I had heard some version of this answer from numerous other restrictionists: there was, they kept telling me, something deeply satisfying about this kind of activism.

At the same time, there was also still something puzzling about this positive characterization. I had been struck by how much physical hardship Rick and the other members of his group, the Soldiers, faced out in the desert. My field notes over the years were peppered with long descriptions of the relentless heat of the day, the bone-chilling cold that came at night, and how wrung-out I felt after even short day trips into the wilderness. "Why do it?" I kept wondering.

The participants' shared positive feelings seemed all the odder given the question of how much their activism *actually* achieved. The Soldiers, like Rick, conceded that their presence in the desert hardly deterred people from crossing the border. That their collective action was not very effective was admitted not only by the Soldiers, but by the other two grassroots restrictionist groups that I studied. The Arpaiositos knew that, despite their best efforts to support cooperation between local law enforcement and immigration authorities, undocumented people would continue to live and work in Phoenix. And the Engineers, confronted by technological bottlenecks, on the one hand, and ambivalence from the media and politicians, on the other, always harbored uncertainty about whether all their work would amount to anything.

In this regard, restrictionism oddly resembled pro-immigrant activism: the actual, external impact of mobilization was only a (small) part of what sustained group members' motivation. People participated for other reasons. As the previous chapter began to illustrate, the meaningfulness that participants ascribed to their collective action stemmed more from how these practices made border activists *feel about themselves* than their by-the-numbers efficacy. That is, no matter where they stood on the political spectrum, activism on the ambiguous border helped participants manage conflictual identities. Collective action allowed volunteers to come to terms with their positions in society.

That said, the dilemma restrictionists struggled with was significantly different from the one that troubled their pro-immigrant opponents. While pro-immigrant activists struggled with being progressive but privileged, restrictionists grappled with being *white but working class*. The average restrictionist hailed from a far more socioeconomically humble background than the average pro-immigrant activist. While pro-immigrant activists wondered what to do with all their power and privilege, restrictionists wondered where theirs had gone.

Just as a typology emerged out of the life histories of pro-immigrant activists, so too does such an ideal-type narrative show through in my interviews with restrictionists. Once again, the climactic moment in their narrative arc was the appearance of a conflictual identity. Restrictionists tried to make sense of the disparity between the in-group status and power they associated with their whiteness (particularly as men) and the sense of disorder and lack of control that accompanied their experience of downward mobility.

Economic insecurity, uncertainty about the future, and generalized anxieties riddled their life stories. Restrictionist respondents returned, again and again, to an acute sense of having lost control over their lives.[1] When their downward mobility was paired with a sense of white entitlement, it produced confusion, anxiety, and deep racial resentment. One scholar deftly summarizes this disjuncture: "[W]hite working class people sense that they have been demoted from the center of their country's consciousness to its fringe. . . . [M]any feel powerless in their attempts to do something about it."[2]

However, my respondents *did* do something about it. Activism at the border presented a resolution to—or, at least, a way to cope with—being relegated from society's center to its periphery. Their feeling of demotion was productive because it created an acute desire for control that restrictionists channeled into their work at the border.

These life histories illustrate a pattern: that a particular perception of state power helped restrictionists manage the dilemma of being white but working class. Specifically, the shared understanding that the state was vulnerable—what I call the "weak-state effect"—transformed the border into a particularly powerful "frontier" for action. These men (and the occasional woman) found consequence in their presence at the borderlands; they saw themselves as sacrificing to prop up a state overwhelmed by the third-world migrant. In a sense, restrictionists projected their own feelings of powerlessness onto the state. Then, by working on the state— by using creativity, skill, and teamwork to try to close the gaps that they identified in the state's power—restrictionists effectively worked on themselves. As they empowered the state, they felt empowered. Strengthening the state brought some certainty, agency, and even a sense of peace into their lives.

FINDING PEACE ON THE BORDER: RICK'S STORY

Rick told me that his initial interest in immigration politics had been sparked on a specific day. It was late 2008 when he realized that his world was falling apart. That day, Rick went to work, expecting to dive right back into the project that he had been working on. His job, he explained, was to build high rises and tunnels. He had been in the construction business for nearly three decades.

> I was the guy who they handed the blueprint this thick [holds his index finger and thumb wide apart] six months before the building even came out of the ground. "Here's your next job; learn it. You've got six months." That was my job: to study this thing from top to bottom and to have to write letters to architects, engineers, and mechanical engineers and plumbers—"why are we doing it this way" and so forth. So that, by the time we were ready to go, we'd be ready to go.

Rick enjoyed the challenges of his job, and he was very proud of what he accomplished. His work entailed tasks that not everyone could perform.

> I built up my stock in myself: I was worth forty or forty-five dollars an hour because not many people want that task. On a thirty-story building, I can be one-eighth of an inch out, per floor, and overall, over the thirty stories, I could only be out two and a half inches. It takes a lot to put up a building. It was a lot of responsibility, and I thrived on it.

But on that fateful day in 2008, when he got to the office, Rick realized that nobody was there apart from some administrative staff. Many of his colleagues had been laid off that morning. "I mean, we weren't even finished with the building yet. [The project] collapsed. They pulled the plug on the money." When the Great Recession took hold of the economy, Rick was in one of the hardest-hit states, Arizona, and one of the hardest hit industries, construction.[3] When he lost his job, Rick was forty-eight years old. To make his mortgage payments, Rick would have to travel the country, taking temporary stints. Two weeks here, three weeks there—often "pounding nails" and making the same wage he had when he was eighteen. Rick said he went from making $80,000 a year to $12,000 on unemployment. He lost his home. He began living out of his car. He started drinking after years of sobriety. His life felt like it was spiraling out of control.

It was not the first time Rick felt like he was losing a grip over his life. He grew up in an abusive household. Rick shared vivid accounts of his father's violent drunkenness, of how he and his brothers were beaten viciously. It drove Rick to alcohol and drugs as a teenager; he did not quit until he got behind the wheel, decades later, and nearly drove his car into a semi. His brush with death was, he later decided, a suicide attempt, a desperate call for help. Rick spent the following year in a sober living facility. Eventually, he started a job that gave him a sense of purpose and built up his feelings of self-worth. Building high rises and tunnels became his salvation. And then, without any notice, he was laid off.

During the subsequent three years, scraping together a meager living, Rick began noticing that no matter how hard he tried, he could never get back up on his feet. He *had* to foreclose on his home. He *had* to settle for low-paying jobs. He *had* to live with the uncertainty of short-term work. Making things worse, he always had to compete for these bad jobs with "Mexicans." Rick began connecting the dots in his head: maybe the reason he was having such a hard time was because there was an endless supply of obsequious "illegal aliens" willing to accept lower wages for bad working conditions. Maybe *that's* why Rick felt like someone had pulled the rug out from under his feet.

Going to the border—first alone, and later, with growing numbers of people—was a way for Rick to regain control over his life. He wanted *to do* rather than be *done to*. And this border work felt consequential. As his border group grew, it reminded him of how he felt when he was responsible for transforming a blueprint into a sound, brick-and-mortar structure. Rick's group had seven core members, but two dozen or more regularly turned up for bimonthly, weeklong operations—the "ops" they organized. The volunteers came from around the country.

When I was with Rick, the op only had seven people. More volunteers were expected later in the week. "But just with those seven people," he explained, "I've closed about five miles of some of their [the cartel's] best stuff [smuggling corridors.] So with twenty-four to thirty [volunteers], I can close up to fifteen miles of the border. And I mean close it, where nothing—not people, not drugs—comes through." Gesturing at the mountainous landscape behind him, Rick continued:

> I mean, look at this terrain. It's nothing but mountain after mountain after mountain. They [the cartel] want to be in this stuff [the mountainous terrain, where they can hide]. They don't want to be in the flat stuff. . . . So we force them into there [the flatter areas] where it's easier to be found and caught [by the Border Patrol].

Just as with pro-immigrant activism, I realized that the actual impact and efficacy of restrictionist activism was questionable. After all, Rick and his group's efforts may have forced the smugglers to move, but it would be hard to argue they actually deterred anyone from trying to cross the international boundary. How could the border be secured at this rate? Did it really take two motivated, dedicated volunteers to secure a single border mile? I asked Rick about my sense that the work was futile, and he responded gruffly, "Then I guess I'll die here. Everybody makes a choice in life about what they do."

I also wondered about the Border Patrol's stance on restrictionist groups. The federal agency never publicly acknowledged the help from Rick's group. In fact, the Border Patrol's official position had always been mild discouragement. They didn't seem to want civilian border-watch groups assembling on the border. Rick nodded:

> Yes, publicly, they [the agency] disavow[s] us. But, when they're down here, they [agents] will stop in and ask you, "What you got? What's happening?" It's an interesting thing. They love us because we're helping them do their job, and we're not even getting paid. I actually *pay* to do this. It's just a decision people have to make on their own.

After a pause, Rick said, "You know, I'm more at peace here, doing this, than I've ever been in my life."

Rick had overcome tremendous challenges: a childhood filled with physical abuse and family dysfunction, the sudden end to a fulfilling career, the uncertainties and economic frustrations of underemployment, the loss of a home, alcohol abuse and drug addiction, divorce and separation from his children. Through it all, he was plagued by a general sense of marginalization. And so, in many respects, Rick's life history could not have been more different from the average, middle-class pro-immigrant participant, who more frequently *relinquished* opportunities for upward mobility to take up activism. For Rick, such opportunities were few and far apart. The feeling of defeat, however, was frequent, omnipresent. The frustration of setbacks, the overwhelming sense of helplessness—all that adversity, and here Rick was, a middle-aged man who said he finally felt "at peace."

Still, I could not overlook the deep racism and sense of white entitlement that colored Rick's worldview. He felt that there were things in life—like jobs, status, and security—that rightfully belonged to *him* and other Americans like him. To Rick's mind, "American" was an identity that was firmly attached to white male bodies. This in-group racial status suggested he felt he was owed certain opportunities in life. But the structural pressures of class, accentuated in the recession, made it feel more and more like he was being deprived of his birthright. The combination of class disadvantage and historic racial privilege generated resentment.

More than a century earlier, sociologist Émile Durkheim had anticipated the kind of self-understanding and feelings that Rick was describing to me. Durkheim discusses how economic disasters can violently unhinge people from their places in society, drive them into a "situation below" without a moment's pause to adjust their self-expectations. The profound suffering that results is enough to drive some to suicide.

> Indeed, in the event of economic disaster, there is something like a "declassification" which suddenly casts certain individuals into a situation below that which they previously occupied. They consequently have to lower their demands, to restrict their needs and learn to restrain themselves more. . . . But it is not possible for society to subject them to this new life instantaneously, and teach them to exercise this additional restraint on themselves when they are not accustomed to it. The outcome is that they are not adjusted to the condition that they occupy and the very prospect of it is intolerable to them. Hence the sufferings.[4]

Notably, Durkheim was thinking about the captains of industry rather than those who toiled on the factory floors.[5] These powerful men could not adjust themselves to their newly bounded horizons, to the experience of sudden failure.

Rick, while definitely not a modern-day Henry Ford, was socialized in a country in which men like him historically had significant material and symbolic advantages over everyone else. The wages of whiteness created a set of expectations about how American society should function, including who should get first pick at good jobs (and who shouldn't); who should be able to use public facilities like hospitals and schools (and who shouldn't); and, more generally, who the public should celebrate (and shouldn't).[6] No wonder Rick was devastated and confused when class pressures began bearing down on him. To be white but working class meant feeling like he was owed power, but also powerless to do anything about being denied that power. Rather than channeling that dilemma into self-harm, Rick channeled it into the border, into feeling strong by strengthening the state.

Thus, the weak-state effect helped Rick assume a sense of control and manage his conflictual identity. Where pro-immigrant respondents saw the third-world migrant as *victim*, restrictionists saw the same migrant as a mighty *victimizer* emboldened by a weak line of defense. Rick demonstrated his sense of mastery here as he explained to me that cross-border migration persisted because there were not enough Border Patrol agents amassed at the U.S.-Mexico boundary, and those who were there weren't there often enough to gain any real mastery of the terrain: "So if you don't get them [migrants] at the line, you're losing x percentage every hour." He continued to tell me that when migrants weren't stopped right at the border, detection became all but impossible, "because ten miles north of the border, there are two hundred places that they could be." Rick lamented that even when the Soldiers called Border Patrol, having seen twenty "drug mules" on their cameras, the response was, "'Okay, we'll be there in two hours.' Okay, now you're two hours behind. . . . And then it gets dark, 'Well, we can't see them. We're going to wait till morning.'" And when agents couldn't find the crossers the next day, Rick said, they would give up.

The Soldiers' tactics were shaped by these logics. Their operations were within a mile or two of the boundary and involved round-the-clock stakeouts. Teams of two men would wait at designated observation posts for forty-eight hours before being relieved, with locations determined by "intel" (camera footage collected in the weeks prior to the "op"). With pride, the Soldiers often told me that Border Patrol field agents genuinely appreciated this extra intel. In fact, one agent was trying to set up a meeting between Rick and the local sector chief. At this conference, Rick hoped to "let them know that we can help, even a couple of percent to get them to be more efficient." The idea that he could help the state restored a sense of purpose to Rick's life. Shoring up the state in this manner counteracted the deprivation, and finally made him feel "at peace" in his white-but-working-class life.

"FREEDOM AND POSSIBILITY" ON THE BORDER:
CONNOR'S STORY

The desire for agency compelled Connor, too. Restrictionist activism turned out to be a kind of deliverance for the forty-year-old former National Guard member as he navigated economic uncertainty. The first time Connor had patrolled the border region in Arizona, it was with the Guard, and he had been ambivalent about border politics. Connor was from Southern California, and had joined the National Guard at eighteen. It was, he said, a "perfect" arrangement, allowing him to work one weekend a month as an infantryman and spend the rest of the time on his passion—computers.

Connor spent his twenties moving up the ranks of the U.S. Army (to E4) while also moving up the ranks of a computer company in Santa Cruz, California (he was eventually promoted to IT manager). As he began to see a lucrative future in computer technology, he felt like he was following his father's footsteps. Then, as he was nearing his thirties, his National Guard unit was activated. Connor was deployed to Fort Huachuca, a U.S. Army installation about fifteen miles north of the Arizona-Mexico border. He spent a lot of time on the Huachuca Mountains doing "perimeter security" for the army base and worked his tech job remotely. Connor recalled watching in disbelief as groups of people he believed were migrants walked through the Arizona mountains: "We're on base, you know. What are these people doing here? This is *our* intelligence center; this is *our* signal command! They shouldn't be here! So, I thought that was interesting." Still, it was a peaceful period for the U.S., and Connor remembered, "I didn't really form any opinions about it," adding, "I didn't like the idea that it was happening, but I didn't get all crazy political about it."

What did make him "crazy political" was September 11, 2001. The stock market was already starting to show disturbing trends in 2000, Connor recalled. The 9/11 attacks were "the final nail in the coffin." The dotcom bubble, which had propelled his California-based computer company to unprecedented success, finally, truly burst. The company shut down.

Connor was startled by how quickly his life plans became irrelevant. Like Rick, he was devastated to find himself in a "situation below." "This brutal economic disaster, for me . . . was just a fall from grace. A *massive* fall from grace." Connor grew depressed, avoiding family and friends, stewing in a mixture of shame, anger, and resentment. "I didn't really have any life to go back to in Santa Cruz," he told me, so he stayed in Arizona.

In 2003, still trying to figure out what to do with his life and working "odd jobs," Connor happened to see a news clip about border security. The clip featured Phil, a leader of a small restrictionist group called the Engineers, discussing the need for technological improvement in border enforcement. Intrigued, Connor reached out.

At the time that I was interviewing him, the Engineers had encountered a severe technological bottleneck and Connor was frustrated. Because their work was on hold, Connor agreed to talk to me. We planned for an hour, but we talked for three. Our conversation seemed to be a welcome distraction for Connor, who reminded me—and himself—that interruptions and delays were normal when tinkering with technology. He admitted that, even if the technical aspects of the project worked out, it remained unclear whether the final product would ever catch the public's notice. Still, Connor loved being a member of the Engineers.

Connor's dedication was evident. In 2011, he was attending paramedic school and doing clinical work in a Southern Arizona border town. All his remaining time was spent at a border ranch that Phil had acquired and was using as a laboratory-cum-testing ground for the Engineers' technological prototypes. To explain his commitment, Connor described a more usual pathway for someone with his interests: "I mean, you go work for Lockheed [Martin, a defense contractor], it's going to be twenty years before you're in charge of anything, and pretty much you're going to be bowing down to everybody else's wishes. Somebody from the top is going to tell you this is what *they* want."

Connor had experienced decision-making power as an IT manager. He knew what it was like to be in charge. Thus, the prospect of "bowing down to everyone else's wishes" while waiting, potentially for years, before "you're in charge of anything" was unappealing. Joining the Engineers could mean having the freedom to steer its projects:

> [As an Engineer], I'm not just working on other people's projects, I work on my projects, you know. The other Engineers and I discuss different ideas, "Let's try this." "Let's do it." Then, BAM! We have a UAV [unmanned aerial vehicle]! We have ground sensors! We have passive infrared sensors! . . . It

was just the *freedom* and *possibility* of developing something really, really cool, like we have now. And working on really neat technology and *then being in charge of it.*

Connor enjoyed reassuming the meaningful pursuits that had accompanied his old job. Against the background of his old company's bankruptcy, the Engineers offered redemption. He felt like he could face his family again. "Now I have a patent in my name for something that is possibly going to secure the U.S.-Mexico border if the politics don't kill it." Being an Engineer, for Connor, was a welcome salve for the pain of downward mobility.

Connor's racial anxieties grew more pronounced as he became more involved in the group's efforts to have a hand in securing the border. He reevaluated his experiences through a prism of white entitlement. Recalling how he'd seen people he assumed were drug mules in the mountains when he was on the Army base, he articulated the memory with vehemence: "This is *our* intelligence center, this is *our* signal command! They shouldn't be here!" He was reassessing his encounters with racialized bodies during his clinical work at a medical facility in a border town, too.

> I can't remember one person that came in that had insurance. None of them spoke English. A lot of them live across the line [in Mexico], and they come there and get free service, because [hospitals] have to [accept them]. . . . There was a guy yesterday, a Mexican gentleman, seventy-six years old, I think. No insurance. Had [a heart attack]. Flew him to [a hospital in a nearby city]. So right there, with the medications and the treatment he got in the hospital, [the cost] was probably upwards of two or three thousand dollars, and then he took a . . . twenty-thousand-dollar helicopter ride, where . . . they're going to put stents in. . . . How much does that ultimately cost? Well, at the end of care, probably close to a hundred thousand . . . that won't be paid, because he doesn't have insurance or anything. He most likely came across the line to get seen. . . . Everybody knows that you can go to the hospital and be treated whether you have insurance or not.

Connor could not have known a patient's legal or health insurance status by simply looking at them, but he *assumed* that the racialized bodies that he treated were "Mexicans" and therefore, undeserving patients. That the patient had experienced a life-threatening medical event, survived, and undergone a procedure that may have lengthened the man's life was not a feat of modern medicine but a costly waste—care given to an undeserving, nonwhite body. As Connor steeped in restrictionist activism, latent racial anxieties bubbled to the surface. The figure of the third-world migrant-qua-victimizer gained sharper focus:

> These people are coming in and working odd jobs for low wages, whether it be in the fields or construction, and no insurance. . . . They're living in less than middle-class conditions, and therefore those neighborhoods bring crime . . . those children are going out and getting involved in . . . Mexican gangs, things like that. The immigration problem has fingers that stretch all over society. But ultimately, it's like in your house. You don't want people walking in and out of your house, so you don't want people walking in and out of the country.

Activism allowed Connor to come to terms with the white-but-working-class dilemma, but in a more generalized manner. Although he never directly linked racist ideas to his own personal economic troubles, as Rick had, Connor was nonetheless overcome by a feeling of deprivation. How could America be experiencing so much hardship? He had been unfairly stripped of a life that he planned for himself, and other Americans (meaning white men) were also being unfairly stripped of the kinds of lives they had imagined for themselves—lives in which there was no shortage of medical resources, neighborhoods were safe, and well-paying, meaningful jobs were plentiful. His was a more generalized feeling of deprivation, but it was still tethered to white entitlement. Connor projected the condition of being white but working class onto American society as a whole.

Mobilizing in response to the weak-state effect, helped restore Connor's sense of agency. Like Rick, Connor blamed the problem of migration and smuggling on a feeble state, though Connor believed the weakness wasn't caused by agents' shift system and locations, but rather the state's incompetent use of technology. Although the Border Patrol had sophisticated technologies, like ground sensors, surveillance towers, and self-guided drones, which generated data about the environment, it simply had no way of analyzing this data accurately in real time. "They have eleven thousand sensors in the ground, and they have a ninety-five percent false alarm rate," Connor explained. As a result, the agency could not deploy its personnel strategically. The Engineers were developing a device that could address these shortcomings:

> Deter them before they've even crossed the line. Make it so they don't want to come across. I mean, if you shadow them [while they're still on the Mexican side] with your lights on in your truck or you send a helicopter and say "I see you," they're not going to even attempt [to cross]. . . . I mean, if they know that they've been seen, they're not going to try and run in and evade the Border Patrol.

He continued, with obvious excitement, claiming that their device would provide "seamless coverage for the entire U.S.-Mexico Border." He said developing tech like this was *"what made it really neat working with the Engineers, because I could use my ideas and I didn't have to ask anybody"* [emphasis mine]. For Connor, the state bungled technology and squandered resources. Working on a solution to this problem empowered Connor. The weak-state effect gave him an opportunity to come to terms with the friction between his racial entitlement and his downward mobility.

PROTECTING HIS FAMILY FROM "MEXICO": DAVID'S STORY

David felt content when he worked on the border. A seventy-three-year-old white man, David had had a meaningful career in the Air Force as an airplane mechanic. He recalled how he first laid eyes on a black B57: "I had never been in love with anything in my life." He waxed rhapsodic: "I fell in love with that aircraft, and I fell in love with that career field. I stayed in it for forty years. Forty years of working on great airplanes." By the time the recession hit in 2008, David had been retired for several years, living in a modest, but comfortable, two-bedroom rental with his wife. He enjoyed bow hunting and attending church. When we met in 2011, David was also going out on reconnaissance missions with the Soldiers on a weekly basis. He told me that he loved the desert, that he wished he could spend more time patrolling it. But just as I had been with Rick and Connor, I grew puzzled by David's dedication to volunteering.

There were many factors that, at first blush, should have made David lose interest in the Soldiers. He did not have any friends in the organization (any camaraderie he needed came from hunting and his faith community) and, oftentimes, he voiced suspicion about other members' dedication to the group's goals. His time with the Soldiers had gotten off to a rather rocky start: on his very first patrol, David skidded on some loose gravel and fell on his back. He was bedridden for nearly a year. And yet, as soon as he was able to stand without excruciating pain, David returned to desert patrols. David did not follow the news and only had a vague sense of which political figures—locally or nationally—he agreed and disagreed with.[7] Politics, in the most mainstream sense, did not seem to interest him, and he had never actually discovered a border crosser. That adrenaline-inducing moment—delivering a supposed person of interest to the Border Patrol—was what I'd assumed sustained members' dedication, but David personally had no such encounters. He explained why that was a good thing: it meant that the Soldiers were actually deterring crossers. Nonetheless, I was surprised that the seemingly distant nature of the group's objective did not dampen his motivation.

What brought him back out into the desert? His dead stepsons, he told me. His comment stopped me cold. We were seated in a bustling diner and a bouncy waitress had just finished taking our lunch orders. His weighty response seemed surreally out of place inside the airy and otherwise forgettable diner. "I still see them dead in my dreams," he continued as tears welled in his eyes. "They died all because they wanted to be Mexican and do drugs and get rich. My wife and I cry everyday over it."

After a few shaky breaths, David told me how immigration and drug trafficking from Mexico had led to a number of family tragedies. David's wife was a naturalized U.S. citizen of Mexican descent. When they married, he adopted her three U.S.-born children. As teenagers, David's two stepsons were killed in separate incidents, one during a drug transaction and the other shot to death by his Latina girlfriend, who was high on cocaine.

David was anguished and felt he should have done more to protect his sons. He hadn't known how, even though there were clear warning signs that the boys were headed toward disaster. As they became teenagers, the boys were increasingly obstreperous. They decided to "become Mexican" and renounce an "American" (read: white) identity. They wore baggy pants and T-shirts. They refused to take school authority seriously and their grades suffered. They peppered their rebellion against their stepfather with hurtful comments about his whiteness. According to David, "the kids that they were running with, all believed in *la Raza*: 'We're Mexicans. We do not have to belong, or socialize with whites.' They don't like Mexican women who marry white men." David was a target for his sons' anti-white feelings.

To David's mind, all this—the anti-whiteness, the drug habits—could be chalked up to the boys' interactions with Mexican kids. David and his wife tried desperately to talk some sense into the boys. When they failed, they enlisted their pastor's help. When that failed, the couple began contemplating moving to another neighborhood—even out of Arizona, to some non-border state—to lessen the boys' exposure to these bad influences. They didn't move because they couldn't afford to move.

Now, David mourned. He believed he had failed to repress the boys' "Mexican nature," thereby ensuring their untimely demise. "My two sons got stupid and used their race to get them murdered," David said bluntly. First, they began associating with "Mexicans," with morally questionable habits. Then, the boys began using drugs and dropped out of school. Soon, they were selling drugs and aspiring to careers in the drug trade. And David had not been able to stop any of it.

Despite being part of a biracial family, David understood his loved ones through a framework wherein racialized people are good so long as they can "bracket" or "ignore" their "coloredness." Only then could they let "the virtue—of a 'noncolored'—or white—self" emerge.[8] For example, he contrasted his stepsons' tragic fates with his stepdaughter's success, saying that she "never used her race," and so she managed to forge a happy and successful life. Steering clear of drugs and crime, she put herself through college, pursued a career in business, and married a nice man with whom she had a daughter.

Nonetheless, a racialized subjectivity still threatened to upset the harmony of her culturally white and, therefore "morally pure" existence. On his last visit with his stepdaughter, David told me, his teenage step-granddaughter had said she was "Mexican." David tried to correct her, saying that she was first and foremost an American. He asked her to say the

Pledge of Allegiance, emphasizing the line about "one Nation under God." Unconvinced, she had humored him. David felt sad and helpless: "I wonder about [her] ... if she's doing drugs, 'cuz they tell you they're Mexican. But then again, who knows?" David's racial anxieties were right on the surface as he described his granddaughter's unwillingness to embrace her whiteness. He feared for her future.

Like any grieving parent, David was tormented: perhaps he could have done more to protect his sons. However, he experienced his remorse through the white-but-working-class lens. He was frustrated that he had lacked the economic means to help his stepsons repress their deviant "Mexican nature" and let their purer, white American selves flourish. As David expressed anguish about having failed to "whiten" his boys, he also drew on the racist idea that racialized bodies can contaminate white bodies.

He tortured himself with the ways he could have distanced his boys from "Mexicans": He could have moved his family to a better (read: whiter) neighborhood. He could have sent his kids to a better (read: whiter) school. He could have disciplined his kids as soon as they started expressing an unpatriotic (read: non-white) identity. He could have put more physical distance between his children and the source of dangerous otherness—Mexico. Many years after their deaths, David mulled over a thousand things he could have done differently. That financial constraints had kept him from making his family "fully white" was a demonstration of his white-but-working-class dilemma.

David's self-torment began to let up when he joined the Soldiers. Patrolling the border, David discovered, allowed him to make peace with himself. Indeed, even a severe back injury would not keep him away from it. Now he could directly protect against Mexican incursions like the ones he believed had claimed his children.

Restrictionist activism was empowering because David, like Connor and Rick, associated the state with vulnerability. The Border Patrol appeared overwhelmed, and, when Brian Terry, an agent, was killed in a firefight with suspected undocumented border crossers in Peck Canyon (eleven miles north of the border), that sealed it for David. "I joined after Terry was shot and killed. My God," he remembered ruefully. It was not only the outcome of the fight that was significant—an American agent was killed, while the crossers, suspected to be Mexican, eluded capture—but also the way the fight had unfolded. As agents fired non-lethal beanbag guns, the crossers responded with real bullets. In 2012, other pieces of what was known as the "Fast and Furious" scandal were coming to light. The guns that the crossers had used to shoot the agents were part of a "gunwalking" operation: The U.S. Bureau of Alcohol, Tobacco, Firearms and Explosives (ATF) had permitted illegal gun sales in an effort to track straw buyers connected to Mexican drug cartels. In addition to losing track of hundreds of firearms and failing to capture any organized crime leaders, ATF's botched operation was believed to have resulted in the death of a Border Patrol agent.[9]

For David, the "Fast and Furious" scandal revealed the state's weakness and incompetence. Now everyone could see that the state undertook risky operations that put frontline protectors in danger. The state was bound by unreasonable protocols—like assigning agents defensive rather than tactical weaponry. And all this while, the third-world migrant was all but allowed to cross the border and wreak havoc. The state needed help defending the border, and the Soldiers answered the call.

To David, monitoring the border felt like atonement, a way to gain a second chance. The color line that he had failed to police effectively in his own household could be policed in the deserts of Southern Arizona. He could not change the past, but he could, in a small way, protect other families. "I don't like the drug part [of immigration]. I hate it. Look at what happened to my children. What about other people's children?" To David's mind, the misfortunes his family experienced were inextricably tied to racialized otherness seeping in from Mexico. When the government failed to secure the border—the ultimate color line—it was a deadly mistake. David believed that he was taking back a little bit of control in a world where racialized dangers threatened to upend the lives of white Americans.

THOSE WHO WORK, THOSE WHO DON'T: MARY'S STORY

Mary was a charismatic and outgoing fifty-nine-year-old white woman from a suburb in Southern California, and again, I was confused as to her motivations. Why was she an active participant in a restrictionist organization?

Mary had joined the Arpaiositos during a lull in its activities. The group had undergone a number of transitions over the years. What had started out as a loose association protesting informal day laborers eventually shifted into a group ensuring that the ranks of the Maricopa County Sheriff's Office (MCSO) posse were filled with enthusiastic enforcers. For reasons detailed more fully in chapter 7, the Arpaiositos had tired of MCSO posse work, and they were exploring other ways to support Maricopa County's restrictionist sheriff, Joe Arpaio, when Mary joined.

In this period, the Arpaiositos met often, and for long periods of time, without necessarily making any decisions about what they should do. I was struck, in the first few gatherings that I attended, by how disorderly and chaotic the meetings felt. Members talked loudly over each other. Discussions frequently spiraled away from the matters at hand. People made obscure references that not everyone understood. Members would arbitrarily call a group vote, but that vote would have no bearing on later meetings. Mary confided in me that she had initially felt really "bored" with the group. But she had patiently weathered the boredom, confusion, and general disorganization to emerge as one of the most active Arpaiositos.

Mary did not think there was an easy solution to "the illegals problem," but she unconditionally supported Sheriff Arpaio's every action. Her Facebook page was covered in tributes to Arpaio, and her profile photo featured her, posing in a sleek black cocktail dress, next to the man himself. It had been taken, she boasted, at an exclusive fundraiser (she had won tickets to attend in a raffle). Mary saw Arpaio as a principled leader and wished there were more law enforcement figures like him, unafraid to take on immigration policing as part of their routine work. Even still, she doubted that more men like America's so-called "toughest sheriff" could stem the tide of "illegals." She paused frequently as she thought it over, concluding, "There's so much you just get when you come in through the back door, you know?"

Like Connor and Rick, Mary articulated a fear that racialized bodies consumed American resources to which they were not entitled. She believed that the widespread availability of jobs, health care, and education enticed unauthorized migration: "They don't work for it, but they get whatever they want," she said disapprovingly. Even though Mary doubted that any amount of collaboration between local law enforcement and immigration authorities could reverse this trend, she was resolute in her dedication to the Arpaiositos.

Mary used a moralizing framework, centered on the sanctity of paid work, to make sense of her own continuous struggle with economic insecurity as well as her understanding of immigration.[10] Mary had spent most of her life in California, where she had raised three children on her own. When she could, she waitressed and tended bar. Despite being at the mercy of customers' unpredictable tipping habits, she enjoyed interacting with the clientele and working hard to earn her tips. The jobs were precarious, however, and there were times when she had to turn to government assistance to make ends meet. "I had to go on welfare, just because I had to deal with deadbeat dads," she confided. Although being on welfare had been a source of embarrassment for Mary, she praised the "workfare" programs that had come in effect by the mid-1990s. Workfare, unlike classic, means-tested welfare programs, motivated Mary to get a job:

> I think Clinton started this program where you won't get shit unless you work thirty-two hours a week, and if you don't, you have to go to these workshops. I love that. To me, that was "okay, cool." So, I'd go to the workshops. . . . Eventually, I didn't want to keep going to these workshops, so I went and got a job. And I made sure that the guy would give me at least thirty-two hours a week. It was a bartending job. A lot of people dropped off the dole because they didn't show up for the workshop or they didn't get a job. . . . I thought that was the coolest program. . . . You had to sign in and you had to call and explain why you weren't coming in. You had to bring a note from the doctor's. It was pretty strict. They were keeping tabs on it pretty good. So I was like, "screw this'" The regimen killed me—driving down and sitting with a bunch of people. "Screw it, I'll go old school and pound the pavement and find a job before my next workfare thing."

Almost wistfully, Mary said of workfare, "They don't do it like that anymore."

In her study of a low-income rural community in California, sociologist Jennifer Sherman (2009) found that community members morally differentiated between various strategies for coping with poverty. Paid work was assigned the highest moral value and welfare and illegal activities—particularly drug dealing—the lowest. A similar code shaped

Mary's understanding of herself and others, including racialized people she automatically associated with socially reprehensible illegality and dependence.

Mary moved to Arizona with a boyfriend; after he suffered a stroke, Mary became his primary caregiver. She told me she was very "antisocial" during this period, and she turned to the internet to pass the time. There, through restrictionist websites, Mary learned how illegal immigration was draining the economy and the American taxpayer. When her boyfriend wanted to move back to California, they broke up. Her father, also in Arizona, had fallen ill and now she would stay to provide end-of-life care.

All this taught Mary that she enjoyed carework, and so she began applying for jobs in hospices. But a drug-related felony charge from her teenage years stymied that plan. "I partied a lot. I was young, I was stupid. I paid for that mistake. I'm paying for it again now," she explained matter-of-factly. Mary hired a lawyer and hoped for a pardon from the governor of California. In the meantime, she took on short-term work at places like the Goodwill.

Although a hard worker, Mary had never known job security. Her work life had been filled with difficulties. Yet whether as a single mother, a low-wage worker, or a person contending with a criminal record from three decades prior, Mary seemed to revere secure, paid work all the more for being denied it.

Her moral code, centered on sanctity of paid work, made Mary receptive to a restrictionist ideology that painted racialized immigrants as a strain on American largesse. She extended her moral condemnation of people on welfare to "illegals." Just as welfare recipients grew dependent on government handouts, Mexicans grew dependent on American handouts:

> And the thing about welfare is that you keep giving it out. Nobody's going to want to do anything. "Okay, the kids are eating and we're fine. But I'm still going to go to the food banks and get the free shit." They're surviving just fine. I don't see poverty when the family has cell phones, and when you have cable, to me that's not poverty at all. . . . It's the same with the illegals. You keep giving them things: a job, school, you know, health care. And for what? You know? For just getting here. Then they tell their friends, they tell their cousins about all the free stuff you can get here. Then [there's] more people! It's not right.

Coming to the United States without papers was like "getting on the dole." Even worse, immigration was tied up with illegality and drug cartel activity. Until America made itself less attractive to migrants Mary did not think illegal immigration would slow down. A "law-and-order" sheriff, like Arpaio, was a small, yet important step toward strong borders. "Arpaio— he's a, like a deterrent. A small deterrent. He ain't gonna solve the illegal alien problem on his own. But still. [If you don't have papers, you] gotta think twice before you come to Maricopa County."

Mary wanted to do her part to publicly support the law-and-order regime she saw as a lonely island in a vast ocean of lax immigration enforcement. Like other Arpaiositos, Mary worried about the emergence of a pro-immigrant Baja Arizona. Shortly after then-governor Jan Brewer signed Arizona Senate Bill 1070 into law in late 2010, progressive groups in Tucson and other parts of Southern Arizona had half-jokingly, but also half-seriously, threatened to secede from the rest of the state. The notion became a useful way for both progressives and conservatives to draw political and regional battle lines. While pro-SB1070 Republican notables like Arpaio and Brewer represented Phoenix and its environs, anti-SB1070 Democratic figures like former Pima County Sheriff Clarence Dupnik represented the political sentiment of Tucson and its environs. Although he later changed his mind, Dupnik initially refused to comply with SB1070, calling the law "unconstitutional" and "unnecessary."[11] Meanwhile, a Tucson police officer brought suit against SB1070, later joined by the City of Tucson. Baja Arizona also seemed to be the national hub of a campaign to boycott Arizona, which progressive activists and politicians there had launched in response to SB1070.

The Phoenix/Baja Arizona dichotomy extended the ambiguous border into central Arizona. Over the years, the federal government had deputized local law enforcement to act as immigration authorities, with Maricopa County among its initial test-sites for power-sharing. But there were questions regarding the acceptable limits of local authority. SB1070 was the lightening rod; in ongoing debate, different groups came to perceive state power in disparate ways. According to Mary, measures like SB1070 and law-and-order figures like Arpaio should be seen as much-needed local efforts to shore up a state's failure to protect. The anti-SB1070 mobilization, especially among enforcement personnel, made no sense to Mary. "I just don't get it," she sputtered. "Why would an officer of the law refuse to go after people who *broke* the law?" In her eyes, the measure spelled out the bare minimum duty of any police officer. "That's why we gotta let everyone know that here in Phoenix, we stand with Arpaio."

In this context of what she saw as state weakness, Mary believed that Arpaio needed all the public support that he could get. "You could sit around and watch TV and throw up your hands," she said, literally tossing her hands up in exasperation, "Or, you could get off your ass and do something."

Later that day, I followed Mary and five other Arpaiositos as they convened across the street from the Maricopa County Fourth Avenue Jail in downtown Phoenix. On the jail side of the street, anti-Arpaio protestors were chanting "We are the ninety-nine percent." Some signs read "Arpaio serves the 1%," while others called for his arrest. Meanwhile, on our side of the street, the Arpaiositos' signs read "We Support Sheriff Joe" and "Sheriff Joe Arpaio = law enforcer." Mary's group jeered and played a bullhorn siren to drown out a speaker on the other side of the street. She yelled "Go back to Mexico!" and then, "Go back to Tucson!" When the anti-Arpaio rally ended, an Arpaiosito suggested dessert at a nearby restaurant. Mary smiled and winked: "We have to celebrate!"

Supporting the state gave Mary a sense of purpose and seemed to restore her moral compass. Throughout her life, she had strived toward economic independence derived from paid work. Oftentimes, she found herself on the wrong side of this morality spectrum, relying on help from family members and boyfriends, unemployment benefits and welfare programs. Even now, her prospects for meaningful paid work were being undermined by a criminal record. The weak-state effect gave Mary a way to live by her own otherwise elusive moral code.

"I CAN FEEL LIKE I'M DOING MY PART": NED'S AND TOMMY'S STORIES

I met Ned, a soft-spoken, forty-eight-year old white veteran, in early 2017. He was a dedicated member of the Soldiers. At the time that I interviewed him, we were out on one of their ops, a few miles north of the U.S.-Mexico boundary. Ned, who worked as an EMT, lived in Southern California with his two teenage daughters and had used his vacation days to fly out to

Arizona. He tried to come out to the Arizona-Sonora frontier as often as he could, because it was important that he did not become just another "Facebook warrior":

> A lot of people just complain about things. . . . [They're] Facebook warriors and complain about this and that. And what attracted me to this group in particular was that we primarily are trying to stop the drug movement. *We can at least be a deterrent.* That way, *I can feel like I'm doing my part* instead of just sitting behind the computer and complaining about it. [emphasis mine]

Ned's friend, Tommy, also a middle-aged veteran from California, shared a similar understanding. Tommy thought that if the op was extended to a month, "we would hurt them [the cartels], like a dent. A small dent," he replied with a grin. "So there's no end in sight?" I pushed. "No," he said. If it was a futile effort, why was it so important for him to participate? Tommy thought before answering, "At least I can say that I did something about it."

Like pro-immigrant activists, the Soldiers and other restrictionists suspected that their mobilizations had a trifling effect. But because the restrictionists rarely had any history of civic engagement, the only alternative Ned and Tommy could imagine was not participating at all.[12] In fact, with the exception of military deployment, neither man had experienced many opportunities to participate in *any* type of collective mobilization. To them, the alternative to being a Soldier was to complain, to be a loud, opinionated, actionless Facebook warrior. So even if restrictionist activism came with caveats and provisos, Tommy and Ned preferred doing *something* over doing nothing at all.

Tommy's empowerment in helping to secure the border had another odd aspect: he was among the few Mexican-American restrictionist activists that I encountered. Tommy admitted that he had undocumented cousins who led quiet lives: "They don't want any trouble with the law. They send their kids to school. Their big day is Sunday, when they go to church, and go to the store, and then they're back at work the next day." If all the migrants crossing the desert were like his cousins, he told me he would not have joined the Soldiers. "I have no problem with that [unauthorized labor migration]. As long as people are productive and being taxed." But, he told me, the involvement of drug cartels could not be ignored.

Tommy also shared other restrictionists' racial sensibilities, freely drawing on the racist trope of the dangerous brown man. A former Marine, he supported himself and his wife by working as a correctional officer in a California state prison. His interactions with the inmate population at work reinforced for him the link between racialized bodies and criminality:

> I've seen them. I work in a prison. They're like, "I don't give a shit." . . . They'll come back in a year or two, hoping that the government has forgotten about it. "I'll go to Oklahoma next time." They don't give a shit. It's not their people. It's not their country.

Tommy had no way of knowing the legal status of the inmates by simply looking at them.[13] Nonetheless, racialized bodies were suspect, un-American. To Tommy's mind, incarcerated Latinos were, by definition, embodiments of deviance and unwanted otherness. Because of their presumed foreignness, he believed that Brown inmates felt no "obligation" to abide by the law. He imagined that they could "go back" and "come back" as they pleased. Imprisonment was only a temporary hitch in their criminal quest. This analysis cast a long shadow over Tommy's role in the prison system, and he knew it: "[T]here's nothing I can do to stop it at my work. We just try to keep them in line, when they're still with us [in our custody]." Awash in racial anxiety, Tommy felt impotent.

Tommy also pointed out that his wife's family lived in a small municipality in the Mexican state of Durango. When they visited his in-laws, Tommy saw signs of how the cartel had taken over the town. A veritable cartel-based nouveau riche emerged. Humvees and "million-dollar mansions," luxury items beyond the reach of "regular citizens," now dotted the streets. "A lot of people think that the cartels are just about drugs and money," Tommy explained, but he saw that cartels also got involved in more mundane businesses, like pharmacies, retail, and manufacturing fake merchandise. Cartels also demanded certain establishments, like restaurants, pay "*derechos de piso*," or permits, in order to continue operating. "They have their hands in everything," Tommy lamented. It had gotten to the point that the cartel could push its way into a new town using only five gunmen and "do whatever the hell [they] want." Civilians like his in-laws were trapped.

> Civilians, in Mexico, they're caught in the middle and they don't know who to go to. From your municipal police to the town mayor, everybody's bought. So what do you do? They just try to survive. That's the only way to do it—not to say anything and live and carry on as much as you can with a normal life. If you do say something, you get labeled and you're going to die.

Tommy felt helpless when he thought about his loved ones in Mexico. Although he had thought about immigrating them to the United States, he had given up as soon as he realized that the process was long, complicated, and cost a lot of money.

Although Tommy identified as Mexican-American—and had, thanks to his family, insights into the immigration experience that other restrictionists lacked—he still struggled with a sense of deprivation engendered by the bundling together of whiteness and working-class status. Richard Dyer has argued that whiteness should be understood as a relational social category, with "fuzzy edges and minute gradations": some groups are more firmly attached to it than others.[14] Although not unambiguously white-Anglo like his friend Ned, Tommy represents a "gradation of whiteness." As a native-born American, a man, a veteran, and a law enforcement official, he was separate and distinct from the "illegal" immigrants he saw behind bars in California or those crossing the desert in Arizona. His subject-position was also separate and distinct from the victimized (civilian) and violent (cartel) bodies he associated with Mexico. These gradations of racial privilege, however, did little to overcome the helplessness he felt in his work life and personal life. If anything, his proximity to whiteness exacerbated the pains of deprivation.

In this context, soldiering in Arizona was an attractive and empowering experience for Tommy.

> I can be home in California, or visiting relatives in Mexico, and just talking about it—"we should do this, we should do that." *At least, I come out here and put my two cents into it. My little help.* We're not going to stop it [the cartel's activities.] I don't think it'll ever stop, but at least I can say I did a little to help. I have the right to say, "Hey, I've been here and I know what's going on." [emphasis mine]

Tommy's analysis suggested a geography of variegated agency: while a concerned civilian could do little in California, and especially in Mexico, Arizona promised something different. There, one could "do a little to help."

During one op, out in the Arizona borderlands, Tommy had spotted a wallet on the ground. In it, he found a Border Patrol agent's driver's license, bank cards, and his pass card for entering the Border Patrol station. "Good thing it was the good guys who found it," Tommy noted, and told me he returned the wallet to a Soldiers-friendly agent. "Yeah," chimed in another of the Soldiers, "they could have extorted the guy [agent]. With that pass card, they could have walked into the [Border Patrol] station." Turning to me, Tommy grinned. "Yeah, out here, we save *their* asses."

CONCLUSION

For the restrictionist activists that I interviewed, the border was a sanctuary from a world in which downwardly mobile people—who were mostly blue-collar white men, but not always—felt helpless, overwhelmed, and ignored. Each activist grappled in their own way with the contradiction and "unfairness" of being white but working class. Each carried a sense of entitlement and expectation. And each experienced, at some turning point, the disappointment and heartbreak of unmet expectations.

The weak-state effect helped resolve their conflictual identity. It was as if activists projected their own feelings of marginalization, uncertainty, and powerlessness onto the state. Law enforcement was as overpowered as men like Rick and Connor. And restrictionists intuited that there were larger inhibiting forces impeding law enforcement, just as there seemed to be larger inhibiting forces impeding them in their own lives.

That the state was weak, uncoordinated, and ineffective was how activists diagnosed society's problems. Specifically, the state's feeble policing capacity was how restrictionists explained the persistence of unauthorized immigration and drug trafficking. It was also how restrictionists made sense of all kinds of other social problems that they associated with the presence of racialized bodies—from labor market woes and problems of resource scarcity to concerns about public health and safety. Connor summed it up: "The immigration problem has fingers that stretch all over society."

Strengthening the state to solve the problem, however, turned out to be a difficult and often frustrating DIY task. Activists rarely saw the results that they set out to achieve, and I was genuinely surprised every time my respondents openly admitted to this fact. Whether staking out unused migrant paths, tinkering with technology that might not work, or coordinating a counter-protest that might go unnoticed, everyday restrictionism was full of defeats, setbacks, and uncertain results.

Yet activism on the border felt as deeply meaningful to restrictionist activists as it did for their left-wing counterparts. I learned that what mattered was not the actual impact of mobilization. What mattered was *how collective action made participants feel about themselves*. Activism soothed, and even countered, the conviction that society no longer had any use for downwardly mobile white people. As they tried to restore the state's diminishing power, it felt like they were restoring their own diminishing power. At the border, they felt useful, decent, and agentic. They could be the people they were supposed to be.

PART II

Contending with Challenges
from the Other Side

Look, humanitarian aid is a crime. Just the other day I was
chatting with a Border Patrol agent and we agreed that the
easiest way to cut two-thirds of drug cartel activity [at
the Arizona-Mexico border] is by putting a halt to
humanitarian aid.

—Rick

I've encountered polite racists. But these people were like,
"Get these fucking wetbacks out of here.". . . I mean, I was
surprised at this movement that wasn't even making an
effort to provide any other justification. It was just like, "We
don't want them here." I was really surprised by that, just the
bald-faced racism of it. . . . It seems to me that the folks that
I've encountered [the Arpaiositos in Phoenix and the
Soldiers in the desert] don't have a nuanced policy position
beyond just racism.

—Mariela

When challenging the actions of their left-wing opponents, restrictionist activists like Rick repeatedly raised the topic of organized crime and drug smuggling. They charged that pro-immigrant organizations, knowingly or unknowingly, aided and abetted those who facilitated extralegal migration and contraband smuggling—the coyotes, or migrant guides; the scouts, or lookouts; and the drug mules, or people who transported drugs for cartels. Pro-immigrant activists, like Mariela, argued that restrictionists were motivated, above all, by their hatred of people of color, particularly people of Latin American descent.

Each side was aware of the other's accusations. In fact, I discovered that all of these activists quietly, but constantly wrestled with their opponents' allegations about their groups. They called upon their specific conceptions of state power to refute such claims.

That is, for the activists that I studied, a state effect was not a singular, static impression of the state. Seeing the state in a certain way was an entire *worldview*. It provided an interpretive schema for understanding the social world and its various actors. It was a shared constellation of ideas that helped activists reconstruct a history of the current moment— including how the border came to be the way it is.

The next two chapters illustrate the inner logic and seemingly unshakeable nature of each side's worldviews. I consider how each group of activists grappled with their opponents' main critique—pro-immigrant activists with the charge that they facilitated cartel operations and restrictionists with the indictment that they were a group of racists. As I went back and forth between my two sets of interlocutors, relaying the criticisms and censures of one side to the other, I witnessed how they "argued" with each other. Through revisits to the field, I gained insight into how their organizations socialized members into the collective worldview.

The state-effect framework helped activists wrestle with their opponents' allegations and justify their own actions. In a setting complicated by the fact that, as one pro-immigrant activist explained, "a migrant and someone carrying a backpack [with drugs] are not mutually exclusive categories," leftist activists quietly struggled to develop collective narratives about the "Other" border crosser. It was especially worrisome for privileged but progressive activists that any criticism of Other border crossers could easily reproduce the power asymmetry they wished to undermine.

Pro-immigrant activists relied on the strong-state-effect lens to navigate this complex terrain. The object-subject dichotomy that activists derived from this framework—the powerless third-world crosser and the powerful state—was key. Regardless of what kinds of people they were and what they did, *all* border crossers were victims of forces beyond their control. Therefore, all were blameless. The American state, by contrast, was *responsible* for the drug trade, unauthorized migration, and all the resulting violence that came with these phenomena. As such, the American state (and *not* cartel workers or their bosses, or any subordinate state, like the Mexican government) was the rightful target of Americans' condemnation and strategic mobilization. As chapter 4 shows, those who deviated from this collective narrative ultimately felt alienated from their organizations and left.

Restrictionist activists also relied on the state-effect lens to dispute the criticism that was most damning for their movement—namely, that they were motivated by "bald-faced racism." To my surprise, right-wing activists did not deny the presence of racism in the Arizona borderlands. Indeed, the numerous precautions they took to vet prospective members stood testament to this concern. What my interlocutors proposed, however, was an alternative way to *define* racism, one that simultaneously drew on the weak-state-effect framework and popular conceptions about the *extremist* nature of racism. The "real racists," my interlocutors claimed, were pushed to the fringes of society. They rarely mobilized as a cohesive group, and they rarely collaborated with state actors like the Border Patrol (some even impeded their work). Contrasting themselves with this definition, restrictionists argued that their own mobilization could not be racist.

Unlike the "real racists," restrictionists claimed they mobilized at the institutional center of society, inspired by respect for the law and the work of frontline state actors. They reinforced an enfeebled state. The fact that state actors regularly communicated with restrictionists solidified these convictions. White-but-working-class activists—who had rarely experienced group life before joining their restrictionist organizations—doubted that the rare camaraderie and the sense of mastery they felt as they helped shore up the state could be based on something as abhorrent as racism.

Exploring how each group wrestled with and repressed the challenges to their worldviews gives us a finer understanding of the logics that sustained their mobilization.

4 The "Other" Border Crosser

HOW PRO-IMMIGRANT ACTIVISTS GRAPPLE
WITH THE TOPIC OF CARTELS

One cold morning in 2017, I accompanied two pro-immigrant activists to a Mexican border town to drop off supplies at a migrant shelter. The shelter, with its industrial-sized stove, long dining table, and barrack-style sleeping area, was designed to accommodate up to several dozen people at a time. On the day that we visited, though, the shelter was empty. A young woman who helped run the place, Carla, said it was the seasonal lull. The numbers would pick up as the weather warmed. We sat at the cafeteria table to chat. Later, behind the closed door of the small office, Carla spoke in hushed tones as she told us how the town was in the grip of two competing cartels.

To illustrate, Carla shared the story of three Central Americans—a husband, his wife, and his sibling—who had arrived at the shelter recently. They hoped to cross the border together, but the cartel—or "mafia," as the locals called it—informed the man that they could not cross unless the man worked first as a *mochilando*, or drug transporter. Speaking rapidly and quietly, Carla recalled that the man had to cross over with drugs four times before the mafia allowed his family to leave together. The mafia did not allow migrants to leave until they had paid a ransom, Carla said, so the man's stint as a *mochilando* might have been in lieu of payment.

Conditions across the state had gotten so bad, Carla said, that prospective border crossers were desperate to find new routes to *el Norte*. A rumor was circulating that some places in Baja California offered "free" passage (i.e., free of any guides). People were willing to take that risk; they would cross without a guide to avoid mafia entanglements. Carla thought border crossing was likely to shift westward, away from the coercive control of the cartels.

Six years earlier, Howard, a pro-immigrant activist, who was neither a Humanitarian nor an Advocate, criticized his leftist colleagues for keeping "absolutely silent when it comes to the drug cartels." I interviewed Howard shortly after Los Zetas drug cartel was reported to have murdered seventy-two undocumented Central and South American migrants in the municipality of San Fernando in Tamaulipas, Mexico. "We [pro-immigrant activists] are selective in our criticism of who we want to vilify," Howard reflected. "We vilify relentlessly the Border Patrol for migrant deaths. We vilify law enforcement. But where is the moral outrage for the seventy-two Central Americans who were massacred by the drug cartels last summer?"

Six years later, reflecting on Carla's experiences, I asked Scott about Howard's critique. Scott was a longtime Humanitarian who primarily volunteered in a Mexican border town, which, like other municipalities across the border, had become a dumping ground for deportees. Scott's organization had been surveying recently deported migrants for years in order to gather data about their experiences, particularly while in Border Patrol custody. While the Humanitarians readily asked migrants about the abuses they endured at the hands of U.S. government authorities, they did not systematically ask about *other* sources of violence.

Scott conceded that cartels were oddly absent in Humanitarian discourse. According to him, that absence severely hindered the conversations activists could have with migrants about their experiences. After all, he continued, the mafia was very much on the minds of migrants. Deportees with families north of the border, in particular, were likely making plans to return to the United States. Returnees were probably more fearful of encountering a cartel than the Border Patrol.

Later, I described my conversations with Carla and Scott to other pro-immigrant activists. On one occasion, my interlocutor was Lucas, a volunteer with the Humanitarians. Certainly, the deployment of Border Patrol resources affected where and how migrants crossed, I began. But in some ways, the demands and threats of organized crime constituted a more immediate—and perhaps even more formidable—concern for prospective crossers. I continued, noting that this emerging reality did not seem to be reflected in the public-facing discourse of the Advocates or the Humanitarians.

Lucas nodded quietly. Then he said, "The potential for actually creating change and accountability exists in one place, where it doesn't in the other." I asked whether he meant that the groups needed to be strategic about choosing their rhetorical targets. "Yeah," Lucas agreed, "As U.S. citizens, we can petition for some modification of behavior" with the Border Patrol. That just wasn't possible with other actors, like the cartels. It was a practical constraint—one set of actors was within the reach of American citizens' purview of strategic action. The other was not.

When I broached the topic with Renee, an Advocate, she too was uncomfortable with publicly acknowledging how cartels harmed migrants. She recognized that there were cartels, but she added that obsessing over them only legitimized restrictionists' racist discourse, which blamed borderland violence on racialized, noncitizen border crossers rather than the American state (itself responsible for the existence of cartels).[1]

As I talked to pro-immigrant activists, I realized that the reluctance to publicly recognize cartel presence was not really a matter of practicality *or* wanting to avoid reinforcing the political opposition's arguments. Rather, activists' *politics of privilege* dictated this systematic evasion. As progressive-but-privileged Americans, my pro-immigrant respondents were reticent to ascribe power and agency to (and, with them, moral judgments against) *any* border crosser—including those who were associated with cartels. So, amid the emerging reality in which drug smuggling organizations *had* made inroads into the migration business, how could left-wing activists contend with the taboo topic?

This chapter begins to address this question. When they tried to make sense of the guides, scouts, and other border crossers who enabled extralegal migration and contraband smuggling, I found that pro-immigrant activists tethered themselves to the strong-state-effect framework. The power of this worldview showed through when activists argued that all border crossers were objects of the state. U.S. government policies were forcing people to participate in crime and violence against their will. And so the only deserving target of condemnation was the state.

"OH, WE DO RUN INTO THEM": PRO-IMMIGRANT ACTIVISTS' EXPERIENCES WITH CARTELS

Despite their unwillingness to speak publicly about cartels, pro-immigrant activists had had many encounters with people they believed were connected to black market organizations. Many even acknowledged that migrants were being recruited to carry out mafia business, making it increasingly hard to disentangle cross-border migration from human and drug smuggling. The activists never really knew what to do during these encounters, and it was an ongoing source of reflection, conversation, and occasional contention within their groups.

Emma and her colleagues developed protocols anchored in the idea of being a responsible ally. A white woman in her mid-twenties, Emma volunteered with the Humanitarians for several years. In a Mexican border town, they provided services like basic medical care to people who had recently been deported from the United States. Because recent deportees were very likely to try to return to the United States, cartel-employed guides would turn up.

"There have been weird interactions on the street," Emma told me, referring to the coyotes—the migrant guides. It was "never easy" to know what to do. Generally, deportees and migrants resisted interacting with the cartel. "People are really frightened and *not* interested." In those types of situations, Emma "tried to intervene" in the unwanted solicitation, then "just walk away." Still, the Humanitarians believed the migrants, not the volunteers, should be making decisions about what to do—even if the volunteers disagreed. "So if someone approaches them on the street," Emma explained, "we don't want them [migrants] to be in a situation that makes them really uncomfortable. If they [migrants] were interested in talking to that person, we're not going to"—she paused—"*stop* them." Being a true ally, she asserted, meant never interfering in a person's opportunity to decide their own path. Ironically, however, this meant that volunteers always had to read the situation and determine whether to "intervene."

Despite these thorny situations and their ambiguous role as mediators between the migration and cartel operations, Emma was one of few pro-immigrant respondents who wanted the movement to publicly comment on cartels. Like Renee, she believed public discourse about cartels was being used by restrictionist groups to justify organized racism. But Emma did not think that silence on the topic was necessarily helpful. No matter how formidable the task, pro-immigrant activists had to eventually change the public's understanding: the U.S. government was responsible for facilitating cartel violence. The fault could not be laid at the feet of migrants. Emma clarified, "I would like us [the Humanitarians] to talk about cartels in a way that's really pointing to [the fact that] the market that they [human and drug smugglers] have, and the violence that they do, is a product of border militarization, of a border security apparatus that has given them power."

When leftist activists hosted visiting delegations of university students, they readied themselves for queries about cartels and drug smuggling. I asked Emma what they said if the questions came up:

> We talk about how a migrant and someone carrying a backpack [with drugs] are not mutually exclusive categories. We talk about how people are coerced into these things. We talk about how, prior to prevention-through-deterrence, people were crossing through the desert ... but it was mainly mom-and-pop shops [independent coyotes] that were doing it [guiding migrants through the desert]. . . . It wasn't this organized network of people that were using violence in order to maintain control.

With visitors, the Humanitarians conceded that the landscape of border crossers in Arizona had gotten more complex. A person that they encountered in the borderlands could be both a migrant *and* "someone carrying a backpack." Activists then pivoted to the effects of American policy, trying to subvert and challenge the kinds of racist discourse that worried Renee. As a result of the prevention-through-deterrence program, Emma explained, border crossers were "coerced into doing these things."

Despite these conversations with small visiting groups, Emma was wary about speaking to larger audiences on the relationship between cartels and the state: "I think it's hard to talk about and hard to create talking points that won't ... I mean, I can just see an interview with a hostile reporter going really poorly. I think that's what people are scared of. Or something being put on the record that reads . . . ." She broke off and finished by summarizing: "Media with the Humanitarians is hard." Even though their work was frequently the topic of local and national news, the Humanitarians were generally reluctant to engage with reporters. Most had the impression that the media were already inundated with discourse that criminalized all border crossers. Talking about a situation where, as Emma said, "migrant" and "someone carrying a backpack" were no longer distinct categories, made it even harder to skillfully intervene in that public discussion.

Other respondents also mentioned encounters with suspected cartel members. "Oh, we do run into them a lot," Silvia told me in 2017. The volunteers, she said, talked about it often:

> Yes, we talk about this all the time out in the field, like the people that we're running into up in [an area for water drops] are all from Sinaloa, which is very interesting to me—that they're all from Sinaloa. I think that probably means that they're being moved through the pathway . . . by a certain cartel. I'm not going to name all the names of the cartels. But yes, often the people that we've run into up there appear, to me, to be guides. I have never run into the same guide twice, but they appear, to me, to be guides or lookouts.

Silvia's caution was clear: she said only that it was "interesting" that so many border crossers were from the same Mexican state, which had a powerful organized crime syndicate. It seemed to her some were cartel scouts and guides.

Others, like Lucas, did not think he had come across cartels in the borderlands, but the issue of cartels had come up in his history of activism. When Lucas worked at a Texas refugee shelter, prior to coming to Arizona, shelter workers had developed a protocol of silence around topics related to cartel activities. "We were increasingly dealing with folks who had been forced to be [drug] mules," he said, but it was not "safe" to broach the topic with their clients or the public. In another volunteer group, which annually rode bikes into Mexico, Lucas recalled, "We were in some of the hottest areas in the Texas-Mexico border, at the height of the [drug] war." In 2011 and 2012, one of those places was Monterrey. It was the site of a turf war between a drug syndicate, Los Zetas, and its former ally, the Gulf

Cartel. "We actually decided not to go back to Monterrey one year because the Zetas were firing heavy machine guns in neighborhoods in Monterrey, fighting for strategic areas there," Lucas revealed. Like Silvia and Emma, Lucas was personally aware that cartels were affecting both migration and everyday life in the borderlands.

Chloe also suspected that she had probably interacted with people involved in "nefarious things" as she fielded the hotline's calls about missing migrants. Chloe's colleague Renee had occasionally spoken with coyotes as she tried to track down the missing. Even by 2010, when I first interviewed Renee, she saw speaking with the coyotes as little different from reaching out to Border Patrol: in emergencies, moral judgments about these actors were beside the point. After all, activists could still leverage their information to save a migrant's life. Chloe worried that the information was not just flowing in one direction: "We were probably helping drug smugglers. I have no doubts about that," she said. But the activists' could not vet callers, because "most of the calls are from devastated people dealing with devastating situations." The occasional calls that *did* worry the group were not the ones coming from suspected drug smugglers. Far more concerning were the ones Chloe described as having a distinct "abuser vibe," like a husband repeatedly calling about the whereabouts of his wife. Those kinds of calls were stonewalled by volunteers.

Taken together, the pro-immigrant activists I interviewed placed their concern with helping migrants. If they also aided the cartels, it couldn't be helped. Most underscored their moral neutrality—often elided into compassion—toward those people doing the grunt work of drug smuggling in the desert. Even Chloe's overreliance on passive verbs conveyed an unwillingness to assign power and agency to smugglers. Why extend moral censure to those who, like regular migrants, are compelled by forces larger than themselves?

I never felt morally wrong about that at all. I feel like it's just part of *what's been created* and I know that there are *a lot of people who are forced to do it, against their will, or willingly also did it, out of whatever*. That's just *what's been created* and it would be unfortunate not to do the work out of fear of helping people who might be doing something that's against the law. I think that . . . I don't know. I feel like drugs is such a complicated issue. I don't have any moral—it's more a health issue for me than a morality issue, which

is *then created by the U.S. government.* I want to continue to trust most people, but be cautious. I think that's the take we had on it. [emphasis mine]

As a privileged white American, Chloe felt it was not her place to pass
moral judgment on what migrants did.

"THE SIXTEEN-YEAR-OLD IN THE DESERT DOESN'T SCARE ME": NARRATIVES ABOUT THE POWERFUL STATE AND THE POWERLESS CROSSER

In 2011, Justin, unprompted, broached the topic of drug smugglers in the
desert. Born in the early 1940s, Justin grew up in rural Minnesota. He
moved around the Midwest before settling in Nebraska. He worked as a
high school teacher and principal for many years, before he became a
family counsellor. Upon retiring in 2007, Justin and his wife, a former
nurse, moved to Southern Arizona. Within a year, they had joined the
Humanitarians.

Justin had a long history of civic engagement, but never on "immigration
issues." Now, several times a week, Justin went into the desert to put out
water along migrant trails. He regularly helped maintain the Humanitarians'
medical camp, located on private property near the border in the desert
wilderness. By the time we met, Justin had been volunteering with the
group for almost three years but was a relatively new pro-immigrant activist compared to many other Humanitarians. He was still trying to work out
the social composition of the borderlands and specifically, the intersection
of migration with drug smuggling.

Camp protocols had recently become a topic of lively discussion among
activists, Justin told me. In particular, the Humanitarians had been debat-
ing what to do when people showed up at the medical camp wanting to
stay for an extended period of time but did not appear to need medical
assistance. "We don't want to become a way-station," Justin explained, but
they didn't want to refuse assistance to a border crosser either. Impartiality
was a core part of the humanitarianism the volunteers tried to practice.[2]
"It brings up that whole issue about some of the people that come into
camp are probably drug smugglers."

The previous summer, some Humanitarians began to suspect smugglers were occasionally coming into the camp. The same border crossers seemed to be circulating through, again and again. Of course, it could just have been evidence of bad luck: certain people who had been apprehended several times and continued trying to cross through the same area. "But how often does that happen, I can't say," Justin added quizzically. Maybe they *had* been working for a drug smuggling cartel. "We're in a drug corridor out there [*chuckles*] for crying out loud, you know?" he told me emphatically.

Quickly, Justin added that "some people actually believe that putting water and providing aid leads to people coming to those very spots, which is just nonsense. They don't. There's so little of it [aid] there that it's just silly." Justin was acutely aware of a discourse, popular among restrictionist activists, partially blaming continued extralegal migration and drug smuggling on the availability of humanitarian aid in the desert. He worried that such "nonsense" could give the Border Patrol a justification to raid the Humanitarians' camp, even though it was on private property. Then, Justin wavered and contradicted himself. Just after calling the area a "drug corridor," he told me there was very little contraband smuggling. He was wrestling with how to even *characterize* the places where he volunteered and the people he encountered.

Six years later, I interviewed him again. I expected that the accumulation of knowledge about the increasing complexities of the borderlands would have made Justin grapple with the topic of camp protocols. I was wrong. He was no longer hesitant, but resolute that everyone deserved aid, no matter who they were.

Justin began by recounting the experiences of a fellow pro-immigrant activist who regularly visited relatives in a Mexican border town that had become a cartel stronghold. "She has these awful stories to tell about people who are held for way long, women and children, a lot of Central Americans." Cartels, he said, targeted Central Americans because they were more desperate to cross the border than their Mexican counterparts.

On his own trips to a Mexican border town (like the one described at the beginning of this chapter), Justin had verified his friend's observations. There, he had helped drop off supplies and food that Carla and other shelter workers distributed to the people staying in the shelter. Other Humanitarian supplies, such as small vials of bleach used to purify water, would help prospective migrants on their journey across the desert. Dropping off supplies at the shelter had given Justin the opportunity to learn firsthand about the conditions that prospective border-crossers faced in the midst of a powerful smuggling organization.

For instance, he found out that migrants were not even in charge of how long they would stay at the shelter before being transported to the border: "They're held, as it were, until they are given the okay [by cartel smugglers] to go into vans and be transported." And the cartel squeezed Central American migrants long before that. Justin said shelter workers reported migrants paying 6,500 pesos (about $300) just to leave town. Justin shook his head. *"That's what gets me—they're so abused and taken advantage of* [emphasis mine]. But that's an old story, isn't it?"

Interestingly, Justin still placed blame for the violence inflicted on migrants with the Border Patrol's rhetoric of criminality, not the local mafia. "They've got to know that ninety-nine percent of these folks are not criminals," he accused. According to Justin, Border Patrol agents told visiting delegations that migrants "are all drug dealers" and that "drug cartels are pushing drugs through here like crazy—you're just naive to think otherwise." Of course, Justin agreed, it was clear there were drugs in the area, but "many of these Central American folks are forced to carry" the drugs. "Let's tell that story, too. Let's *also* tell the story that cartels control human trafficking. Now, you mix up to the two, you've got a real mess."

I pushed back. If it was increasingly difficult to separate cartel activity from the business of migration, and if there was mounting evidence that the cartels were highly coercive, then wasn't humanitarian volunteers' role in the "mess" worrisome? By adopting a neutral stance—both in their public statements and in their daily protocols—were pro-immigrant groups ignoring migrants' misery? Why was it not reasonable for American activists also to feel morally outraged by a coercive cartel?

Justin said I wasn't the first to lodge this argument; just a few days earlier, he had received an angry email from some friends who disapproved of the Humanitarians. They chastised Justin for doing water drops in a known drug smuggling corridor. But, he insisted, their outrage was misdirected. The cartels, in exploiting a high-profit market niche, were

not the cause of the violence in the borderlands, but a symptom of the
political economy of violence the U.S. government had created:

> To me, there's no argument with someone who chooses to believe that we're
> aiding the cartels. There's no argument, other than when you go down and
> meet these folks in person, you actually sit with the migrant who's got hope
> in his or her eyes, you begin to understand how connected we actually are.
> They want what I want, or rather, what I already have. What I'm doing, in a
> very minimal way, is providing aid, like food and vials of bleach [to sterilize
> water]. [*Laughs.*] If it wasn't for this really oppressive policy, they [migrants
> and/or cartels] wouldn't be in the desert anyway, and we wouldn't need to
> give them these [water sterilizing] kits. I'm not even sure if they [the kits]
> do any good at all. We have no proof that those kits are saving any lives. We
> hope they do. The cartels mostly make their livelihoods—well, they're trying
> to provide a service, I guess you could say. But they're certainly not giving
> them [migrants] any amenities.

As the conditions around him changed and he grew more knowledge-
able, Justin became more resolute in his moral neutrality toward cartels.
During the years that separated the two interviews I conducted with
him, Justin had amassed a lot more experience in the borderlands. He
had seen the growing effects of cartel activity in the desert. He actively
participated in his organization's efforts to develop protocols about how
to interact with border crossers who activists suspected were involved
with cartels. He had learned about how cartels controlled different
Mexican border towns. He heard about the strategies that cartels used to
exploit migration for their benefit. He grew increasingly appalled by the
misery that these syndicates forced migrants to endure. At the same
time, years of group participation also meant years of group socialization. Justin internalized the dominant framework among pro-immigrant activists.

According to their strong-state worldview, public contempt toward
smuggling organizations allowed the culprit (the state) to go unpunished
and further criminalized its victim (the third-world migrant). Over many
decades, American policies had deliberately perpetuated migration over a
highly militarized and deadly border. This ultimately coercive power and
these coordinated actions were responsible not only for migrants' collective desire to escape to the United States, but for the profitable black

market in cross-border smuggling. Cartels, just like migrants, were responding to the conditions created by the American government.

Nina also tied her moral appraisal of cartels to the strong-state effect. Drug smuggling was only profitable because of the way the state—*her* state—had built up the U.S.-Mexico border.

> My understanding of it from working in the desert is that the cartels can't exist without militarization of the border. *We've* created the market. *We* continue to create the market as *we* militarize the border. Prices go up as it becomes harder to cross. *We're just handing the smugglers more money,* which I think is something that people don't think about a lot when they think about militarization of the border.

Nina's narrative echoed the anxiety among progressive-but-privileged activists that they themselves were complicit in the oppression of others. By using the pronoun *we*, Nina associated herself with the government's actions. She shifted culpability away from the "other" crossing the border and onto a powerful category of actors including Americans and their state apparatus. Under these circumstances, it was unremarkable to her that cartels used violence to secure their share of the smuggling market.

Later, Nina revived a familiar dichotomy to make sense of the border crossers who do "bad things": the powerful state versus the powerless third-world migrant. As she tried to find her analytic footing, Nina tethered her argument to the morality that this framework dictated:

> The coyotes, the smugglers who are running the desert, are *like sixteen to twenty [years old]*. [*Laughs.*] They're not getting paid a lot. And this is not to absolve folks from really horrible things that happen in the desert. *But it is to say that those folks are getting paid very little,* their bodies are being criminalized, the market that was created by another country is being criminalized, *there's no other economies in their communities*. So, they're participating in this thing because they can get paid, but they're not. . . . [*pauses*] For the most part, I don't think they're bad people, I think they are people who have probably done bad things. [emphasis mine]

Nina seemed to stumble a bit here. As she asserted that some people weren't "bad," she acknowledged that "they are a very small part of a much larger system where a lot of bad people do really exist." It's just that "we don't necessarily go after those folks." Nina continued,

I don't know when the consciousness is going to change around that, to be like, "I don't need to be armed for this sixteen-year-old. I don't. I might need to be armed if I was going to go bust down Chapo Guzmán's door. But a sixteen-year-old in the desert doesn't scare me." Also, people who are really concerned about their interactions with criminals should take their money out of banks right now. I don't know. It's weird to think about people not wanting to support black market business. But what about the white-collar businesses that are laundering the money?

According to Nina, those who were entangled in the everyday, on-the-ground business of the trade were ultimately victimized by the conditions in which they found themselves. It was not entirely appropriate to blame them for their actions. Nina made this assertion in several ways. First, she emphasized smugglers' youth, a claim contradicted by at least one study.[3] However, in this rhetorical move, Nina drew on a public narrative that infantilized migrants and extended it to the people who *facilitated* migration.[4] In this way, she downplayed smugglers' agency and the threat they posed ("a sixteen-year-old in the desert doesn't scare me").

Second, she speculated that teenagers were forced into the business because they lacked other economic opportunities. Moreover, she thought that within the profitable drug trade, the cartel's rank and file workers were making little money but getting all the attendant criminalization and stigma. To the extent that there *were* blameworthy actors in the "larger system," they were people like the former head of the Sinaloa Cartel, Joaquín "El Chapo" Guzmán, or the (American) banks and white-collar businesses laundering money for drug lords. To Nina, the average smuggler, like the average migrant, had little agency or power and deserved none of the public's moral censure.

Finally, Nina's linguistic inclinations stand out in this narrative. For instance, she uses the passive voice to describe smugglers ("they're not getting paid," "their bodies are being criminalized"), reinforcing the idea that all border crossers are *objects* rather than subjects of their circumstances. Similarly, she separates actors from their actions: Instead of saying that she did not want to "absolve folks from really horrible things that *they do* in the desert," Nina said "really horrible things *that happen* in the desert." The dichotomy of powerful state and powerful crosser even saturated her speech.

Lucas never characterized smugglers as teenagers, but he, too, discussed their lack of agency:

I see it—the [cartel] activity—through a class analysis, where the foot soldiers of these organizations are poor people who are being poorly paid and [who] suffer. The people at the top are well paid and living a life of luxury, in collusion with U.S. banks and U.S. government officials and the corrupted peoples at all levels of government in the U.S. *I feel like I have empathy for the people on the ground.* At one point, I heard that *sicarios* [cartel assassins] at the border, they [the cartel] would pay them like five thousand pesos a month, and a truck and a pistol. That's like five hundred dollars a month. They would end up no doubt *carne de cañón* [cannon fodder] and end up dying. *So, like, even those people committing those crimes, especially south of the border, they're being treated as expendably as capitalist drones in some transnational corporation, you know?* [emphasis mine]

Like Nina, Lucas distinguished between the different organizational layers of a cartel, assigning little power and agency to those at the bottom of the hierarchy. He emphasized that their labor and their lives were cheap, that they were precarious workers who endured tremendous risks.

Despite his effort to "empathize," however, Lucas grappled with the morality of drug smuggling. "I feel like the leaders of these organizations are just as evil as the CEOs of other major corporations that lead to death and suffering of lots of people." He referred to the drug trade as a variant of "turbo-capitalism," wherein "the people at the top are benefitting with insane amounts of wealth at the expense of the suffering of the working people." He paused, as if to gather his thoughts, then returned to the idea that it didn't matter who you were, participation in the cartel was not fully voluntary. "I suppose the people at the top of those criminal organizations probably have less of a choice in their business model than the people at the top of other corporations. Everything is enforced with bribery, *plata o plomo* [money or bullets]." The real decision-making power, Lucas explained, lay with the *U.S. government.* If only there was a program of legalization—"legalization of everything"—then resources would be shifted away from criminalizing groups and toward treating substance-abuse problems. Lucas was not certain how legalization would affect the cartels, but thought it might alleviate the circumstances faced by both migrants and "foot soldiers."

The politics of privilege dictated Lucas's meandering argument. He began with a "class analysis" in which he equated clandestine drug distribution rings to regular multinational corporations and challenged the public scorn accrued by "foot soldiers" (similar to how Nina deflected blame by emphasizing the youth of smugglers). Like CEOs, drug lords oppressed those lower in their organizations. Then, however, Lucas seemed to falter before returning to the framework of the powerless crosser versus the powerful state. While Nina had used the pronoun *we* to widen the "powerful state" category so that it encompassed both the state and Americans like herself, Lucas broadened the category of the "powerless crosser" so that it came to encompass cartel leaders, too. Even these men, compared to CEOs, had "little choice in their business model." They were *forced* to participate in unsavory actions like bribery and violence. The blame, in both Nina's and Lucas's line of reasoning, migrated north, too.

When it came to people she suspected were not "ordinary" migrants, Silvia initially used the boundaries of her medical profession to maintain her moral neutrality. Later, like her activist colleagues, she referred to the powerful state–powerless crosser dichotomy to downplay the (moral) significance of smuggling in the desert. "Frankly, I don't have a problem with the individual," she said matter-of-factly. A person's identity, their intentions, their profession—none of these were important. When a person's life was at stake, Silvia was simply a doctor.

> When I run into you in the desert and you've been walking for nine days and you have holes in your feet, I'll take care of you. I don't care if you're with a cartel, if you're not with a cartel, if you're the guide, if you're the migrant. . . . You know, that's not the problem right now. My problem is that you don't die in the desert.

Like Justin, Silvia struggled with the critique that putting out water and medically attending to border crossers in the desert meant aiding and abetting human and drug smuggling.

> I think that, without stating it explicitly, when we do take care of people on the trail who are pretty obviously guides or are pretty obviously traveling under the auspices of a cartel, I think that sends a message that we're not supporting your bad behavior but that we are going to provide aid to these migrants, even though they're traveling with you guys.

By medically attending to a migrant who was in a cartel's jurisdiction, the Humanitarians were, Silvia tried to impress upon me, relaying their disapproval of cartels. By the same token, distributing water was a public critique of the state.[5]

Silvia mentioned at one point that, when it came to cartel involvement, she cared about it "at home," just not in the field. Even "at home," however, Silvia dismissed the moral significance of crossers' activities by referring back to the state. "Would these guys have jobs if it wasn't for the border militarization and for the marketing of drugs in the United States?" Silvia asked rhetorically. "No!"

> Are these little guys walking across the desert with backpacks—are they responsible for the tons and tons of drugs coming in the country? Hell no! You know? They're smaller than me. Can you carry fifty pounds of drugs? Good for you. That's not going to last a day in the streets. It's ridiculous.

Silvia ultimately cleared her concerns about potentially helping drug cartels by returning to the trope of the powerless border crosser against the powerful state. She made this claim in two ways. First, she described how smugglers, like migrants, were also reacting to circumstances not of their own making ("Would these guys have jobs if it wasn't for border militarization?"). Second, she suggested that the power disparity was literally *embodied*. Rather than stressing their youth (as Nina had) or their expendability (as Lucas had), Silvia emphasized smugglers' petite bodies ("they're smaller than me").[6] She downplayed the practical impact of drug smuggling that occurred in the desert, between official ports of entry. The amount of drugs that any one person—especially one as "small" as the average smuggler she saw—could transport across the wilderness would barely make a dent in the American market.

The narratives of Nina, Lucas, and Silvia represented one tendency among progressive-but-privileged activists: to *challenge* but not *dispense with* dominant moralistic characterizations. These analyses still featured the good and the bad, after all. Gail, by contrast, represents the tendency to assign all responsibility to the U.S. government, thereby refusing to morally typecast the border-crossing "other."

After I completed the interview and switched off the audio-recorder, Gail, unprompted, brought up smuggling. We had been discussing the conditions that migrants faced in the borderlands. Along with the Border Patrol's brutality, Gail added that prospective border crossers could no longer avoid being implicated in the cartels. There were no more "mom-and-pop" guides; hiring a guide meant hiring someone who worked for a cartel. And, more often than not, transporting drugs was part of the cost of crossing the border. The U.S. government's stringent enforcement of the borderlands had conveniently jacked up the price of crossing. It was now very lucrative for cartels to control the passageway. They did so. Viciously.

I asked, "Shouldn't these organizations—now with more power than ever—be held accountable at some level?" Gail held her ground, saying that people crossing the desert with bales of pot on their backs are at the bottom of the socioeconomic totem pole and that we should be thinking about the poverty that got them to that point. Gail remained careful, because she did not want to fall into the trap of saying that every crosser that her group encountered in the desert was necessarily *good*, though: Saying they're "good" was just as racist as making a blanket statement that all crossers are bad or suspicious.

Robert grounded his commitment to moral neutrality in historical precedent. He explained that the Humanitarians and other groups that provided aid in the desert were following the dominant principles of the Sanctuary movement of the 1980s. During that period, there was simply no way for Sanctuary workers to help every person fleeing the wars in El Salvador and Guatemala; there were simply too many who wished to escape into the United States. As a result, Sanctuary workers developed a triage system based on "human rights standards." Volunteers asked them-selves how likely it was that each potential Central American client would encounter grave harm if they were forced to return to their country of origin.

Not everyone in the Sanctuary movement was on board, however. Robert explained how some wanted to ask, instead, whether each person was "politically useful" (read: a leftist) in the struggles in Central America. Robert told me that the "human rights" proponents eventually won the day: "If they're threatened from the [political] right or the left, we'll help them. If their lives are on the line, [we'll help them]. And so, we don't have political criteria, we have human rights criteria." The analysis was predicated on the shared understanding that whatever their political affiliation, all Guatemalans and Salvadorans were, to some degree, victims of the U.S. government's aggressive foreign policies. As such, anyone in harm's way deserved help.

To Robert, the Humanitarians' work with border crossers grew out of the same commitment to human rights and the political neutrality that it entailed. His group had a "blanket policy" of "simple medical aid" for everyone. Just like the Central American refugees in the 1980s, everyone who crossed the desert today was, to some degree, an object of the U.S. state. Further, he added, injury and death were not evenly distributed among border crossers:

> And I can also tell ya that there is little or no evidence that the drug cartels are dying out there. In fact, there's none. The folks who are dying out there are poor migrant workers. So, that's where we focus our attention. It's why we continue with the same criteria because there's no evidence that we have been assisting the drug cartels at all.

Indeed, Robert said, cartels "stay the hell out of our way." Yet, he circled around a particular scenario: What should volunteers do when they encountered a group of migrants being led by a coyote?

The experienced participants, Robert told me, immediately knew that the "one guy in the group who has tattoos all over his arms and teardrop from his eye, tattooed on, that's probably the coyote. And some of 'em [the coyotes] will be honest enough to tell us [their identity], from time to time." In all likelihood, coyotes worked for a cartel. However, the service that they provided to migrants was an invaluable, indeed potentially life-saving, one:

> We know that the major cause of death out there is groups, people [migrants] who get separated from the coyote. So, you're caught in that question: how do we distinguish humanitarian aid assistance out there from *coyotismo*? And, there's a whole set of little issues around that which has to do with, well, yeah, how do we help the people who need medical assistance and not get associated with coyotes who always bring groups through? And what do you do with the coyote in the group that's healthy while you're giving medical assistance to someone else? And we've tried to, and struggled with, how do you do that? And we've tried to come up with some criteria and some protocols and some ways of doing that . . . but it's a great question

and we're trying to operate with as much integrity as we can under the circumstances.

Despite the neutrality that he wanted the Humanitarians to uphold, Robert found the coyote—particularly the healthy coyote not in need of medical assistance—very troubling. Unlike Nina, Gail, Lucas, or Silvia, he could not bring himself to downplay the coyote's power by referring to their life circumstances. He never mentioned their youth, small physical size, or expendability. To him, the coyote seemed to wield a lot of life-and-death power. So, Robert circled back to the progressive-but-privileged activist's guiding principle—what would a responsible ally do? A responsible ally would never endanger a migrant. In some circumstances, this meant leaving a border crossing group in the custody of a disreputable figure because it was safer than leaving them to their own devices.

THE OUTLIERS' NARRATIVES

Not every pro-immigrant activist was on board with this analysis of the coyote-in-the-camp scenario, however. Larry told me that, after five years of volunteering with the Humanitarians, he had stopped going to the desert. He disagreed with the group's actions.

Born shortly after the end of World War II, Larry grew up in a white, upper-middle-class household in the American South. After a career in the book publishing trade, Larry had moved to Arizona for drug and alcohol treatment. Then, through his volunteer work with the homeless, he learned about the Advocates and the Humanitarians. He instantly fell in love with the work in the desert and went out as much as three or four times a week for water drops. "If we weren't there, there would be many more people dying," he told me, adding, "I'm a walker and a birdwatcher and even if there were no Humanitarians, I'd still be walking out here in the wilderness." It was "just a perfect fit" for Larry.

Larry started feeling alienated from the group when he began wondering if they should be more discerning about the people they treated in the desert, particularly at their medical camp. "I fear that we're too open," he began. It was "foolish to pretend that all travelers in the desert are equal." In earlier years, the coyotes were independent entities: "They were good kids, from Sasabe or Nogales, just making money on the side." Over time, as the cartels entered the migrant-smuggling business, he had gotten wary. "Today, they're all—I think the term I've used is 'murdering rapists,' because they are. If they're not murdering rapists themselves, they work for murdering rapists." Larry hastened to say he was not opposed to providing food, water, and basic medical aid to everyone, "Anybody who's thirsty deserves water, even if they're carrying cocaine on their back." However, it seemed "foolish" to encourage people who were clearly not ordinary migrants to stay at the medical camp. If Border Patrol ever raided the camp and discovered patients linked to a cartel, the Humanitarians might have to close down their desert operations.

Larry's colleagues responded that it would be too hard to discern migrants from cartel members. "But, that's not so," Larry insisted. "I've done that work for five years, and I know that you can tell who's who." Some of the telltale signs he listed were ones Robert had shared: tattooed men showing up at camp, time after time, and those who arrived without backpacks (probably drug mules who stashed their bales of marijuana outside camp) were obviously suspect. Any reasonable person should be able to identify them, Larry thought.

Despite his unconventional contention that some border crossers were "murdering rapists," Larry believed, like Lucas, that the U.S. government should change its marijuana laws and suggested that the people actually moving drugs across the border were underpaid, ill-treated, and disposable—not kingpins deserving prison sentences:

> Let's not punish the poor guy . . . being brought into the country, and they're carrying the backpacks—and I've heard stories of these folks in Nogales—that when they get to the truck to unload their drugs, the driver of the truck pulls out a gun and takes the drugs and leaves them there. They're getting left out in the middle of the desert and not getting paid anything. They made it to *el Norte*, but . . .

Larry trailed off and then smiled. His smile implied a qualification to what he had been saying. Although he agreed with other pro-immigrant activists about the vulnerability of rank-and-file smugglers, he also seemed to suggest that it was acceptable, and perhaps even just, if the "poor guy" met his demise before he reached *el Norte*.

Larry was a dedicated member of the organization. He happily volunteered. He worried about the sustainability of the Humanitarians' operations in the desert. He even remained attached to the powerful state–powerless crosser dichotomy. Yet rather than resort to moral neutrality, as Gail or Robert did, Larry used characterizations that were far more common among restrictionists, eventually leading to his alienation from the group. That Mexican cartels were products of the U.S. state and, as such, not the rightful targets of public censure was so foundational a belief among activists that participants like Larry who did not fully endorse these ideas faced ostracism.

Amanda also stopped volunteering with the Humanitarians. A twenty-nine-year-old woman from an Arizonan border town, Amanda was not as well off as many of her white colleagues, but she too was the product of generational upward mobility. Her grandparents had immigrated to Arizona from Sonora, Mexico, to work in mining. All had successfully naturalized, including a grandfather who joined the military and served in the Vietnam War. Amanda's father had managed to avoid the mines— work that was "super dangerous"—by securing a job as a police officer, and eventually moving his family out of a trailer park into a "nice neighborhood." The extra income that her mother brought home as a secretary at a big company allowed the family to lead a "comfortable" life, especially compared to her relatives. Her family's economic well-being seemed particularly pronounced, and even disturbing, when she visited the neighboring Mexican border city "to have a good time."

> When I was fourteen, we'd go to [a Sonoran border city]. Everything was so cheap. We would drink. We would have fun. And then when we were done making our mess, we'd just cross the border [back to the United States]. When you're drunk, you can ignore the poverty in Mexico, but it still kinda brings you down. And you see people your age, or even younger, just suffering, looking older than what they should be. Then, we would just cross the border and the roads are paved, everything is fine. I felt like there was something wrong, and that I needed to escape where I was from.

To "escape," Amanda left home for university and became the first college graduate in her family. Later, she worked as a paralegal and made plans to apply to law school. Soon, however, studying for the Law School Admission Test and making other related preparations took a backseat to her civic engagement. She became a regular volunteer with the Humanitarians.

Amanda attributed some of her most "intense" life experiences to her work in the desert. "I mean, to be part of an enterprise to help a person who's, like literally dying in front of you, it's life-changing." But she grew increasingly uncomfortable with some of the interactions that the powerful state–powerless crosser dichotomy engendered between the Humanitarians and the people they set out to serve. Amanda was often the only fluent Spanish speaker as well as the only person of color volunteering at the medical camp. The group's racial homogeneity was confusing:

> I kept wondering, like, where are all the other Latinos? Like, how come there aren't a lot of people like me? I wanted to relate to *somebody*. I wanted somebody with my color or a darker color, with a thicker accent—somebody who wasn't wealthy or white to participate. It drove me nuts.

For Amanda, the "weirdness" came to a head one day when two well-dressed men showed up at the camp with a group of migrants. She overheard their conversation and realized they were coyotes, yet "I was grateful to them, because they brought people that were lagging behind, for aid." Still, it was clear they'd brought the migrants for help not because they cared about their well-being, but about losing profit if the migrants died. As the migrants rested, Amanda noticed the guides interacting with several new volunteers.

> Young Christian [white] women, who are, like, "Oh, poor Mexicans, give 'em a hug." Then, all of a sudden, these men were, like, touching their legs and being flirty, because what they were doing, culturally, they were . . . the girls were flirting too much . . . totally did not realize their boundaries. They were too into, like, "saving the Mexican" and hugging them, that when the other person started to act inappropriately and started touching back, they were, like, "Oh, what do we do?"

Amanda intervened, asking the men to go to the other side of the camp. She also stopped volunteering with the Humanitarians.

To Amanda, this incident encapsulated the bothersome dynamics between white activists and racialized border crossers. "I felt like, if you [the female volunteers] realized that we're all people, that there's no, like, 'us and them,' something like this could have been avoided." After a moment's pause, she added, "It just frustrates me when people [. . .] think that they're better than them." At camp, one could catch a glimpse of the state violence that migrants endured, violence that was otherwise invisible to Americans, particularly privileged ones. Yet, the very same experience could also reinforce a white savior complex: "'Oh, I'm a humanitarian, I saved this Mexican today.'" The image of the powerless crosser, which had been so compelling to other Humanitarians, felt like a racist trope to Amanda. "I just quit after that," she told me.

Though their views were significantly different, both Larry and Amanda stopped participating because they could not accept pro-immigrant activists' moral consensus around the trope of the "powerless crosser." Larry did not think the contexts of a guide's life circumstances necessitated his sympathy. Amanda worried that some activists' sympathy was actually based in a deep-seated, condescending racism.

CONCLUSION

This chapter illustrates the resilience of a worldview, a particular impression of the state that serves as an interpretive schema for Americans trying to navigate a complex space in which migration and the illicit drug trade are inextricably linked.

The identity conflict that grew out of their progressivism *and* their sense of personal privilege led left-wing activists to maintain public silence about drug smuggling, even as they privately struggled over how to make sense of it. Just the simple admission of the fact of drug smuggling, they feared, might reinforce the power disparities about which they already harbored so much personal guilt.

However, even as early as 2011, and certainly by 2017, cartel presence in the borderlands was a topic of private reflection and internal group discussions. Activists struggled to develop protocols around encounters with suspected cartel members. In a complex, uncertain space, pro-immigrant activists found their bearings with the help of the strong-state framework.

The strong-state effect offered activists a historical narrative about how the borderlands came to be, as well as a moral guide by which to assign certain actors agency and blame, and others none. This worldview pitted the powerless, third-world border crosser against the powerful American state. By doing so, activists managed to evade the tempting but problematic binary between the good and bad immigrant that was salient in public discourse and even in the larger pro-immigrant movement.[7] Variously, activists discussed the youth, expendability, and physicality of the imagined cartel member. These assigned attributes helped activists empathize. Some activists went even further, collapsing Latin American drug kingpins and their rank-and-file "foot soldiers" into oppressed "others" and the power of the American state and the privilege of ordinary Americans into an oppressive subject. Other activists used the dichotomy to justify their moral neutrality toward guides and smugglers. Those leftist activists who failed to internalize the implications of this strong state–weak subject dichotomy felt alienated and, eventually, stopped participating.

5 "We Work with Border Patrol"

David inched closer to the audio-recorder. It was loud in the diner, and he wanted to be heard. "This should go on the record," he said carefully. "I have a hate for bigotry and racism." I asked if he wanted to elaborate, but he told me that was all he wanted to say.

Restrictionist activists were profoundly aware of the allegation of racism. David, whom we met in chapter 3, was a white septuagenarian and an Air Force veteran. The premature deaths of his two Mexican-American stepsons had led him to join the Soldiers. After I switched off the recorder, waiting for our check, David seemed to be studying me. Unprompted, he said, "Don't write anything bad about the Soldiers, okay? We work with Border Patrol. We're not the Ku Klux Klan, you know? If the Soldiers were the Ku Klux Klan, I wouldn't be a part of it. I wouldn't."

Distancing himself from the KKK while embracing the Border Patrol captures the work that the weak-state-effect framework did for restrictionists as they wrestled with the topic of racism. Just as pro-immigrant activists danced around the uncomfortable subject of cartel violence by referring to the state's power, restrictionists relied on the weak-state-effect framework to make sense of race and racism, to dispute that their work was racially motivated activism.[1]

Restrictionists like David borrowed from conventional, bipartisan beliefs about racism as "essentialist racism" or a body of ideas that overtly claims the biological inferiority of people of color.[2] In this conceptualization, racism is a relic of the past only harbored by those on the fringes of society. Racists are extremists, marginal loners. By contrast, when David referred to the fact that his organization worked with (or, at least, strived to work with) the Border Patrol, he was pointing toward how restrictionists saw themselves: *as actors operating, collectively, at the institutional center of society—and therefore, not racist.*

This chapter shows how restrictionists rebutted "racism" claims in two main ways. First, they emphasized wanting to *collaborate* with frontline state actors, not get in their way. Their groups were set up to empower an emasculated state, they were inspired by respect for the law. "Real racists," meanwhile, were those who eschewed the law. They interrupted and interfered with everyday state practices. They annoyed Border Patrol agents. Sometimes, racists even tried to usurp law enforcement, further weakening the state. Second, restrictionists claimed that rather than being racist, their mobilization exemplified civic engagement and camaraderie. The exclusionary nature of racism, to their minds, was at odds with the fraternity and solidarity that restrictionists *felt* inside their groups. They were simply doing what other concerned Americans do when they want to see change—join groups, volunteer time, work together. The change that my conservative interlocutors wanted to see was a stronger, more authoritative state that could uphold the law.

By framing the "real racists" as outsiders and extremists, restrictionists once again drew on the conventional understanding of racism as a marginal rather than pervasive, interpersonal rather than institutional phenomenon. In this framework, racists were not guided by any clear cause, like ending unauthorized immigration and drug smuggling. They were motivated by personal greed and irrational hatred. Restrictionists would even imply they could spot a racist simply by the fact that he joined an activist organization in order to "play" with guns and tactical equipment, without considering how these actions could jeopardize the state's ability to do its work in the borderlands.

In distinguishing themselves from the "real racists," then, restrictionists drew on the weak-state-effect lens alongside conventional (and liberal) understandings about the extremist nature of racism.

TACTICAL VERSUS TECHNICAL

The restrictionist respondents contended that racists were people who overly focused on tactical operations, flouted the law, and impeded law enforcement agencies from carrying out their work. Boundary-making mechanisms like these were very important to the people I interviewed; like the pro-immigrant activists, restrictionists also worried about how the public talked about their mobilization.

Restrictionists described a particular scenario that they feared: a discrete act of violence by a right-wing activist against a border crosser leads to a loud, public condemnation of restrictionist groups as racist, thereby bringing their mobilization to an end. As if in anticipation of such an event, restrictionists differentiated among themselves, and the most significant marker of legitimacy and reputability was whether an organization had ties to state actors. For instance, when I first interviewed Connor the Engineer in 2011, he explained how he had been exposed to the full spectrum of restrictionist activism over the previous decade: "I've seen the good, bad, and the ugly. And the ugly gets real ugly." He painted a scenario that he believed could happen to another like-minded group, the Soldiers, if they weren't careful:

> They go out there with their guns and camouflage and get all . . . like the Soldiers, the guys in the camouflage. I was talking to them. . . and I was like, "How you guys going to alert people when you see somebody? *You guys don't have communicational capacity to alert Border Patrol.*" And the guys say to me, "We don't have too much range [on the satellite phone] . . . so we're just going to fire shots in the air." "That's illegal," [I said]. "No, it's not." "Yeah it is," I said. "You can't just shoot your guns in the air! It's against the law! Where's that bullet coming down?". . . [The Soldiers] really haven't thought about what they're actually doing out there in the desert and how they could really hurt somebody. And it really freaks me out. . . . God knows that these people are getting out there with their guns, and if they get in a bad spot, someone's going to get shot, and then somebody's going to get prosecuted, and then it's going to be [in news anchor's voice] "Ah, this Minutemen-type group kills illegal aliens. They're all racist hate groups." Vroom! There goes the whole thing! There goes the whole thing just down the tubes, because someone blew it.

Connor worried that the Soldiers mobilized without the right training to match their equipment ("guns and camouflage") or a clear protocol for contacting the Border Patrol in case of an encounter with a border crosser. He worried that the Soldiers' lack of expertise endangered lives and risked media scrutiny and charges of racism. He feared their rash actions could affect what people thought of his own group, the Engineers.

In another moment, Connor referred to the kind of "ugly" mobilization that could easily be depicted as racist and probably *was* motivated by racism. Once again, he emphasized that group's relationship was a prime indicator of its race neutrality.

> Honestly, I think they [the Soldiers] have more of penchant for *being tactical than for catching illegals.* They like to use all this cool gear they have, and they want to go out and play guns . . . because maybe they couldn't get in the army or something. I don't know. I don't want to talk too bad about these guys, but that's taking it a little bit far, going out all tactical like that. That's why it's cool being on the technical side, because we can stand up and watch and detect instead of being right on top of these people, because that's too much. *And really, Border Patrol DOESN'T like it. There might be a couple of agents who think it's cool, but the people at the top DO NOT want you out there doing that* because it's—somebody's going to get killed out there. And it's going to be bad. It's just a matter of time, you know. Remember what Shawna Forde did, you know? That's the perfect example. [emphasis mine]

Setting aside, for the moment, his Forde comment, we can see that Connor broached an important boundary-making theme often raised by restrictionists: those groups that were overly "tactical" were thought to have nefarious motivations. Arming yourself to go out into the border wilderness was not inherently wrong or racist; Connor told me he always armed himself "to the teeth" whenever he ventured into the desert, even though his organization, the Engineers, did not undertake patrols in the borderlands. Instead, the critique was that being tactical was not supposed to be an end in itself. It was a method, rather than an objective. The *actual* objective was to collaborate with, rather than try to replace or get in the way of, state actors. So the border groups that were fixated on the *means* were worrisome. When they swapped critical foresight for fancy military-grade equipment, these groups failed to prioritize their relationship with the state.

By way of example, Connor referred to Shawna Forde. At the time of our interview Forde had just been sentenced to death for murdering Raul

Flores Jr. and his nine-year-old daughter, Brisenia, in the Arizonan border town of Arivaca. Forde and her two accomplices were members of a border group that had splintered from the Minutemen; according to news reports, one accomplice, Jason Bush, had long-standing ties to the white supremacist organization, Aryan Nation. The three had impersonated law enforcement to enter the Flores home, hoping to find drugs and money to help finance their border group.[3] The would-be burglars shot Raul and Brisenia before escaping with some jewelry.

"I don't think that they were *that* motivated about illegal immigration," Connor continued. "They were just some racist rednecks who went on a shooting rampage. I heard they even dressed up like the cops!" To Connor's mind, being "motivated by illegal immigration" or the aim of "catching illegals" or even arming oneself in the desert were separate and distinct from "racism." But public discourse collapsed all these categories together. What mattered to Connor was the group's relationship to the state. Those who valued tactical operations were not trustworthy. They were probably racist. Those who understood that tactical equipment could come in handy when working *with* the state were just being good citizens.

Ian, a fifty-two-year old white man, agreed with Connor. Early in our conversation, Ian referred to groups like the Soldiers as usually having the "right motivations." But this diplomatic characterization began to waver. People who went out into the desert, he said, were, at best, "playing cowboys and injuns, you know, just having fun." At worst, they were the next "Shawna Forde waiting to happen." Taking on risky endeavors that could get all border-watch groups crucified as racists seemed like a particularly bad idea because "border militias" were not actually forcing the government to change how it protected the boundary.

You can tell that I have various degrees of burnout, because I have been doing it for so long. It's just that nothing changes. The government's not going to change, let you really do something. So I figured instead of telling them they're stupid all the time—which is kinda what those border militias are doing—let's give them [government officials] something that will solve their problem. Let's see if they'll use it. You know, if we give them a good tape [recording of a demonstration of the Engineers' technology], if they run with this technology, if they [install] it, . . . what's going to happen? Arizona will be the first to put it in; Texas will be like "Holy crap, that's cool.

We want one!" They'll put it in. . . . And if it works out, that'll solve it. That'll look great on my *résumé*. [*Laughs.*] Oh yeah, "That was me. I solved the border problem. No really, it was just me."

The difference between their group and those open to charges of racism, these men insisted, was that their group was actually trying to "solve" the "border problem." Even if the federal government was unresponsive, there were still opportunities to collaborate with state and local governments, Ian explained. Racism, to the extent that it existed, was a fringe phenomenon; the Engineers, by contrast, operated at the rightful center of society.

Interestingly, the Soldiers utilized the same boundary-making mechanism to dissociate themselves from *other* organizations that patrolled the border. Linda explained that the Soldiers had to be careful about what they allowed participants to bring into the desert on patrols. Scopes for guns, for instance, were not allowed; when someone donated scopes to the group, Linda auctioned them off on eBay. When I asked why, she said scopes were considered "tactical, like you're aiming" your gun at someone. Certain types of long guns, like AKs, ARs, and shotguns, were not allowed either. Though the guns were legal to carry in Arizona, Linda explained that the guns, like the scopes, could still put volunteers in legally precarious situations. "Let's say that the cartel is out there and all of a sudden," Linda narrated, "you hear gunfire, and you have one of those [*points at a donated scope*] and you're shooting back. That's the difference between murder and self-defense."

The Soldiers soon realized that their protocols served a second, potentially more important, purpose: they helped the group vet new volunteers. A prospective volunteer's response to the gun and equipment guidelines could tell the Soldiers a lot about their worldviews and mental health. Some applicants, for example, flatly refused to participate when they found out they could not be as tactical as they wanted to be. "Well, we don't want you around, anyway," Linda said, "So peace out." She told me the group had "gotten rid" of someone who had wanted to bring along his AK and who had referred to "scalping Mexicans." "That's what I consider racist," Linda snapped.

Billy, a thirty-year-old white volunteer who worked as a software engineer in Southern Arizona, and Dougie, a retired, white participant from

Mississippi, expounded on what made the Soldiers different from militia groups. Billy was an enthusiastic participant who went out into the desert with the group twice a month, and he had been volunteering for a little over a year. On a few occasions, I overheard Billy explaining to newcomer Dougie how "things were done." When the three of us spoke together, we sat in lawn chairs under a foldup shade, about a mile north of the border in the middle of desert wilderness. At midday, the base camp was quiet. There was nothing to do but pass the time until dinner.

Dougie leaned back to put his feet up on a cooler. Before arriving in Arizona, Dougie had volunteered with a border group in Texas, but he said Texas was full of militias and he did not want to be part of one. I asked him what distinguished the Soldiers from those groups: "I see the difference as [militias] being more aggressive, more tactical. We're not aggressive. We're very not aggressive, as you can see." He chuckled and gestured to the way he was lounging. Billy jumped in: "Militias have a mentality that they're going to come out and perform law enforcement duties. . . . *Whereas we . . . are operating within a set parameter of rules and regulations that are not law enforcement. We're not out here to take the law into our own hands*" [emphasis mine]. By way of example, he likened the Soldiers to defense contractors, like Triple Canopy and Blackwater.

Dougie picked up, "Yeah, we don't carry handcuffs. We don't detain them [border crossers]. If they sit down, they sit down. We give them water, something to eat, and we call Border Patrol." The men were briefly sidelined discussing a border crosser ("one Mexican," in Dougie's words) whose knee had been hurt and how the Soldiers had provided medical help and then called Border Patrol. The militias, they contended, would not have provided humanitarian aid like that. Billy continued, saying of militias,

> They're not disciplined. They don't actually answer to anybody, whereas we do. As Rick was telling you, we do converse with Border Patrol. [With us,] there's a chain of command, and there is oversight. Whereas militias, anybody can call themselves a militia, grab their rifles, come out here, and perform border security. There's far less oversight of what they're doing.

Dougie added, "It's a camaraderie thing. You're going to watch my back and I'm going to watch your back. I think, on the militia side, they watch their own backs."

Billy disagreed. He retorted, "I think the militias have camaraderie among themselves as well. I think they're going to watch each other's backs as well. *But they're not going to take their relationship with the law into the same consideration*" [emphasis mine]. Dougie agreed. As if to settle the issue that the Soldiers were no militia, though, he said, "We're an intel-gathering group—that's it. Now, if we're tracking them [border crossers] and they drop their bags, by all means, *please* drop your bags. We'll just call it in, Border Patrol will come pick it up and pick them [the border crossers] up hopefully."

In the conversation, Billy drew a starker boundary between his own group and militias: "I think that a lot of the people that you talk to around here [who say], 'Oh, someone was killed and we don't know who did it,' they're thinking about the militias, not us when they say that." Billy may have been referring to Shawna Forde's group, or maybe the case of Jason Todd "J. T." Ready out of Gilbert, Arizona. Ready was a former neo-Nazi who helped found a restrictionist desert patrol group that called itself U.S. Border Guard. In 2012, during a violent domestic dispute, Ready shot and killed four people, including a toddler, before killing himself. Whoever he meant, though, I could see that Billy was acutely concerned about the infamous people the public might associate with Arizona border groups. As if coaching Dougie, the Soldiers' newcomer, and maybe even performing colorblindness for me, Billy had also interrupted Dougie to correct a racialized assumption earlier in the conversation. When Dougie referred to the man with the knee injury they encountered as "one Mexican," Billy had said quickly, "There's no proof he was Mexican" and "we *think* he was illegal."

Most importantly, the nature of one's relationship to law enforcement was the principal boundary-making mechanism that the men harnessed in order to dispute the claim that their actions were racist. Certain kinds of equipment (handcuffs) and protocols (like the use of a rank structure) were coded as "tactical" and "aggressive." Importantly, being "tactical" got a group dangerously close to vigilantism. Although the Soldiers were armed and uniformed when they went out into the desert, and could easily be mistaken for Border Patrol agents when seen from a distance, the Soldiers nonetheless maintained that they were not trying to *be* agents. Moreover, the issue of ranks had almost caused a schism among the

Soldiers a few years prior: one faction wanted a rank system based on military experience. The fight had been about a key aspect of the group's identity: how civilian (and inclusive) would the Soldiers be? And, by extension, what kind of relationship would the group have with state actors? Eventually, the rank-system advocates were ousted and the Soldiers avoided becoming more like a typical militia.

The Arpaiositos did not raise the issue of tactics or even militias as reference points, but they, too, worried about being tainted by the racism of "fringe" figures. The Arpaiositos primarily organized in urban regions in the Greater Phoenix area. At one of the first meetings that I attended, the Arpaiositos were discussing recruitment and their relationships to others in the field of struggle.

Cheryl, a forty-five-year-old Latina, was trying to convince her colleagues that they had to "drop the Tea Party brand." Specifically, she wanted the Arpaiositos to leave a Tea Party–organized forum and create a new website, outside the umbrella group. The group's online forum was an important line of communication for like-minded local groups in the area; this way, for example, Sedona Tea Partiers stayed aware of events that Phoenix-area groups were organizing and vice versa. It was particularly instrumental in quickly assembling for public events, raising money, and recruiting new members. The Arpaiositos were among the most active groups on the forum.

Now, Cheryl told her colleagues, it was time to rethink the group's affiliations with the Tea Party. She didn't "trust" them. Speaking rapidly, Cheryl noted that local Tea Parties were overly besotted with State Senator Russell Pearce, who had been elected president of the state senate a few months earlier (in 2011). Pearce's relationship to J. T. Ready, the neo-Nazi, was well known. Despite public denials, Pearce and Ready had been friends well before they appeared together at a 2007 political rally, Cheryl explained: "The rumor is that Pearce ordained Ready as an elder in the Mormon Church. . . . That's a big deal in the Church, you know?"

Rafael, a Latino in his forties, jumped in. He, too, had heard the rumor, and he had read online forums suggesting that "Even the militias don't trust Ready anymore. . . . He's too *out there*. He's crazy." According to the forums, people were leaving Ready's border patrol organization because of the "crazy" things he was saying and doing. Ostensibly a group of "patriots," it appeared Ready's group was actually a front for his bigger, neo-Nazi project. So, Rafael suggested that instead of using the Tea Party forum, perhaps the Arpaiositos could rely on other right-wing forums in which he participated. Cheryl liked the idea.

Months later, the Arpaiositos were still using the Tea Party forum, but the topic was raised at almost every group meeting. I noticed that it seemed the group's inertia, rather than their ideological views, was the only barrier to a final break with the Tea Party brand. The ongoing conversation also indicated how the Arpaiositos understood racism: to the extent that racial bias existed among restrictionists, the Arpaiositos maintained, its sources primarily existed on the margins of society.

In the minds of my restrictionist respondents, they *couldn't* be racist because they were helping frontline state workers carry out the law. Billy, not unlike Connor of the Engineers, argued for the legitimacy of his group by referring to defense contractor's relationships with the government as precedent. A contractor worked with, and at the behest of, the state; the contractor allowed the state to more effectively carry out its policies, without losing sight of the fact that it was not officially *part* of the state.

As chapter 7 explains in more detail, there was a material basis for this perception that restrictionist groups were prospective security contractors or civilian extensions of Border Patrol. The Border Patrol's official discourse discouraged private citizens from intercepting border crossers. However, I witnessed how rank-and-file agents readily worked with the Soldiers and how deputies worked with the Arpaiositos through the Maricopa County Sheriff's Office civilian posse. Restrictionists were appropriating a tendency in public discourse—including some leftist discourse—to locate organized racism at the margins, rather than the center of society. Racism lived *outside*, in fringe groups that had completely disavowed state institutions, not *inside*, working with the state.

"WE'RE ALL BROTHERS, NO MATTER WHAT COLOR YOU ARE"

Restrictionists distanced themselves from claims of racism by referring not only to the trust and relationships that they cultivated with frontline state actors but also to the trust and friendships that they cultivated among themselves. "It's a camaraderie thing," Dougie had explained. "You're going to watch my back and I'm going to watch your back. I think on the militia side, they watch their own backs." James, a reserved and thoughtful forty-five-year-old white man, told me the friendships and sense of group solidarity that bloomed among the Soldiers was colorblind: "We're here, we're all brothers, we watch each other's backs, no matter what color you are."

It was a cold winter morning, and James and I huddled by a dying bonfire at the group's base camp. James was waiting for some of the other men to return from the previous night's stakeout before he departed. His demeanor was generally serious, yet James seemed to be in a more somber mood than usual. He was "kinda dreading" going back to his "boring life" in Central Arizona. About two years before, the Marines Corp veteran had left California and moved to a town about an hour and a half north of Phoenix. He was following a young woman—his future ex-wife. James eked out a living fixing cars, his occupation indelibly marked on his oil-stained fingers. It was dirty, low-paid work, and James flirted with the idea of going back to school for an associate's degree. But the prospect of taking classes was daunting; he had barely gotten through high school. So here, with the Soldiers, it was a respite.

James eagerly looked forward to going out into the desert. He had, at times, even borrowed gas money from friends to make the drive to the border. On this particular trip, James had come down to the border for just two nights. He greeted fellow participants with warm handshakes and enthusiastic hugs. The circumstances, James mentioned later, forced the men to get to know each other well. Two-person stakeouts lasted a minimum of twelve hours, and you had to stay awake and focused; talking kept them alert. When the men sat around the bonfire in the evening, joking and telling stories, they got closer.

At one point, James asked me what I, personally, thought of the Soldiers. A little startled, I told him that as a sociologist, my job was to set my assumptions aside and try to understand why people did what they did. But, I told him, the Soldiers' presence at the border made me "uneasy." When he pressed the issue, I talked about how the circumstances were highly racialized: most of the Soldiers were white men, most of the people they were trying to catch and detain were Latin American. If their work was not racist, if it was not at least *racialized*, I asked, why weren't there more people of color volunteering with the Soldiers? James jumped in.

> But you know that's wrong, right? Every op is different. I grew up in L.A. I love Hispanic people. I love Mexican food. I have a lot of friends that are from Peru, Mexico. I don't have any issue with anybody. Tommy is Mexican. His wife is from Mexico. We have another guy who was out here, he's Native American. We've had some Asian guys out here. The majority is white, maybe. But it's not really about that. And that's the problem I have with this whole issue: it ends up being about race. It's like, we're not out here to shoot Mexicans. It could have been a Paki who came across the border. It could have been a white guy from South Africa coming across the border. Because Mexico is a point of entry, people come from all over. So, it's not. . . . It's just that, flying directly into the U.S. is very difficult. So, Mexico is the easiest— it's like the center point for anybody who wants to come to America, from any country. It's a lot easier to come through Mexico rather than directly into the U.S.[4]

I circled back to the most observable indication of racial dynamics. "But you do recognize that it is overwhelmingly people from Mexico and Central America [crossing through Southern Arizona], right?"

"Of course, of course," James conceded.

"And the people who are out here," I said, pointing to the men around me, "doing this work are mostly Anglo." He nodded in agreement, but insisted it was geographic happenstance that created these racial patterns.

> But that's also the majority here in the U.S. If you look at it proportionately, that's just the way the coin fell. But there are guys from other races here. I mean, if we're on patrol and we see two white, pasty, redheaded guys walking through the bushes with big ol' packs and camo[uflage] and water jugs, are we going to treat them any different? "Where are you coming from? Why are you carrying those packs?" The same thing. It's not *who's* coming through. It's "why" and "what" and "how." . . . You get, mostly Hispanic, because this is the Mexican border. In Spain, they get a lot of the people from Africa, you know, crossing their borders. You're not going to be catching Mexicans crossing the border in Spain. Geographically, we have borders with Mexico, so the majority of what's coming through here are people from Central and South America.

Going further, James told me that the friendships and sense of camaraderie that he felt among the Soldiers were incompatible with racial hostility.

> That's the part for people to understand, that it really isn't about race. I've been out here, every time I come out, I meet different people. And I'm not just telling you this, honestly, not because you're doing research and I'm trying to say the right thing—this is not a racist group at all. *We all have friends of all different kinds of colors. You get Marines—they're brothers whether they're Black, white, Chinese, Native American, they're all brothers.* We operate the same way here. We're here. *We're all brothers. We watch each other's backs, no matter what color you are.* [emphasis mine]

In line with other conservative restrictionists, James attributed the racialized nature of unauthorized migration in the Arizona borderlands to "the unintended consequences of demography and geography."[5] Moreover, the Soldiers and other groups offered a precious opportunity to build community and cultivate friendships in ways that were totally inconsonant with racism.

Bob, a lanky man in his late sixties, also believed that the multiracial camaraderie he felt among the Arpaiositos was anathema to racism. Compared to the Soldiers or the Engineers, the Arpaiositos did have more activists of color in their ranks. Bob, who identified as white, was like James, never really a "joiner." But soon after he attended his first Tea Party rally in downtown Phoenix, Bob joined two restrictionist groups. One, for dedicated motorcyclists, was almost exclusively white men. Bob did not like the group's emphasis on "education" rather than "action," and he almost immediately began skipping meetings. But he rarely missed an Arpaiosito meeting. In his black leather Harley-Davidson vest and black boots, Bob stood out next to Arpaiositos like Cheryl, who preferred brightly colored shirts, puffy vests, and no-nonsense khaki pants. Bob's ears were pierced, and he often wore black nail polish. At meetings, he hung back, leaning against his cane as other group members talked with and, often, over each other.

At one particularly animated meeting, Bob turned to me and asked whether I knew anything about La Raza movement. I shook my head, inviting him to explain. In his steady manner of speaking, Bob explained that we were living in "dangerous times."

There's a lotta La Raza people that are actually talking about civil war. It's gotten to that point. They want to kill all white males and white females under a certain age. They keep saying we're the racists, because we want to defend the constitution and uphold the law [*chuckles*]. But, you know, they're the real racists. They want to slowly wipe the country clean of white people. They [the Raza movement] recruit in the schools, with the Raza studies programs. It's really scary, when you think about it.

I pushed Bob for details. He said that Raza groups, like the ones that congregated in front of the State Capitol building to protest SB1070, were trying to turn non-racial issues into racial ones. Instead of promoting unity and lawfulness, they were creating false divisions among Americans and joining forces with "illegals" on the basis of race. Provocatively, he claimed some members of this so-called Raza movement were in favor of white genocide. More moderate movement people simply wanted to use their demographic advantages to marginalize white people. "But look at us!" Bob exclaimed, gesturing at the loud Arpaiosito meeting unfolding in front of us. "You know, I never really had Hispanic friends or Native American friends before I joined this group," he said.

The collective solidarity that people like James and Bob felt in their organizations seemed antithetical to the divisiveness and acrimony that they associated with racism. They pointed to the multiracial membership of their organizations. They also fell back on the idea that civic engagement and racism existed in very different, *opposite* domains of society. When people got together to discuss and advance a cause, as Bob and James did, they were exercising good citizenship, not racism. Such opportunities for civic engagement were rare for the average restrictionist, who, as a white-but-working-class man, felt so marginalized in other parts of his life.

HELPING THE STATE PROTECT WOMEN

The Soldiers also relied on a gender-protectionist logic that ironically tied into racist tropes about dangerous men of color in order to dispute the claim that theirs was a racist endeavor.[6] Rick, for instance, used the relationship between geography, gender, and racism: "According to the media, we're [the Soldiers are] a bunch of racists with guns, shooting women and children, when [in fact] we haven't seen women and children here in years. *You* see this terrain! Do you want to drag a child through this thing?" Rick professed that women and children preferred crossing through Brownsville, Texas, because the terrain was less rough there. Arizona, where it was more rugged, had become the territory of drug smuggling—an activity that the Soldiers associated with men and masculinity. Trying to interdict women and children was potentially racist, but interrupting drug smuggling was not. Thus, by being in Arizona, the Soldiers were, by definition, not motivated by racism.

Staying within this logic, I wondered what the Soldiers would do if they came across a female border crosser carrying drugs or accompanying a group that was carrying drugs. Sometimes drug transportation is part of the fare of passage, I said to Rick. Anyone—including a woman—might be coerced into smuggling drugs. Rick conceded that it could happen, but it seemed very unlikely. The cartels, he replied, preferred "professional" (read: male) smugglers to civilians (read: female). "They're called [drug] 'mules' for a reason," he said. Smugglers were "professionals" who had to be in "tip-top" shape to brave the 120°F weather while loaded down with "twenty-five kilos of dope, plus another twenty kilos of food. . . . These guys are frigging animals."

Rick paused, then shared an anecdote that would become very familiar in my research. To the Soldiers, this story illustrated how the Arizona borderlands had become uninviting for women crossers and how the Soldiers were justified in supporting law enforcement efforts in the region:

> About two years ago, I was coming out here and right down the road, there was a nineteen-year-old Ecuadoran girl standing in the road. I stopped and got out and asked her if she wanted help, and she said "Yeah." She had a black eye, blood coming out of her nose, and her lip was busted. She had dried blood all over her face. So I got her in the truck, started heading back in. She told me it took her six months to get to the fence, and the night before, she came across with twenty-three guys. And when they laid down to go to sleep, that's when they beat her and gang-raped her. They took all of her money and her ID and just left her. So, as soon as I could, I called Border Patrol and they came swarming in. They were like, "When? Where? How long?" It was like eight or nine hours before. They put out, basically, an APB [all-points bulletin] to find these guys. I don't know if they ever did. It happens *all* the time out there.

I was never able to independently confirm or contradict the veracity of this story. While there have been many reported cases of sexual assaults against migrants en route to and in the U.S. borderlands, I never found this particular story mentioned in the local media.[7] More than its actual truth, however, the story's importance lies in the work that it does for Rick and the other men. First, the story illustrates how the Soldiers use gender to understand the landscape. According to Rick, to the extent that there *were* women border crossers in Southern Arizona, they were embodiments of victimhood. All the details reinforced female vulnerability and, concomitantly, the dangerous nature of the borderlands: she was nineteen years old, barely an adult, a "girl." She had been traveling alone for a half a year, and was again alone, presumably left for dead, when Rick found her. She had been robbed. Her abuse was detailed and graphic—there was "blood all over her face," having been gang-raped by as many as twenty-three men.

Two other aspects of this narrative are noteworthy. The first is that, in his telling, Rick and the Border Patrol teamed up; they were the white saviors of a brown woman from brown men, bringing to life a well-known racist trope.[8] The second is that Rick does not claim to work with the agency as an equal partner. After getting the woman into his truck, Rick reported that he "head[ed] back in." While it was unclear where exactly he transported her, the destination was presumably away from the desert (understood as a site where racialized sexual predators lurked) to a Border Patrol post (understood as a site of safety.) Rick did not take matters into his own hands, the way a "racist vigilante" might have. He deferred to the Border Patrol so completely that Rick never even learned what happened afterward.

Rick shared the burden of white male protection with the Border Patrol, and so he alluded to the idea that the state needed reinforcement. The agents had not found the girl; Rick had. Without him, the woman may never have been found. The possibility that the perpetrators were never located, alludes to the state's weakness.

Military activities tend to be gendered and sexualized, with women participating in nationalist politics as "signifiers of ethnic/national differences."[9] Although the U.S.-Mexico borderlands are not officially a warzone, many actors—from Border Patrol agents to television shows—nonetheless utilize this metaphor to describe the relationship between border crossers

and law enforcement.[10] Borrowing this metaphor, restrictionists additionally described *sexual* violence by male smugglers against female migrants
and attributed this aggression to the state's feeble enforcement apparatus.
In this narrative, women were either entirely *absent* from the Arizona-
Sonora border or they were *present, but raped*. Either way, the gendered
logic helped restrictionists paint a moral picture of the borderlands
wherein they—along with Border Patrol agents—were heroic, masculine
protectors not only of the country, but of victimized women.[11]

Their gendered and sexualized coding of the borderlands helped
restrictionists dispute allegations of racism. Within the stark context of
"war"—between masculine protectors and rapacious, racialized demons—
the question of racial intolerance was beyond irrelevant; it was ignorant.
In a context of war, you had to take a side—either you protected female
border crossers (like the restrictionists) or you condoned sexual violence
(like the pro-immigrant activists):

> I've asked the humanitarians before [about sexual assaults].[12] The humani-
> tarians are the ones who leave all the water on the drug trails. Do you know
> what their answer was to me? "Well, they're told to take birth control pills
> before they come across." I was like, "So that makes it okay [that female
> migrants get raped]?" And they're like, "Well, no, but at least they won't get
> pregnant." So, I ask them, "Well, if they're doing it out here [raping women
> in the desert], they'll do it in the city." What if they rape your mother or
> daughter or sister? What are you going to say? "Oh, you should've taken
> birth control"?

To Rick, pro-immigrant groups were oblivious to the gendered and sexualized realities of the "war" unfolding in the borderlands. They were morally
indifferent to cartel violence; they *condoned* the rape and abuse of female
crossers by putting out water on migrant trails, by aiding and abetting cartel
activity. Pro-immigrant activism weakened an already-emasculated state
and thereby increased gendered violence. In an us-versus-them context,
restrictionists thought it made no sense that pro-immigrant activists cried
"racism."

Ned also used the logic of gendered protectionism to dispute the claim
that race and immigration politics necessarily intersected. On numerous
occasions, Ned insisted that his concern about drug smuggling was his
motivation for border work. I asked about a hypothetical scenario: What

if there were no drug smuggling in the Arizona borderlands? What if the only illegal activity was simply the cross-border movement of people? Would he continue to come out into the desert? Ned took his time to think before explaining that the gendered consequences of the human smuggling trade still bothered him. Migration involved cartels.

> No, I wouldn't say that I wouldn't be out here. Not so much because of the people being smuggled but because of the people *doing* the smuggling. We've all read horror stories of what happens to them. . . . *Women get raped.* One of the times that we were out here, a couple of people came running up to us and said that they were robbed two days ago at gunpoint. They took everything. They had no food, no water. They'd been stranded for two days. Um, those guys [in the cartel], they're trafficking people. They're trafficking prostitution. . . . A lot of times, they bring these women over and they make them pay it off in sex trade. It's still wrong. They're still bad guys. It's all cartel related. They make money however they can. . . . The same guys who are responsible for human trafficking are the same groups that are moving drugs. They just have different facets of the business. But in the end, they're all the bad guys. They don't care. I read a news story a while back where they found a six-year-old girl on the side of a river wash, just abandoned. Dying. They don't care if you're a kid, as long as they've got their money.

To Ned's mind, migration was morally problematic because the cartels had taken over as guides, and they were sexual demons that victimized women. His mention of the six-year-old girl is significant: Ned assumed her abandonment was the result of sexual violence committed by cartel-employed smugglers. He did not entertain other scenarios; perhaps the child was dying of dehydration and the parent could not carry their daughter to safety. Restrictionists' gendered logic dictated that women and girls were the victims of violence, male-typed cartel affiliates were the perpetrators, and the violence was sexualized. This framework allowed restrictionists to challenge claims that their mobilization in the borderlands was racially motivated.

"I'VE BEEN CALLED A RACE TRAITOR"

The resilience of the weak-state effect became most clear to me when I asked Tommy about the racial aspect of his mobilization. A devoted restrictionist, Tommy was one of the few Soldiers who identified as a Mexican-American. He also drew on the group's boundary-making strategies. Like his fellow participants, Tommy argued that there was a vast social distance between state-reinforcing *collective* work undertaken by the Soldiers and the extremist actions of racist loners.

Tommy was so aware of race that he answered my question before it was finished. "Do you get people saying to you, 'Hey you're Mexican-American, why'"—Tommy stopped me. "Yes!"

"What do you say to them?"

"It's not about the race!" He spoke with a staccato emphasis on each word: "It is not about the race." He went on: "I go, 'My wife's Mexican. My parents immigrated to the United States and became citizens. I have cousins who are illegal. I still have relatives in Mexico, and I go to Mexico and visit them.'" He continued, "We had a journalist out here who said, 'You're racist.' Man, I'm not racist! It's not about stopping a race. It's about," he paused, "the drugs coming in, the really bad stuff going on."

Tommy said, "Oh I get it all the time, especially at work." Many of his coworkers at the California prison were also Latino. One such coworker, who realized that Tommy was accumulating his vacation days to go to the Arizona-Mexico border, had confronted him. Just as other studies about conservative Latinos have revealed,[13] Tommy responded to his co-ethnics' social sanctions by positioning himself as "Latino, but American":

> I'm proud to be Mexican. But I'm not a citizen of Mexico. I was born in America. I was raised in America. I was in the military. I was given a free education in America. So why would I support another country that hasn't done anything for me? . . . I do have relatives in Mexico. I'm glad to be of Mexican-American heritage. I'm proud of it [*chuckles*]. I've been called "race traitor." I mean, come on! [*Laughs.*] How can I be a race traitor? "You're out there stopping, you know, poor guys or ladies or kids." No! How many ladies or kids walk through here? If you don't believe me, you try it. We'll see how long you last out here. Do you think it's really safe? Go stand there at night and see what happens. People are so naive. People will believe what they see on the news. They'll believe what they want to hear.

With obvious frustration, Tommy disputed the idea that his racial heritage required him to feel solidarity with immigrants. The label "race traitor" suggested to Tommy that Latinos should trade their loyalty to their own country for loyalty to a foreign nation or to a race.[14] To him, that was absurd. His allegiance lay not with people committing a crime by crossing into the country illegally but with the nation in which he had grown up and served. Above everything else, he was "American."

Like the group's white participants—and sometimes even more emphatically—Tommy drew on the gender-protectionist logic to assert the irrelevance of race to their actions. He insisted that people who deserved sympathy—regular civilians who were not affiliated with the cartels, particularly women and children—were not in the areas where their group operated. He dared an ambiguous "you" (by which he may have meant an unsympathetic co-ethnic coworker, a woman, or specifically me) to try surviving in the desert alone. Its cruelty kept "regular" people out of this desert. Only professional drug smugglers would be found in this rugged terrain.

At times, it felt like Tommy was talking as much to himself as to me. He struggled with the theme of race. Like other restrictionists, he argued for the racial neutrality of the Soldiers by associating them with law enforcement and distancing them from "fringe" racist actors:

> We're out here. What are we going to do when a lady with a child comes walking in? Of course, we're going to give them humanitarian aid; we're going to give food and do medical assistance on them. There's obviously the human side to it, the sanctity of life, yeah, I think about that too. . . . *Other [border watch] groups out there, the militia guys, they're like, "They're Mexican, screw 'em."* I mean, come on, dude. [emphasis mine]

I pressed on. "So, if there wasn't drug smuggling going on and if it was entirely human smuggling, you wouldn't be out here?" Tommy said, "Probably not, probably not." I continued, asking, "What do you say to people who want to come to the United States, want to assimilate, want to be productive, but don't have the means and that's why they might get roped into transporting drugs. What's your response to that?"

"It's a bad situation," Tommy admitted. "I mean, if they mean well, I mean, there's the right way to do it and there's the wrong way. The economics . . . ." Tommy trailed off, and so I picked up again.

> EFE: But you know that for many Mexican citizens it's very, very hard to even get a visa to come to the U.S.

TOMMY: Not really. Not really. Because my wife's relatives, they just came to visit. They're business owners. Okay, yeah, they have to have certain documentation, paperwork, okay, "We have land. We have a business going on."

EFE: Not everyone has land. Not everyone's a business owner.

TOMMY: That's true [*pauses*]. But the reason why *I* am here is 'cuz of the drugs.

I gave Tommy some time, thinking he might elaborate, then asked whether he'd come across anyone among the Soldiers who was a white supremacist. "*No,*" he insisted. "*I mean, I use common sense to figure out who's who and who's not. I wouldn't associate with them at all, especially if they're obsessed with race. I'm not going to name any names, but certain groups. I tell this to my friends at work. It's not about the race. It's about the drugs on the streets*" [emphasis mine].

One of the consequences of this colorblind and "power-evasive discourse" about race is "flight from feelings."[15] Respondents, often after contradicting themselves several times, ultimately downplay their feelings about racial difference to the point of even minimizing their *own* experiences of marginalization.[16] This happened with Tommy repeatedly.

In sum, Tommy fastened himself to the weak-state effect so as to find his footing in these confrontational moments. His group wasn't interested in stopping the "good immigrants," like women and children, but in bolstering law enforcement. The Soldiers, if they came upon women and children, would emulate the state's protectionism, providing them safety, water, and medical assistance. By contrast, militias' "obsession with race" muddled their motivations. Racists were not trying to be civilian extensions of the state, but fringe actors. Rather than cultivating camaraderie, encouraging civic engagement, and recruiting more people into the restrictionist cause, the "real racists" alienated concerned Americans like Tommy.

CONCLUSION

This chapter uses a bottom-up approach that attends to actual racial utterances, and in doing so, contributes to extant scholarship about how right-wing activists "neutralize" charges of racism.[17] In contrast to some scholarship's assumptions about restrictionism and race,[18] I find that

activists are not comfortable with the racial aspects of their mobilization. Even those who wanted to reinforce racialized social systems nonetheless struggled with the stigma of the label "racist."[19] They understood
that mainstream discourse defines racism as exclusively "essentialist racism" (rather than also colorblind, institutional racism), and it tends to
equate "racist" with being a "bad person."[20] Within this context, restrictionists responded to the label "racist" the way *most* Americans do: with
distancing.

To distinguish themselves from racists, restrictionists leveraged the
weak-state-effect paradigm in conjunction with mainstream ideas about
racism. David, for instance, stated that his group was "not the Ku Klux
Klan" in the same breath as "we work with Border Patrol." In referencing
the Klan, David was conveying the idea that racism was an extremist, and
even bygone, phenomenon. Racism was a set of *individual* affective dispositions harbored by *fringe* social actors. Logically, such marginalized
actors would have a hard time working with formal institutional actors
like Border Patrol. By pointing to their efforts to shore up the state, therefore, restrictionists were actually arguing for the legitimacy and mainstream nature of their work.

To underline the idea that theirs was a legitimate and race-neutral
rather than marginalized and racist form of mobilization, respondents
also linked their actions with the celebrated American tradition of volunteerism. In the United States, distinctly American moral values like individualism can be used to justify racial resentment.[21] My right-wing
respondents were doing something similar. In this variant of racism,
restrictionists argued that the masculine camaraderie that they felt as they
cooperated with state actors to protect racialized women and even cultivated interracial friendships was antithetical to the extremism and exclusionary nature of racism. How could they be racist vigilantes if state actors
agreed to work with them? How could they be racists qua bad people if
they were trying to protect "girls" from assault? How could they be fringe
actors when their activism was collective, even including people of color?
These boundary-making mechanisms allowed restrictionists to discard
the relevance of race in what they were doing.

Although volunteering is widely celebrated in the United States, the
restrictionists I spoke with had rarely encountered such opportunities,

making grassroots restrictionism even *more* attractive to them. For many restrictionists, the military was the only other institution in which they had experienced any kind of group solidarity or teamwork. Their activism reminded veterans like James, Rick, and Tommy of the kind of fellowship that had been celebrated while they were in the service. It also was a powerful contrast to the alienation they felt in the rest of their lives.

To varying degrees, scholars have documented the absence of associational life among white working-class people.[22] Unlike other studies, however, this book illustrates that there are important links between racial politics and the desire for collective action among white-but-working-class people. To right-wing interlocutors like James, it seemed genuinely impossible that this rare occasion for inclusion and camaraderie could accommodate racism. Such boundary-making mechanisms, which James harnessed so easily, should give sociologists pause. We should rethink our tendency to celebrate all instances of volunteerism. Instead, future research must take seriously the *content* and *political effects* of civic engagement and social movements, just as much as, and perhaps even more than the forms that they take.

PART III   Practicing Symbolic Politics

The state effects that activists perceived informed which strategies their organizations used. The next two chapters describe the elaborate tactical repertoires of each group. More importantly, I illustrate how activists' methods of mobilization—their day-to-day practices and long-term strategies—gain meaning *only* in relation to participants' worldviews, the organizations' political programs, and the broader immigration struggle in which activists were embedded.

Social movement and political sociology scholars' preference for studying form (*how* groups mobilize) over content (*why* they mobilize) is not unusual. This empiricist preference is, in fact, motivated by a noble goal: to overcome the deadlocks that accompany contentious topics and possibly foster more mutual understanding across conventional political divides (rather than reproducing partisan positions by spotlighting content).

Certainly, the focus on form has generated rich empirical insights. We have learned, for instance, that right-wing groups no longer have a monopoly on religion in America: immigrant rights advocates and other progressive organizations increasingly rely on faith to make their demands. Empirical studies about right-wing mobilization methods have also helped illustrate how conservative activism is neither collective hysteria nor corporate-sponsored astroturfing, but the ordinary ways that ordinary men and women participate in political life. Still, studying the means without the ends gives us a woefully incomplete picture of mobilization.

Divided by the Wall brings *politics* back to the study of political struggle. While quotidian tactics are clearly important, *why* participants select them in the first place and *what meanings* they hold are not immediately self-evident. Describing and enumerating tactics also overlooks the seemingly non-instrumental moments of collective action. Absent activists' conceptions of the world, it is hard to understand why organizations prefer tactics that are, at least ostensibly, ineffectual.

In Arizona, I found that two divergent orientations toward the state drove mobilization. In chapter 6, I demonstrate how pro-immigrant activists' strong-state views were translated into strategies to *weaken* the state. For the Humanitarians, this meant claiming the borderlands as a domain of international humanitarian aid and fashioning themselves into a Border Patrol watchdog. The Advocates confronted the state more indirectly, trying to boost civil society's resilience to the immigration state by training noncitizens to avoid encounters with the state and working to stop local institutions, including local law enforcement, from cooperating with immigration authorities.

Chapter 7 turns to the weak-state effect and how it shapes restrictionist mobilization. The Arpaiositos, the Soldiers, and the Engineers tried to *strengthen* the state: The Arpaiositos tried to shore up the ties the pro-immigrant Advocates tried to sever between local law enforcement and federal immigration authorities. The Soldiers and the Engineers mobilized to expand the Border Patrol's scope of activity, even as the Humanitarians attempted to track and curtail the agency's work. Thus, by using the state-effect framework, we see the relations of collaboration and opposition—or the field of struggle—that unfolded between these five organizations.

The state-fortifying or state-destabilizing potential of their mobilization made participation meaningful to activists. It sustained old members and attracted new ones; by working to reshape the state, they also worked to reshape themselves. This *political* program—reconfiguring state power at the ambiguous border, even just a little—mitigated the tensions in activists' identities.

6 Weakening the State

In 2012, I walked a seventy-five-mile route that began just south of the U.S.-Mexico border, in the community of El Sásabe, Sonora. We meandered north across a small, quiet port of entry flanked by twelve-foot steel posts, through the western edge of Buenos Aires National Wildlife Refuge to Robles Junction along highway 286, then eastward past an old Border Patrol station. We finally stopped, amid ceremony and prayer, in a park along the southern rim of Tucson's sprawl. This "migrant pilgrimage" took a week to complete.

The core organizers—which included members of the Humanitarians, the Advocates, and other local pro-immigrant groups—had carefully designed the pilgrimage to emulate the route a migrant might take, crossing from just south of the Altar Valley toward Tucson. When they first organized it in the early 2000s, the two groups had presciently anticipated how much the event would resonate with participants. In 2012, fifty-some pilgrims made the journey. Most were seasoned participants who returned to Arizona for the event year after year. Many were faith leaders. Most were white.

The pilgrimage clearly exemplified the religiosity scholars have documented in pro-immigrant activism in the United States.[1] Indeed, the markers of Christianity were ubiquitous. The event itself was inspired by

Christianity's Ninth Commandment ("Thou shalt not bear false witness against thy neighbor"), and it was framed as an opportunity to "bear witness" to the plight of "our Migrant brothers and sisters." The journey began in a small church, with a pastor's blessing. Throughout the week, we slept, ate, and socialized amid dozens of small, wooden crosses that we carried with us. Once a day, we intoned the migrant prayer ("Loving Creator, I want to ask you: have pity on my Migrant brothers and sisters"). Then, on the final day of the pilgrimage, in a reference to the ministry of Jesus's disciples, twelve participants' feet were washed ceremoniously.[2]

Religion was certainly pertinent in the pro-immigrant activism that I studied. My day-to-day ethnographic fieldwork with left-wing activists involved countless vigils and collective prayers. I grew accustomed to faith-inspired discourse: activists frequently referred to their "moral mandate" to act, as described in chapter 2. Yet the religiosity of these tactics, while important, should not be the only or even the primary lens through which we analyze pro-immigrant mobilization. A singular focus on religion would simply return me to a description of these events, rather than their sociological analysis.

So, I wondered, what did all these rituals have to do with what the Humanitarians and the Advocates did the *rest* of the time? How did these religious moments fit with the worldviews of progressive-but-privileged activists?

Chapter 2 showed how pro-immigrant activists' perception of the state reflected their self-conceptions. The unease they experienced when they considered the state's power was closely related to their unease about their *own* social power. Just as they, as upwardly mobile Americans, possessed an oppressive power, so too did the state.

Pro-immigrant activists came to understand the state's strength as the main reason for unauthorized migration: the third-world migrant was merely an object that the formidable American state volleyed back and forth across the border. The adversity that the migrant faced was the state's doing. Activists believed that it was morally incumbent upon them, as progressive-but-privileged Americans, to devise ways to weaken the state.

Analytically speaking, this weakening took two forms. First, left-wing activists tried to curb the state's reach. This endeavor was largely the terrain of the Humanitarians. By claiming that the borderlands necessitated humanitarian intervention, the organization challenged the legitimacy of how the state managed the region and tried to limit its scope. Over time, volunteers began documenting Border Patrol's practices. Eventually, the group fashioned itself into a human rights watchdog.

The second strategy was to buffer the third-world migrant from the state. This venture was what primarily occupied the Advocates, who trained immigrants to make themselves less vulnerable to deportation. They also worked to extend this buffer to other institutions that had ambiguous relationships with the immigration enforcement arm of the state. In some instances, the Advocates tried to stop these third parties from collaborating with the state; in others, they used third parties to broadcast the pro-immigrant cause.[3]

The migrant pilgrimage, I realized, encapsulated both of these state-weakening strategies. As a procession moving deliberately through spaces normally occupied almost exclusively by the state, the pilgrimage exemplified the Humanitarians' struggle to use participants' privileges to check the state's reach. At the same time, the pilgrimage also epitomized the Advocates' efforts to reinforce the buffer against the state. Despite being socially distant from migrants' lived experiences, participants emerged from the event feeling equipped by a visceral, embodied knowledge of migrant suffering. They harnessed that knowledge to discuss the urgency of the pro-immigrant cause with other Americans in the schools, churches, and other institutions to which they were attached.[4] The pilgrimage therefore cohered with the larger pro-immigrant strategic repertoire, oriented toward weakening the state.[5]

THE HUMANITARIANS:
RESTRICTING THE STATE'S REACH

Challenging the "Antagonist" State on the Frontier

On a hot, sunny day in late fall of 2010, I accompanied Lori and Alyssa to help distribute humanitarian aid in Arizona's Sonoran Desert. Both women were white and relatively new to the southwest. Lori, twenty-two, had transferred to a college in Central Arizona from Oregon. Her friend Alyssa, eighteen, had moved to Arizona from the Midwest just before finishing her senior year of high school. She wanted some time off from schoolwork, and was training to become an emergency medical technician. Both women had moved to Arizona in order to volunteer with the Humanitarians.

Today's water drop was momentous for Lori and Alyssa: it was the first time they were going without a more seasoned volunteer. This meant they had acquired enough experience in the desert to independently undertake the task that had attracted them to Arizona in the first place—humanitarian work.

The term *humanitarian* saturated the organization's public-facing discourse as well as members' self-conceptions. Lori and Alyssa were not just two civilians going into the desert, but "humanitarian workers." The plastic gallon-sized jugs of water, the canned beans, the socks, and the chlorine capsules loaded into their SUV were not, as law enforcement agents insisted, "litter," but humanitarian aid. Moreover, if the Border Patrol detained Lori and Alyssa, it would be "interfering with humanitarian work." Gary, one of the group's founders, told me how they had strategically adopted the term *humanitarian*:

> Framing it [our work in the desert] that way is a way of showing how ridiculous and how abusive the government, as the antagonist, is. Because as soon as you say that, [people] have immediate sympathy because it isn't a crime— that kind of humanitarian aid, like giving a ride to migrants who are about to die, giving them a ride to medical care is not a crime. Giving water to migrants is not a crime. And so when you're transporting and quote "littering"—that's what the government is saying—it shows their inhumanity.

As discourse and practice, humanitarianism challenged the idea that the border region was the exclusive domain of state agents. It allowed the group to frame the border as a place where an "abusive," "inhumane," and even "ridiculous" "antagonist" state operated. The conditions the strong state created on the border were dire; just as a conflict zone or an earthquake-blighted region necessitated immediate relief, so too did the border. Moreover, the framework of humanitarianism imbued the group's practices with a moral urgency that transcended the state.

Relatedly, *humanitarianism* also suggested that activists, as well as their practices, the objects they brought with them, and the people they treated, were outside of the purview of any single state. To them, the desert was subject to international law, and the Humanitarians were members of the global human rights community charged with documenting the state's transgressions. The group often referenced international institutions' codes, reports, and rulings—such as the Inter-American Court of Human Rights (IACHR) 2003 ruling that the United States violated international law at its southern border[6]—to justify actions the authorities construed as "law-breaking" (like "transporting illegal aliens," "conspiracy", and "littering.") The Humanitarians characterized Border Patrol interference as violations of *international* law.

Perceiving the state as the "antagonist" informed everyday protocols. Group members were continually working out how to interpret these protocols. On the day that we drove out into the wilderness, Alyssa encouraged me to look through a manual for new participants. One section adumbrated what to do in case of an encounter with law enforcement. The Humanitarians were legally obligated to answer a Border Patrol agent's questions about their legal status. However, it was the participant's legal prerogative to then say, "I'm doing humanitarian aid work," and then to "walk away and keep walking." It was acceptable to be rude in this "legal" rather than "social" encounter, because, while it was the Border Patrol agent's job to interrogate anyone they deemed suspicious, it was the Humanitarian worker's job to distribute aid.

Individual Humanitarians devised their own protocols for navigating quotidian state antagonism. On another outing into the desert, I noticed that Jane, a white woman in her late twenties, kept one hand on the steering wheel, and the other on the window control panel. It was scorching, and the air conditioning was broken. Still, Jane, with a neutral expression, rolled up all the windows whenever we drove past a Border Patrol van on the narrow dirt roads into the wilderness. Staring straight ahead, she hoped, would allow her to bypass "any unnecessary chit-chat" with agents. Annie, a twenty-five-year-old white activist, told me that, whenever she went through Border Patrol checkpoints, she kept her car's windows halfway closed, her doors locked, and her camera handy in case the agent became "belligerent." If an agent wanted to make small talk by asking how she was, she responded simply with "I'm fine."

A volunteer in her fifties, Silvia, tended to handle these interactions differently, presumably informed by her intersectionality. As a lighter-skinned

Latina, Silvia said she could usually pass for a "middle-class white lady" by assuming an overly loquacious, friendly demeanor:

> I'm very fair skinned and I can talk like a middle-class white lady, so when I run into Border Patrol or the Sheriffs—I mean, this happened when we were out at camp just last week. This sheriff drove in with some people from Friends of the Parks or whatever. . . .[7] They were going to have an event. And we [the Humanitarians] are all there with a bunch of kids and crusty punks [younger volunteers]. But I know how to talk to these people. So, I walked over, [*imitating an exaggerated Midwestern accent*] "Oh, sure. I'm on your mailing list and blah blah blah." Half an hour later, we were back on the [migrant] trails.

Ironically, amid the younger, white participants, Silvia had been able to divert the state's suspicious gaze away from their group by mimicking white bourgeois femininity.

Lori and Alyssa, newly minted Humanitarians in 2010, were trying to work out what encounters with the state would look like for them. The volunteer instruction manual (which would be changed by the time of my site revisit in 2017) described the Border Patrol and the Humanitarians as having a "working relationship." When I asked my two guides what they thought about this characterization, Lori shook her head, saying that Border Patrol's stance changed with each new sector chief. It wasn't really a working relationship, but "a relationship that worked," she said, necessitated by the agency's efforts to improve its own public image.

Their cynicism about the group's relationship with the agency was based on the law enforcement terrain that they believed surrounded their humanitarian intervention in the borderlands. Alyssa explained that field agents were not educated about humanitarian aid work, even though agency officials claimed otherwise. At best, agents were confused, at worst, deeply suspicious when they encountered Humanitarians in the field. Neither boded well for volunteers, especially since the agents had broad discretionary power. The charge of "aiding and abetting," for instance, was purposefully vague. The legal doctrine could easily be used to prosecute the Humanitarians for any number of acts in the field.

For this reason, the Humanitarians consulted with a team of lawyers and developed protocols for operating in terrain they perceived as hostile.

In case of an encounter with a migrant, volunteers could provide food, water, and basic medical care. They could even provide a lost border crosser with "general orienting directions" and other relevant information, including the risks associated with the immediate surroundings. They could not, however, provide maps, because that could be considered aiding and abetting.

Most importantly, the Humanitarians trained volunteers to describe the options available to migrants and solicit their "informed consent" before undertaking any action on their behalf. Offering choices and looking for informed consent—instead of automatically calling the Border Patrol, as the Soldiers would do in case of an encounter with a migrant—could be read as the Humanitarians' attempt to carve out a small space of autonomy from the state. These options were limited, however. So too were the chances of actually bypassing the state altogether. Nonetheless, making these choices available to a border crosser was paramount to the organization's self-understanding as a state-weakening entity.

As the Humanitarians understood it, a migrant could continue on or return south, ask to summon an ambulance and be evacuated to a hospital, agree to be transported to the Humanitarians' field medical camp under the supervision of medically trained volunteers, or simply ask to call the Border Patrol. Humanitarians harbored deep reservations about following through with that last possibility, and some volunteers took it upon themselves to describe the hazards of being in Border Patrol custody. Of course, the more attractive options also risked exposing a border crosser to law enforcement. A Border Patrol agent could always intercept the call to the paramedics, for instance. On at least one occasion, the Border Patrol had searched and arrested migrants staying in the Humanitarians' medical camp. Thus, it was highly likely that any of the options the Humanitarians presented to migrants in the field could end in detention and deportation, just as a direct call to Border Patrol would. Therefore, the significance of giving an opportunity for informed consent lay not in its measurable effectiveness but in its symbolic offer of autonomy to both volunteer and migrant under the specter of a powerful state.

Early that fall morning in 2010, it was hot and blindingly bright as Lori, Alyssa, and I carried water jugs and a medical aid kit up a small hill. It took about fifteen minutes of hiking before we found the first water drop site. Six jugs, still filled with water, sat on the ground. They were decorated with hearts and crosses and the words *buena suerte* ("good luck") scrawled in blue. The jugs seemed untouched. The women decided that we should return to the car with our water to find the next drop site. We repeated this process several times over two hours. In two cases, we decided to leave additional water, but the rest of the time, seeing the previous drop's supplies intact, we simply trudged back to the car.

Sweaty from the difficult hiking, I grew increasingly annoyed. Were all our efforts in vain? Had migrants' routes through this region shifted? Were these sites out of use? Lori and Alyssa seemed unperturbed: the routes probably had not changed. It was just the regular ebb and flow of the season, they insisted.

That the Humanitarians were pushing up against an "antagonistic" state triggered anxiety for Lori and Alyssa, even though we never saw a migrant, a Border Patrol agent, or anyone else for that matter. Nonetheless, the two volunteers were noticeably nervous throughout the day. Their jumpiness was particularly apparent on our lunch break, as we settled down on some large rocks near the dirt road where Alyssa had parked the SUV. Lori said that she would rather encounter people where we were sitting, near the main road, rather than on a walking trail far from the car. Yet every time a distant vehicle came into earshot, the two women fell silent, straining to hear whether it was coming nearer. As we drove, we passed several Border Patrol vans, but they didn't even slow down.

Neither Alyssa nor Lori had shared my frustration, but anxiety pervaded their experience of that autumn morning. Alyssa explained that there had been several instances of water vandalism in the past. Plastic water jugs left out for migrants had been slashed, wasting the water. Possible suspects included the Soldiers and other restrictionist groups, as well as neighboring ranchers and hunters who frequented the area for sport. In most cases, however, Alyssa concluded the "water vandals" were probably the Border Patrol. Lori added that a couple of Humanitarians had recorded a video of an agent following their car to a water station and, later, committing water vandalism. Alyssa reflected, "Look, putting out water is not just about putting out water. I mean, it is, but it's also a symbolic thing. When we put out water, it's telling the world that these are migrants. It's a message we're sending to Border Patrol, to hunters, to

Minutemen, to everyone." Activists came to see the desert as conflict zone in which they tried to establish a domain outside of the state. Robert explained how maintaining this domain of humanitarianism required his group to constantly push up against the state. "Every year," he told me,

> We get new young people and they're gung-ho and they want to push the boundaries. So we started in the early 2000s. We knew where two trails were and a year after [the organization was founded], we knew maybe where six trails were, and now [we know] scores of trails all over.

Lori and Alyssa were a pair of these young people, heading out into the desert and anticipating that the Border Patrol would try to upend their efforts.

Alyssa's remark about the communicative aspect of the jugs of water is important. Humanitarianism offered a way to denaturalize state discourse and convey an alternative set of ideas about migrant suffering. In this regard, humanitarian aid was meant as a way to challenge the configuration of power relations between the state and the third-world migrant. The jugs of water were intended not only to quench thirst, but also to remind state agents and American civilians that the well-being of humans was being jeopardized at the border to the extent that relief efforts were necessary. Even the "good luck" messages, ostensibly meant for border crossers, were more importantly aimed at state actors who might discover the jugs.

That the jugs carried literal and symbolic meaning goes some distance toward explaining why Lori and Alyssa had not been frustrated to see that the water drop sites had gone without visitors in the previous weeks. I fixated on the absence of migrants. But they fixated on the absence of water vandals. Every time they saw that the supplies remained intact, Lori and Alyssa felt relief. True, they wanted migrants to find their drop sites. However, it was also equally—and perhaps more—important in that moment that the state had not answered the Humanitarians' political challenge with water vandalism.

In the years that followed, I witnessed how the Humanitarians worked out other ways to maintain and expand a domain outside of the state. In 2012, I attended several meetings during which activists discussed ways to keep the Border Patrol from interfering with their efforts in the desert. Robert had been instrumental in organizing these conferences. At one, he

explained to me that that agents would "sit up on the hill with their binoculars, watching [the medical] camp" in which activists treated dehy-
drated border crossers. Once, alleging that activists were harboring illegal
aliens, more than two-dozen Border Patrol agents raided the camp on
horseback. There were at least three more raids in those years, and the
agency threatened more. Many Humanitarians believed these raids were
direct retaliations for their release of a report on the Border Patrol's abusive treatment of migrants (more on that to come).

In response to the raids, the Humanitarians brainstormed ways to keep
agents from entering their camp. One suggestion entailed organizing
members of the city's medical community to acknowledge that the desert
region where migrants crossed was a humanitarian disaster. Following the
international principles of humanitarian aid, this coterie of doctors,
nurses, and other medical professionals would then be asked to publicly
ordain the Humanitarian tent as an official medical unit, outside the purview of enforcement agents. In this manner, the Humanitarians could
counteract the commonplace thinking that the organization was harboring criminals. It would establish their desert camp as something akin to a
Doctors Without Borders care unit—a space safe from state intervention.

These efforts culminated in a partnership with the International
Federation of Red Cross and Red Crescent Societies (IFRC). The
Humanitarians adopted the IFRC's code of conduct, which defended the
"right to receive humanitarian assistance, and to offer it."[8] It also entreated
"governments of disaster-affected countries" to "respect" nongovernmen-
tal humanitarian bodies and grant them access to "disaster victims."[9] The
code stated that it was "the duty of the host government . . . not to block
such assistance, and to accept the impartial and apolitical action" of non-
government humanitarian organizations.[10] The Humanitarians erected a
Red Cross flag in the camp.

With the help of other similar organizations, the Humanitarians then
developed a proposal for the Border Patrol's local sector leadership, arguing that this area of the borderlands fit the Red Cross's definition of disaster. As evidence, they cited the medical community's 2012 declaration and
quoted the section of the Red Cross's code of conduct that dissuaded governments from impeding humanitarian efforts. The proposal concluded by
demanding the agency refrain from surveilling or entering the medical

camp. The sector chief tentatively agreed, but the Humanitarians remained skeptical about the assurances of an "antagonist" state.

Robert and Justin, the very activists who had led the multiyear diplomacy effort, were among the skeptics. When I interviewed him again in 2017, Justin said the agency had agreed to refrain from "invading" the camp, but that raised two problems. First, the Border Patrol had said that they would only refrain from raiding camp unless they were in "hot pursuit." That rationale could easily be used to justify *any* raid.

There was also the problem of institutional memory in an agency that experienced high turnover. "What we realized was that Border Patrol agents change so often that it made no difference" whether they had an agreement, Justin explained. "They'd say, 'Oh, who are the Humanitarians? What's this about?'" Just a year earlier, the Humanitarians had photographed a Border Patrol agent standing on top of his truck conspicuously surveilling the camp with binoculars. This kind of "power play" was not uncommon, Annie added: Agents simply did not want the Humanitarians there. Whether they were or just claimed to be ignorant, the agents had the power of the state in the borderlands. Against them, the Humanitarians remained stalwart.

Becoming a Watchdog

Framing the border region as a humanitarian disaster area was only one way the Humanitarians worked to circumscribe the state. Over time, service provision in the border area led the pro-immigrant group to become a watchdog group, more systematically interviewing crossers who had been apprehended by the Border Patrol and deported to Mexican border towns. Based on these data, the group wrote and circulated several reports. Each maintained that the agency egregiously violated basic human rights in its day-to-day practices.

In two of these reports, the Humanitarians concluded that Border Patrol "processing centers" were not just waiting rooms where apprehended crossers stayed until they were deported. Instead, these spaces, where migrants could be held for up to seventy-two hours, were detention facilities where agents systematically abused their charges. Agents habitually kept the temperature inside holding cells very low, for instance. There was also a tendency to refuse detainees, including children, adequate food or water.

One Humanitarian, who had medical training, described having treated dozens of deportees after they had been in custody; the injuries, for which they had not been treated while in Border Patrol custody, included sprained ankles and severe dehydration. The Humanitarians also charged that agents physically and verbally abused the people in their custody. Agents reportedly pushed their charges into cacti and beat them up, exacerbating the injuries migrants may have incurred while crossing the borderlands. These incidents were not random events. Nor were they the work of a few rogue agents. Rather, the reports argued, this kind of treatment followed such a stark pattern that it should be considered intrinsic to the agency's standard operating procedures.

The Humanitarians launched a drawn-out campaign to disseminate the report. They presented their findings at well-attended hearings organized by the IACHR, where representatives of the Department of Homeland Security were present. Activists also gave interviews to English-language and Spanish-language media. The Humanitarians organized public forums, including one sponsored by the Advocates. A few years later, the report provided the basis for a class-action lawsuit alleging that Customs and Border Protection (CBP) detention facilities in Southern Arizona were unconstitutional and even violated CBP's own guidelines about confinement. The report generated negative publicity for the Border Patrol.

Eventually, the group assembled another report that focused on the apprehension tactics that Border Patrol agents used in the desert; once again, activists underscored state violence. This report focused specifically on agents' use of high-speed chases to capture border crossers in the brush. Chasing suspects into remote areas, the Humanitarians argued, was a form of punishment, because when the agency let a border crosser run until the point of exhaustion, it increased the chances of injury and death. Capture did not necessarily bring respite; agents were reportedly more likely to use excessive force on those who had tried to flee. Meanwhile, migrants fled because they were well aware of the agency's reputation for abusing the people they captured.

The Humanitarians' report further charged that the Border Patrol routinely used low-flying helicopters to scatter groups of migrants traveling together; this tactic also deliberately increased the risk of injury and death by separating guides from those in their care. Disoriented migrants, left to their own devices, would die from dehydration following such a separation. Fleeing border crossers were also more likely to drop their supply of food and water, further jeopardizing their chances of survival. Scattering a group could easily be a death sentence for people in this harsh desert.

Since these tactics could just as easily *reduce* the chance of capture as help with it, the Humanitarians alleged that the moment of pursuit, much like the moment of detention, was an opportunity for the state to terrorize and kill migrants.

By becoming a watchdog group, the Humanitarians worked to bring public attention to the state's day-to-day practices and to reframe these practices as egregious human rights violations. With the publication and dissemination of each report, the Humanitarians publicly challenged the idea that the agency was a politically disinterested and reactive entity. Instead, they claimed that the Border Patrol's active hostility toward border crossers was at the center of the prevention-through-deterrence policy program. Migrant suffering and death were not unintended policy consequences. They were consequences that were *engineered* by a formidable state. The Humanitarians hoped public pressure would restrain the Border Patrol.

Unsettled Questions

Despite their shared commitment to curbing the Border Patrol's power, the Humanitarians grappled with whether and how they should interact with the agency. Should progressive-but-privileged Americans, who allied themselves with the third-world migrant, forego all dialogue with state actors? Or was an effective ally one who, at times, gave information to the state? Or asked the Border Patrol for help?

It even remained unclear *how* volunteers should conduct themselves if they encountered an agent. Was it best to be cordial, even friendly, with agents? Or should the committed activist be brusque, perhaps hostile, with agents? Volunteers were continuously working out what it meant, ideologically and tactically, to be privileged Americans, who could be *heard* by the state, but also progressives who recognized that the state was ultimately untrustworthy and oppressive. Disagreements over these questions were sometimes severe enough to strain relationships among the Humanitarians.

It was exactly this kind of rift that Gary and Barbara described when we first talked in 2011. The fault lines, the spouses believed, could be chalked up to age. Gary, a former pastor, and Barbara, a retired teacher, were among the Humanitarians' founders. They had witnessed the group's evolution, including a tendency among younger, newer volunteers to be more "aggressive" than previous cohorts of Humanitarians. "There are more [participants] that are openly hostile to government," Gary remarked, "more aggressive on how they think things ought to be run." Meanwhile, septuagenarians like themselves favored more measured approaches to interacting with state actors. This age-based tension was starting to manifest itself in the desert. Although, the group had developed protocols for volunteer-agent interactions, in the heat of the moment, it was not always clear what activists should do.

Gary told me about lively debates at the Humanitarians' meetings: should members remove any stickers bearing the group's name they might have on their vehicles? Some Humanitarians, including Alyssa, wished to make the group less blatantly visible to the Border Patrol. They feared for their well-being in remote regions of the desert. The water they transported already clearly indicated the group's intentions. It seemed unnecessary, and even dangerous, to further advertise their identity by emblazoning the vehicles with the Humanitarians' name. Other members, including Gary and Barbara, vehemently disagreed. They believed that transparency was the only way to ensure the group's ability to maintain their peaceful presence in the desert without being charged with a crime.

To further illustrate the debate around transparency, Gary recounted a recent Border Patrol raid on the Humanitarians' field camp. Having completed a water drop, Gary was returning to the camp, where activists attended to injured migrants. He got a call from another volunteer saying, "'There are a whole bunch of Border Patrol cars out here. What do I do?' And I said, 'Well, they can come in if they want to.' Like I said, 'Tell them that you've got three migrants, if they ask you.'" The volunteer agreed to follow Gary's instructions.

Later, however, Gary discovered that the volunteers who had been in charge of the camp that day—"two young adults, who are experienced, smart people"—had decided the week prior that if there was a Border Patrol raid, "they were going to hide the migrants in the bushes." Gary shook his head disapprovingly. "If they had done that, it would have been all over! There were twenty-five officers on horseback. And they would have found the migrants, and it would have been all over for our camp." Hiding migrants from the agents might have had devastating legal consequences for the Humanitarians; volunteers would have been arrested, accused of harboring undocumented people, and that charge would cause irrevocable damage. The Humanitarians might have had to give up their mission.

Although the Humanitarians all shared a similar view of the state, Gary disagreed with his younger colleagues about how to interact with state actors. He described the state as "abusive" and "inhumane" and believed the agency was retaliatory. The Humanitarians' report about the conditions inside Border Patrol facilities had attracted a lot of negative media attention to the agency, and Gary thought it made the camp more vulnerable to agency surveillance and raids. Nonetheless, Gary wanted the Humanitarians to cultivate a relationship with the Border Patrol that was neither hostile nor guarded. This was not merely a matter of principle; it was tactically shrewd. To be a morally responsible ally to the third-world migrant, Gary believed that the Humanitarians had to ensure the long-term sustainability of their organization. This meant cordiality and transparency when interacting with frontline state actors. Hiding a migrant, by contrast, was irresponsible and even selfish—the kind of action that was motivated more by personal distaste for authorities than any genuine effort to help migrants.

The younger volunteers I interviewed tended to be more guarded in their everyday encounters with agents and more skeptical about whether officially communicating with agency leadership could be helpful to the Humanitarian cause. In 2011, I asked Mariela, a twenty-four-year-old volunteer, about the raid Gary had described. Mariela had not been at the camp that day, but she knew what had transpired and agreed with Gary. At the same time, however, she "understood" the desire to hide vulnerable people from law enforcement. She helped write the report about the Border Patrol's abusive treatment, and it was on her mind. "What we learned is that to do successful border enforcement, agents *have to be* abusive to migrants," she explained. "Abuse is a deliberate part of the agency's strategy."

To illustrate her point, Mariela recalled her participation in the "medical evacuation" of a young man suffering severe dehydration after four days of crossing the desert without water. The medically trained volunteer accompanying Mariela at the time said the migrant was at risk of kidney failure, so they called 911 and summoned an ambulance to the Humanitarian camp.

> The paramedics agreed with the volunteer's medical evaluation. So they took the migrant to [the nearby town's] fire station, and we followed in our own vehicle. We were met by Border Patrol agents who spent about half an hour harassing us: how the work we do is illegal, how we treat terrorists, how we had concocted this elaborate story for why this person had to go to the hospital, and on and on. At this point, the paramedics had already started an IV for him [the migrant]. And the ambulance drove away with the Border Patrol after it. . . . The migrant's brother called us the next day to tell us what had happened: Border Patrol had said, "You got everything you're going to get out of this country," had ripped out the IV, and had deported him to Nogales in the middle of the night.

Mariela agreed that it was important to be transparent with law enforcement about who was present at the camp at any given time. On the other hand, she sympathized with the younger volunteers. Gary had described the volunteers' motivations as immature, self-centered, and even selfish. To him, the younger colleagues had neglected to think about the organization's well-being. Mariela, by contrast, suggested that the desire to hide migrants from law enforcement, far from being an immature impulse, could just as easily be the result of years of hearing about agents' abusiveness.

From her own experience, Mariela felt there was a layer of cruelty to everything the agency did and the young volunteers' plan to hide migrants was not unreasonable. In her story, agents questioned whether a medical evacuation was necessary, even though both medically trained volunteers and independent paramedics recommended it. Agents did not wait for the migrant to recover before deporting him—they had not even waited until the following *day*. They took a person who was already vulnerable (a migrant), in a position of extreme vulnerability (possible kidney failure), minimized the significance of the man's health and humanity ("You got everything you're going to get out of this country"), and deported him in circumstances that increased his vulnerability (having "ripped out his IV" and deported him "in the middle of the night"). Wanting to protect migrants from this kind of treatment was not to her mind, self-centered or selfish. She might not recommend it, but she could understand the volunteers' impulse.

Internal struggles reveal an ongoing preoccupation: Humanitarians wanted to limit the state's reach. The disagreements matter insofar as they reveal the organization's efforts to maintain (and expand) an independent domain of humanitarianism in a region they believed was the stronghold of a formidable state. All Humanitarians agreed that the *ultimate* goal was to push back against the Border Patrol. Every time they went out onto migrant trails with water, activists were effectively reasserting that the state had created a crisis in the borderlands necessitating the intervention of international humanitarian groups. Every time they released a report about the agency's activities, activists declared the state was purposefully violating human rights. Over the years, the Humanitarians continuously worked out how to pursue these state-weakening aims as effectively as possible.

THE ADVOCATES: BUILDING GROUPS' RESISTANCE TO THE STATE

Helping People Avoid (and Escape) the Clutches of the State

One Sunday afternoon in early 2011, I pulled up in front of a house in a predominantly Spanish-speaking neighborhood in Tucson for a "know-your-rights" training organized by the Advocates. Four women were seated in the living room. As I greeted everyone, I learned that one woman was the homeowner. The other three were neighbors on the block. I sat down and waited for Magdala, an Advocate, to begin the session.

While the Humanitarians trained their focus on the state and its agents in an effort to reduce its reach, the Advocates were more concerned with building up immigrants' everyday capacities to protect themselves from the state. When the Humanitarians interacted with undocumented people, it was usually to provide a one-time service: medical care or water, for instance. The Advocates, by contrast, tried to give immigrants tools to become less vulnerable to law enforcement and immigration authorities. The know-your-rights sessions were one such effort. In these trainings, the Advocates described the state's reach and how to avoid it. They also tried to reduce a person's vulnerability to the state in the event that he or she attracted its attention. People were taught how to avoid deportation proceedings even after they came into contact with an officer.

This session focused on what to do if one was pulled over in traffic. After everyone had settled, Magdala began speaking in Spanish. Traffic stops were now among the most common situations funneling migrants into deportation proceedings. By knowing their rights, a person could potentially protect themselves and their loved ones against this outcome. "If you are the driver, you're only required to show your driver's license, registration, and proof of insurance," Magdala stated. "If the officer asks you questions about your country of origin, don't answer," she continued. "If you're a passenger, you can tell the officer your name, but you're not required to provide identification or answer any of their questions." Magdala added that it was important to ask for the police officer's name and badge number: "This way, you can communicate to the police officer that you're not going to be pushed around, that you're ready to assert your rights," she explained. Later, Magdala passed around little slips of paper to put in our wallets, instructing that we try to memorize this simple script for talking with a police officer: "I am exercising my right to remain silent."

We broke into pairs to role-play. I was paired with Teresa, who sat on a chair, pretending to be a driver. There, in the middle of the living room, I stood over her, playing "the cop." Teresa smiled, pretending to hand over her driver's license and registration. In English, I asked where she was from, and she looked ready to answer. Then, she clamped her mouth shut. A moment later, she had retrieved the little piece of paper and read the script out in English. I grinned, asking if she wanted my name and badge number. She cracked a smile back, "Yes." Our impromptu skit ended in applause. When Magdala asked Teresa how she had felt, she quickly said "Nervous." That was normal, Magdala assured us. She encouraged everyone to keep role-playing at home: "The more you practice it, the better."

Later, Magdala told me about other know-your-rights training topics. For instance, she trained people about what to do if law enforcement suddenly showed up at their doorstep. "Your instinct might be to open the door," she said, "because here's this big guy, with a uniform, telling you to. But you don't have to and you shouldn't." Ask for a warrant first, she prompted, and even then, step outside and close the door behind you rather than inviting them in. It wasn't something that most people would think to do. And if you were arrested and put in an immigration detention center, "We tell them not to sign anything without talking to a lawyer first," Magdala said. Correctional officers were known to pressure their charges into signing "voluntary removal" forms. If they signed, a detainee could forfeit their chance to appear before an immigration judge, and they could be expelled from the country in a matter of hours.

Magdala and the Advocates had no way of knowing how often these trainings protected people from the deportation state. It was not clear, for instance, if asking for a name and badge number actually discouraged a police officer from pursuing a case with immigration authorities; surely, it might *also* make an officer more aggressive. Nonetheless, occasional anecdotes of successful encounters with the state infused the Advocates' work with meaning. Magdala said, of being an Advocate, "Even if I only save just one person—that's enough for me." She shared the story of one woman she had "saved," who had recently approached Magdala to thank her for conducting a know-your-rights training in her neighborhood. It turned out that two weeks after the training, the woman had been stopped in traffic and wound up at an immigration detention center. She was detained for three months.

And [at the training] I talked about how when you're in detention, they will talk about taking away your kids. They'll tell you a bunch of lies to get you to sign [the voluntary return form]. So she remembered me, and she said, "Every time they [the correctional officer] said something, I would hear your voice: 'Don't listen to them, they're making it up.' So I didn't sign anything." . . . She said, "Thank you; if it wasn't for you, I would have signed [the form], and I would have been deported to Mexico." And those are the moments that matter, when you know that at least one person got to stay [in the United States]. That's your job.

The Advocates also tried to build up the protective buffer against the state through *prepárete* or "prepare yourself" workshops. These, too, were often held in people's homes, and they were usually organized on the heels of a know-your-rights training. In these workshops, the Advocates explained the basics of immigration law and encouraged attendees to create emergency plans in case they or their family members were detained. These plans were intended to mitigate the confusion that could ensue if a household member suddenly disappeared. For instance, the Advocates urged household members to grant power of attorney to trusted others so that their affairs could be handled in their absence. Activists also encouraged people to compile important documents, such as birth certificates, marriage certificates, passports, and any immigration-related documents, in a place other household members could easily access. They advised households to find immigration lawyers with experience in deportation cases and memorize their contact information.

In a radio interview, Renee explained how sometimes immigrant families took even more extreme precautions. In one family she had come to know, the parents commuted separately even though they both worked the same night shift at a factory. "The father drives his car while the mother gets a ride with friends," she told the interviewers. The couple, she said, told her that, if one of them was stopped and picked up by immigration authorities, this way their children would still have at least one parent left behind. "This is the degree to which immigrant communities are being terrorized. . . . Imagine having to plan to that level."

The Advocates also worked with the other end of the spectrum of non-citizens—legal permanent residents—through citizenship fairs. The Advocates and other trained volunteers helped applicants fill out the cumbersome N-400 Application for Naturalization forms. Then volunteer immigration lawyers would check the forms. The service was free to applicants. Renee remembered that the Advocates began organizing citizenship fairs soon after Arizona Proposition 200 was passed in 2004. Reminiscent of California Prop 187, Prop 200 required proof of citizenship to register to vote and to cast a vote.[11] It also required state and local agencies to verify the immigration status of applicants before dispensing non-federally mandated public benefits and to report any applicants who were out-of-status to immigration authorities. The citizenship fairs were a response to this measure: Naturalization was a way for individuals to protect themselves and their families.

Citizenship fairs also buffered immigrants from having to interact directly with the state before knowing it was safe to do so. Just like a traffic stop encounter with a cop, the process of changing one's legal status required a state-interaction that could potentially trigger deportation. Thus, the Advocates used the fairs to find and warn individuals who wanted to naturalize but were risking deportation if they initiated the process.

Prior to one such citizenship fair, I attended a training that the Advocates had organized for volunteers who would help applicants fill out naturalization applications. Renee told the volunteers about one time the Advocates had advised an applicant *not* to naturalize. Apparently, a man had committed a deportable offense, and the group feared that bringing this incident to the government's attention would lead to his deportation. So, the group refused to give him back his application. Angry and desperate, he promised the Advocates that he would not mail his application in—he would take it to a pricey lawyer to have it checked over again. Renee had told him that the lawyer would certainly take his money and help him turn in his application; afterward, however, he would probably still get deported. Advising the man to remain a legal permanent resident, the Advocates had not returned the application. In this way, like prepárete workshops and know-your-rights trainings, citizenship fairs also gave noncitizens the tools to protect themselves against the state.

The Advocates' networking function helped strengthen undocumented communities' buffer against the state, too. For instance, the contingency plans they advocated relied on linking individuals to "protection networks"—relatives, friends, neighbors, immigration lawyers, and others who could step in and take care of a targeted individual's immediate concerns. If someone in the network was detained during an immigration raid, for example, the chain of communication cautioned others in the network to stay away from that area for the time being.

Gabriela remembered that when SB1070 was first signed into law, a handful of police officers began pulling over drivers they believed were not in the country legally. The Advocates noticed that the officers were carrying out this kind of enforcement in particular neighborhoods, often targeting cars with families. The group quickly created and widely advertised a twenty-four-hour hotline, asking for tips on sightings of the cops together with the Border Patrol. When the hotline got a tip, the Advocates would send text alerts out to their protection networks. Those members of the protection network who had irregular status could avoid the place where law enforcement had been spotted with Border Patrol. In these ways, the social capital that protection networks generated was supposed to shield noncitizens from contact with the state.

In her radio interview, Renee had described how deportation "imposed mass confusion on people." Such chaos and uncertainty was a severe "form of punishment" for the family and community of the individual who was apprehended. Know-your-rights trainings, prepárate workshops, citizenship fairs, and protection networks were all important pieces in the Advocates' mitigation program. As the Humanitarians tried to curtail the state's reach, the Advocates taught immigrants just how far that reach extended—and how best to avoid it. It was all part of the same struggle: to create a protective buffer against an unforgiving, punitive, powerful state.

Forging Alliances

Whether training people to avoid the state or plugging them into protection networks, the Advocates worked directly with undocumented people and other noncitizens. The purpose of these efforts was to help potential victims of enforcement steer clear of the state as much as much as possible. However, the Advocates also cultivated another approach, this time targeting third parties.

These third parties were relatively powerful institutions and social actors with ambiguous relations to the immigration enforcement state. In that sense, the third parties "floated" in civil society. They were largely unattached, able to align with the state and reinforce its capacity or, just as easily, side with pro-immigrant groups and serve as an additional layer of resistance to the state. The Advocates targeted two important third parties, which had frequent encounters with migrants and the Border Patrol: the Medical Examiner's Office and the city police.

The Advocates often asked the chief medical examiner to present a talk on the process of identifying human remains recovered from the desert.

The doctor usually complied, though the working relationship hadn't been forged so easily. Other Arizona medical examiners' offices (MEOs) were averse to even basic cooperation with the Advocates; depending on who was at the helm at the moment, some of the offices would not even give out information on how many bodies had been recovered in the border area over the prior year. When I interviewed him, I asked the medical examiner why his staff worked so closely with the Advocates. The group, he explained, had been instrumental in helping the MEO identify family members of the deceased, particularly if they were undocumented people living in the United States who did not want to talk to a government office. Sometimes kin were unwilling to even speak with their home countries' consulates. However, they were far more willing to speak with the Advocates. As unidentified bodies from the desert piled up in their morgue, and later, their auxiliary morgue, MEO staff became increasingly grateful for the Advocates' help. Over time, the Advocates successfully requested that MEO staff present their work to the public.

When two prominent members of the Congressional Hispanic Caucus organized a community hearing in an Arizonan border town, I later learned that it was the Advocates who convinced them to invite the doctor as a guest speaker. Other speakers at the forum included the town's mayor, the county sheriff, the CEO of an American firm that conducted business in Mexico, and a self-identified DREAMer who had started his own business.[12] The relatively large conference room was packed, flanked with reporters and news cameras. The speakers were supposed to represent the diverse array of stakeholders in the border region. However, most of the hearing was framed around the ways in which increased border security conflicted with American values, particularly the freedom to do business.

Only the DREAMer and the doctor spoke about the experiences of undocumented immigrants. The DREAMer discussed the effects of enforcement on young undocumented people like himself, while the doctor discussed the scale of migrant deaths in the desert. The doctor's presentation prompted a congressman to ask whether the deaths on the border constituted a humanitarian crisis. The doctor responded with an analogy: "It's like a mass disaster, like a plane crash that happens every year. . . . But unlike a plane crash, there isn't a list of missing identities. So we end up with hundreds of bodies that are never identified." A clip featuring the doctor's response was aired on the local news that evening—a boon for the Advocates, who had successfully and strategically used their ties to the MEO to broadcast their message more widely.

The MEO itself was an ongoing target for the Advocates' messages. I witnessed how the Advocates, while carefully managing this relationship, were always trying to push the MEO toward a more openly pro-immigrant stance. When I visited the MEO, I asked the doctor about his own personal outlook on migrant deaths; he responded that he and his staff sympathized with the plight of migrants, but wanted to uphold the "professionalism" of their office so that they could keep doing their work as effectively as possible. Thus, he refrained from making political comments in public.

A few months after that visit, the Advocates asked the doctor to present his work to a small group of artists and Advocates. The presentation would be video recorded so that the group could show it to others. The doctor agreed. Toward the end of his presentation, Sandra asked the doctor to reflect on what impact his work had had on him "at a human level." The doctor skirted the question, saying that despite the best efforts of his office, many human remains would never be identified, which was "not easy." Gabriela then asked the doctor what he thought should be done in response to these deaths. The doctor shifted uneasily. Afterward, Gabriela seemed to verbalize a collective wish: "I wish he would be less clinical and more human in his presentations to the community."

Another ambiguously aligned third party was local law enforcement. The Advocates were aware that these local actors were increasingly becoming key players in immigration enforcement. Certainly, in Arizona, sheriffs like Joe Arpaio of Maricopa County were very vocal about their restrictionism, and the Advocates frequently heard rumors about how certain officers were zealously working with Border Patrol. At the same time, however, local law enforcement had resisted such tendencies around the time that Senate Bill 1070 was under discussion. One police officer had brought a lawsuit challenging the measure. The chief of police publicly criticized the bill as burdensome for officers, adding a task that would hinder their other duties.

Realizing there was room to maneuver, the Advocates looked for ways to pressure police to be more loyal to the city's denizens than the federal government's mandates. For instance, as they publicized the hotline for tip-sters who saw police interacting with Border Patrol or ICE, the Advocates both warned noncitizens *and* pressured officers to stop cooperating with those agencies. The Advocates also launched a campaign targeting the police. By spring of 2011, the U.S. Court of Appeals for the Ninth Circuit had upheld the preliminary injunction against the enforcement of SB1070. The decision was met with optimism from pro-immigrant activists, who raised the possibility that the Supreme Court would find the immigration statute unconstitutional. In the meantime, the Advocates were certain that the local police were working more closely with immigration authorities than they had in the past. This campaign was a coalition effort bringing together Advocates and Humanitarians.

The coalition aimed to instate an arrest moratorium on Fridays, Saturdays, and Sundays. Their goal was that, for three days of every week, city police would refrain from checking immigration status and from com-municating with Border Patrol. They worked to mobilize clergy and other faith leaders as liaisons to the city council and the police department, even approaching the pastor of the church that the police chief attended. Together, the faith-based leaders (including the chief's pastor) drafted a resolution that, emphasizing the need for people to be free to worship without fear of arrest and deportation, called on the city police to make the enforcement of immigration laws of lowest priority on Fridays, Saturdays, and Sundays. Further, the resolution called on officers to refrain from asking about the immigration status of vulnerable popula-tions, including minors, students, and crime victims and witnesses.

When the clergy presented their resolution to the city council, "The city council and the police chief dug in their heels," Robert, a member of the coalition, recalled. The city's charter prevented the city council from directing law enforcement activity. Still, the city council *did* enact a reso-lution about being an immigrant-friendly city. Without authorizing the moratorium, this resolution noted that the police *were* committed to pro-tecting the public safety of all the city's residents, regardless of immigra-tion status.

Robert recalled that the city council also began putting "quiet pressure" on the chief, particularly as police and sheriff's departments around the state came under scrutiny for civil rights violations. In *Arizona et al. v.*

United States (2012), the Supreme Court upheld the most controversial provision of the statute, Section 2(b), which allowed officers to stop and arrest anyone that they "reasonably" believed to be undocumented. In doing so, however, the Court explained that the provision's future would depend on its interpretation and implementation. If local law enforcement relied on race and national origin as the basis of their "reasonable suspicion" about a person's immigration status, the question of constitutionality could be revisited.[13] In response, the Advocates and other local pro-immigrant organizations began to document cases of collaboration between local law enforcement and the Border Patrol.

In late 2013, at the behest of the Advocates, the Humanitarians, and coalition members, the American Civil Liberties Union (ACLU) filed a notice of claim (the precursor to a lawsuit) against *another* nearby police department. It alleged that three officers had been involved in the false arrest and detention of a man based on his perceived race. The notice was the first of many that the ACLU filed in Arizona municipalities, all related directly to Section 2(b). By 2014, the police department had averted a formal lawsuit by agreeing to change its policies around immigration enforcement. New guidelines instructed that officers could *not* consider a host of factors—including race, dress, level of English fluency, accent, or lack of identification—in forming "reasonable suspicion" about a person's immigration status. That the lack of a form of identification was explicitly included was particularly significant, Renee noted. On numerous occasions, she had witnessed how an officer could use lack of identification as justification for calling the Border Patrol.

The coalition leveraged the ACLU-approved guidelines the other police department had adopted to demand, again, that the city council revisit the issue of immigration enforcement. According to Robert and Renee, the police chief's 2015 retirement came early—hastened by the coalition's dogged efforts to change police policy. The city then appointed a community advisory board to help select the next chief. Many members of the coalition, including the leaders of several local pro-immigrant activist organizations and the ACLU lawyer who had been instrumental in bringing the notice of claim in the neighboring city, were on the advisory board charged with appointing a new chief. The incoming chief stated, upon his appointment, that his department would not cooperate with immigration authorities if it violated best policing practices. A month after Donald Trump was elected president, the city passed another resolution proclaiming that it would not participate in mass deportation campaigns. The police, Robert concluded, "just realized, 'We can't do our basic job, which is public safety.' Now [in 2017], the city's finally declared itself to be a sanctuary city in everything but name."

The Advocates also cultivated contacts with Border Patrol Search Trauma and Rescue (BORSTAR), a volunteer unit within the Border Patrol. Recall that the Advocates had been working closely with the MEO to help identify remains, because the kin of missing migrants showed a greater willingness to speak with the Advocates than to the ME or law enforcement. As the calls about missing family members came in, the Advocates developed a system to try and determine individuals' whereabouts. The system was based on three possible scenarios. In the first, perhaps, most straightforward scenario, the missing person had died while crossing and their remains had been found. The Advocates could call the MEO to determine whether this was the case. The next two scenarios were trickier to investigate. The person in question might have been apprehended and had been or continued to be in Border Patrol custody. Or the missing person was still in the desert, dead or alive.

To investigate these trickier possibilities, the Advocates turned to BORSTAR. The Advocates were deeply critical of the Border Patrol. Yet Renee conceded there was a "truce" when it came to missing migrants. "[W]e're not best friends out there," she said of the Advocates and Border Patrol, "But then in the area of missing people there's like this weird truce that we have where none of that matters." Renee regularly called her contacts in the BORSTAR unit to determine whether a missing person had been apprehended and was "in their system." In other, rarer instances, if she had enough information about the possible whereabouts of someone she believed was still somewhere in the desert, Renee requested searches. In one instance, an agent agreed to go out in search of a diabetic man believed to be lost in the desert. "This agent was out there on an ATV in the middle of the night looking for him for me." The man was found. But she cautioned, "We very rarely have enough information for BORSTAR to do a search."

Within two years, by the time Chloe took over the missing person hotline, two significant changes had occurred. First, the Advocates were working with the Humanitarians. Given their constant presence in the wilderness, the Humanitarians had both knowledge and resources that could come in handy during a search and rescue operation. Second, Chloe and other Advocates had grown frustrated with BORSTAR. The agency had developed a more centralized system for working with the Advocates on missing persons cases. Instead of five contacts, the Advocates now only had one agent with whom they could partner. "We didn't want to rely on this one person, who we didn't trust and who was embedded within a system that was problematic and racist," Chloe emphasized. "No matter what, the priority for any agent is enforcement and not rescue." She worried that the agency was just using their partnership with the Advocates to improve their public image.

Chloe recalled one illustrative instance. The agency had "co-opted" a successful search initiated by the Advocates and the Humanitarians. "Border Patrol held a press conference about how they rescued a man, which they did," Chloe explained. "But it was because of our help. . . . Never gave us the credit, even though we did all the legwork," she said. Annie, the Humanitarian, had participated in the search and recalled the tense atmosphere between agents and volunteers as they searched for the missing man. She felt patronized: "'Oh, we'll humor you kids in your rags and your beaten-down trucks, but let the grownups work,'" Annie laughed. Later, the press conference had neglected to mention that the man was released from the hospital long before he had fully recovered from dehydration—and he was promptly deported.

Increasingly disillusioned with the agency's search and rescue unit, the Advocates and Humanitarians decided to develop an alternative set of procedures to respond to missing persons cases. Their response system eschewed reliance on any one agent—ideally, Chloe explained, they would avoid working with the Border Patrol altogether. When activists wanted to determine if a missing person was in Border Patrol custody, they did not call the senior contact person in BORSTAR. Instead, they cold-called individual Border Patrol processing centers and immigrant detention facilities. The group assembled a team of Humanitarian volunteers for on-call shifts for search-and-rescue operations. The new plan gave activists more flexibility to execute a search on less information than what BORSTAR agents required, and they could more easily avoid cooperating with authorities.

CONCLUSION

As I write, activists in Arizona have finished organizing the annual migrant pilgrimage for the sixteenth consecutive year. Religious entities studded the sponsor list, including a group of Franciscan friars, a Buddhist monastery, and two Presbyterian congregations. This event was clearly in keeping with what many scholars have noted: that religion is an integral part of pro-immigrant mobilization, particularly at the U.S.-Mexico border.

Yet, the sociological significance of the pilgrimage only gains clarity when it is put in conversation with everything *else* the movement did. In fact, the pilgrimage was a précis, summarizing the Humanitarians' and Advocates' state-weakening strategies. Like the Humanitarians' water drops, the pilgrimage temporarily created a civilian domain, defying the state's monopolistic hold over particular geographic spaces. Like the Advocates, the pilgrimage also provided an opportunity for activists to reach out to relatively unattached third parties—such as faith leaders— and welcome them into the pro-immigrant fold.

The goal of pro-immigrant activism was to weaken the state. To this end, the Humanitarians largely relied on a two-pronged approach. By framing the borderlands as a humanitarian crisis zone and the Border Patrol as the cause of that crisis, the Humanitarians called into question the legitimacy of the state's presence at the border. In response to the crisis, they established a domain of humanitarianism in the desert, challenging the state's attempt to monopolize interactions with migrants at the border.

Over time, the provision of aid allowed the Humanitarians to fashion their organization into a Border Patrol watchdog. As they delivered aid, activists documented the agency's practices. In openly damning reports, the Humanitarians concluded that the Border Patrol, as an institution, violated the basic human rights of migrants.

The Advocates were just as critical of the state's power. However, by comparison to their desert-based colleagues, the Advocates primarily trained their focus on the state's potential victims, rather than its agents. Specifically, they tried to build up noncitizens' *resilience* to the state. Without being fully versed in their rights, activists argued, undocumented people could hardly avoid being ensnared by the state's deportation apparatus. Activists taught people how to manage everyday encounters with state actors. They facilitated naturalization, striving to protect even the relatively privileged strata of noncitizens (permanent residents) from the deportation state.

The group also targeted relatively powerful actors with ambiguous relationships to the immigration enforcement apparatus. In some cases—like the Medical Examiner's Office—the Advocates tried to get third parties to engage directly in their activism. In a context where people were fearful of any entity attached to the state, the Advocates provided a safe conduit for the exchange of information that could help find a missing migrant. For several years, the Advocates even worked with a surprising third party—a Border Patrol unit—to locate missing migrants. When this relationship eventually deteriorated, the Advocates, working with a team of Humanitarians, tried to create an alternative system of search and rescue. The effort fed into both groups' strategies. By introducing civilians into search-and-rescue operations, the Humanitarians were trying to create yet another nonstate, humanitarian domain in the desert. The Advocates, meanwhile, were extending a protective buffer that benefited the kin of missing migrants, who might be rendered vulnerable if they interacted with the state.

Just as each campaign the pro-immigrant movement organized makes more sociological sense when analyzed with respect to the rest of the movement's repertoire, pro-immigrant strategy takes on more meaning when considered in relation to restrictionist efforts. When Alyssa put out water in the desert, she thought of her action as conveying a message to the entire field of actors—not only the state, but also groups like the Soldiers, the Engineers, and the Arpaiositos. Pro-immigrant activists diligently worked to weaken the state because they knew their opponents were working diligently to shore up the state.

7 Strengthening the State

THE RESTRICTIONIST STRATEGY

In 2011, the man who had spearheaded the restrictionist cause in the Arizona state legislature and been a lead sponsor of Senate Bill 1070, State Senator Russell Pearce, was recalled from office. The event prompted the Arpaiositos to begin discussing how to protect Maricopa County Sheriff Joe Arpaio from a similar fate. The group that had been instrumental in the Pearce recall campaign, Citizens for a Better Arizona (CBA), had their eyes on the controversial sheriff.

Valerie scoured CBA Facebook posts, calling an emergency Arpaiositos meeting at a diner. Through her internet sleuthing, Valerie had deduced that CBA planned to attend the Maricopa County Board of Supervisors' meeting to demand the Sheriff's resignation. The board held the purse strings for the Maricopa County Sheriff's Office. "Humph," snorted Bob, "as if that's ever gonna happen!" Though they doubted Arpaio would ever retire, Cheryl urged, "We have to be there. Who knows how many people they're going to bus in from Tucson!" Mary, Valerie, Alex, and Bob agreed to go to the Board of Supervisors meeting.

Cheryl leaned forward, brow furrowed: "I'm glad we're doing this," she began, "but we have to think more long-term, *like* the communists. We have to plan, step by step. Protesting their meetings is a good way to show our support; it's not going to get Joe [Arpaio] reelected." Jason nodded enthusiastically. He had somehow gotten on the CBA email listserv, and mentioned that CBA was working on a voter registration campaign. "Including illegals!" Alex inserted. "We've gotta do the same," Mary declared. "Registering illegals?" Valerie asked incredulously. Mary chuckled. "No! I mean, we also have to do a get-out-the-vote with American patriots. Otherwise, Arpaio will be the next one to go down, and you know that others will follow." Everyone agreed.

A few months later, a grainy image of Dale's lanky figure was projected onto a screen inside the Arizona State Legislature. Dale was a longtime Engineer. That day, he was standing a few hundred feet from the Arizona-Mexico border, while a group of conservative state representatives in Phoenix watched a livestream of Dale and his colleagues showing how some of their technologies worked and might be used at the border. It was a sort of second chance, after an invitation to do a demonstration like this was rescinded, last minute, the year before. Phil, the group's leader, had been thrilled. "It was a blessing in disguise, really, that we got another year to work on it," he told me.

"It" referred to the Engineers' system of ground sensors, which Phil had first showcased at a security conference in Phoenix a few months prior. He told an audience of security company reps, journalists, and low-level DHS officials how the sensors, aided by a network of drones and cameras, could provide a more accurate assessment of the number of people crossing the border than the DHS had managed. The message was the same in the capitol building. This time, however, the rapt audience was a coterie of state representatives.

Years later, in 2017, I met Dougie, a smiley Southern man. He recounted his very first night shift with the Soldiers. Dougie was an Army veteran, but he was still getting used to the Soldiers' tactics during this "muster" in the Arizona wilderness. His overnight adventure, less than a mile from the border, had been an important learning experience. Dougie and another Soldier had been assigned to an observation post on a steep hill overlooking a migrant path. They silently hunkered down with their long arms and night vision equipment, struggling to stay warm and awake. At the crack of dawn, a dozen border crossers came into view. Nine, Dougie said, were carrying "dope"—big bales of marijuana—on their backs. The others wore regular backpacks. "I guess they were the reserves," Dougie surmised. Sheepishly, he remembered that they hadn't known what to do, so they called in to the Soldiers' "base command." "We wasn't told to engage them, as far as stop them. I guess we misunderstood." People on observation posts were not supposed to move: "They stay still, observe, report." Still, Dougie realized afterward, they should have moved to "drop in behind them and track them" until the Border Patrol arrived. "So the idea is to keep an eye on them until the Border Patrol shows up?" I asked. "Or, if we can get them to drop their bags," Dougie replied, "We wanted to be silent, camouflaged. . . . I'm sure if we had hollered 'stop' maybe two or three of them would have dropped their bag and hauled ass in different directions." Dougie's sheepish smile returned: "Now I know [what to do]. These guys [the Soldiers] are doing a really good job out there," he said admiringly.

What was at the core of restrictionist mobilization? This was the question I grappled with as I shadowed my respondents in the middle of the desert wilderness, in Phoenix streets, and inside convention centers. On the surface, the Soldiers, Arpaiositos, and Engineers' quotidian activities were widely divergent: the Soldiers patrolled the desert at the U.S.-Mexico boundary, clad in military fatigues and carrying AR-15s. The Engineers tinkered with gyroscopic drones and computer software. Nearly two hundred miles north, the Arpaiositos took up bullhorns and homemade signs, trying to keep a controversial sheriff in office. Despite the differences in their everyday work and the variations in the problems each group tried to solve, all these activists mobilized around the same *strategy:* to strengthen the state's coercive ability.

As chapter 3 explained, restrictionist activists saw themselves in the state—just as their pro-immigrant counterparts did. But while pro-immigrant activists understood themselves and the state as occupying positions of *power* in relation to racialized immigrants, restrictionists experienced relative deprivation. People like Dale, Mary, and Dougie struggled with the seeming discrepancy between their in-group racial status (and all the prerogatives that this status had once implied) and a fading sense of agency. White-but-working-class restrictionists came to believe that their experience of losing control was not unique to them. At a broader, institutional level, a loss of control, an erosion of power was afflicting the state, too. What else could explain the "illegal immigration problem"?

This chapter describes restrictionists' efforts to strengthen the state's coercive capacity by analytically distinguishing between two mobilization strategies. The Arpaiositos, I argue, strove to *empower groups to assist the state*. In this way, their tactics can be contrasted with those of the pro-immigrant Advocates. The Soldiers and the Engineers tried to *expand the state's reach*—an endeavor that combated the state-limiting efforts of desert-based pro-immigrant groups like the Humanitarians.

Conventional analyses of nativism as a type of vigilantism are not accurate. Despite restrictionists' deep-seated criticisms of the Obama (and later Trump) administration as well as nearly all federal lawmakers, their grassroots organizations were not anti-state. Nor did the Soldiers, Arpaiositos, and Engineers operate on the fringes of society.

Rather, restrictionists actively tried to forge working relationships with state actors. In fact, such collaboration was an important source of legitimacy for these activists, as chapter 5 showed, allowing them to make moral distinctions between themselves and the "real racists." This was a grassroots presence on which state actors could—and sometimes did—rely. The Soldiers strove to become a civilian extension of the Border Patrol in the desert; the Engineers to be a border security contractor for the Department of Homeland Security; and the Arpaiositos to be a protection posse for local law enforcement and its restrictionist sheriff.

THE ARPAIOSITOS: BUILDING SOCIETY TO REINFORCE THE STATE

To Valerie, Maricopa County was one of Arizona's last domains of law and order. A fifty-eight-year-old white woman, Valerie had lived exclusively in the Southwest: New Mexico, Southern California, and, finally, Arizona, where she had settled with her then-husband in the early 2000s. Valerie, a high school graduate, worked in low-level retail positions until medical problems forced her onto disability benefits. In 2011, when we first met, Valerie spent most of her time volunteering with the Arpaiositos. Her eyebrows shot up in surprise when I told her where I was living; shaking her head, she told me there was really "no hope for Tucson." New Mexico,

California, most of Arizona—*especially* Southern Arizona—had, in her estimation, no chance against the juggernaut of sanctuary politics.

Valerie thought city officials, under pressure from "illegals and their supporters," had transformed Tucson into a sanctuary city in practice, if not in name. Neither Tucson nor its neighbor, Southern Tucson, had even adopted the more politically palatable label "immigrant-friendly." Still, Valerie told me, the Tucson Police Department could no longer uphold the law (read: perform immigration enforcement). Their leadership was appalling: When SB1070 was first introduced, she remembered, the police chief had plainly stated the measure was a terrible idea and his department would refrain from checking immigration status in lawful encounters. Valerie heard that a Tucson-based Tea Party group rallied in protest, but its efforts had been in vain. As we talked, SB1070's fate was unclear, however, Valerie doubted anything would change even if the Supreme Court ultimately upheld it. Tucson, she repeated, was a lost cause.

As Valerie fell silent, Bob piped up, voicing the Phoenix-based group's collective concern: "If we're not careful," sanctuary policy, "could happen here!"

That fear animated the Arpaiositos. They believed immigration had negatively impacted American citizens, and it was being aggravated by tepid municipal-level enforcement. Sheriff Joe Arpaio was the exception: After ICE granted immigration enforcement authority to his Maricopa County Sheriff's Office (MCSO) in 2007, through the 287(g) program, the sheriff enthusiastically poured local law enforcement resources and know-how into immigration control. But the Arpaiositos worried that even Maricopa County was in danger of de facto sanctuary. At the end of a three-year Department of Justice civil rights investigation, DHS, under Secretary Janet Napolitano, began curtailing MCSO's 287(g) powers in 2009.[1] With every federal criminal investigation and grand jury probe into the MCSO, the Arpaiositos grew move convinced it was a systematic effort to undermine an arrangement that actually worked. Thus, they took it upon themselves to work with the MCSO.

The key members of the Arpaiositos—Bob, Valerie, Cheryl, and Alex—first met in 2006 at a protest against the presence of day laborers in East Phoenix. For years, these day laborers had gathered each morning in the parking lot of a local Home Depot to solicit work. In 2005, however, Home Depot stopped allowing this practice. The day laborers thus assembled farther up the street, near Pruitt's Home Furnishings. The storeowner solicited the help of the Phoenix Police Department to chase the day laborers away, but pro-immigrant groups' pressure had stopped the cops from openly policing the area. When the storeowner hired off-duty Phoenix officers and MCSO deputies as private security guards, pro-immigrant activists began to assemble every weekend, claiming the guards were racially profiling the area. They videotaped the security guards. They held up big signs denouncing racism. They chanted.

Valerie saw the furniture store protestors on the news and remembered feeling infuriated. It seemed unfair that a small business owner had to bear the brunt of "illegals," especially during the holiday season. She found it even more disconcerting that the police seemed unable to intervene because of the "pro-illegal" supporters. One Saturday, Valerie drove to the store. She was surprised at the sight of *another* group of men and women—a group that had barely gotten any coverage in the "lamestream" media. *This* group, Valerie said approvingly, held "patriotic" signs. They were "orderly." She quickly realized she was not the only one frustrated by the situation. Other Americans were frustrated that a small business suffered because of "illegals." Other Americans were frustrated that the police could not "do their jobs." Other Americans were frustrated with troublemakers "bused" in from Tucson.[2] Valerie returned the following week, proudly carrying a sign proclaiming "No Open Borders." In the weeks that followed, she met the men and women with whom she would later form the Arpaiositos.

The events Valerie narrated were unfolding against a backdrop of change in immigration policing practices. The years of the furniture store battle (2006 to 2007) roughly overlapped with an important shift in Sheriff Arpaio's attitude toward undocumented immigrants. It had been prompted by the Illegal Immigration Reform and Immigration Responsibility Act (IIRIRA) of 1996. Section 287(g) of IIRIRA enabled the federal government to bestow state and local employees with the powers of immigration officers, pursuant to a written agreement with the federal government and immigration enforcement training for the deputized public servants. Police could make immigration-related street arrests, while correctional officers could issue immigration warrants (or "detainers") in jails. As chapter 1 described, the 287(g) program marked a radical shift away from a system in which civil immigration enforcement fell under the sole jurisdiction of federal officers and toward a system of harnessing local law enforcement networks.

The 287(g) program came into effect in the mid-1990s, but none of Arizona's sheriffs seemed to be aware of its existence. Indeed, as recently as 2005, Arpaio seemed ambivalent about immigration enforcement—undocumented people were simply not a priority. *The Associated Press* quoted the sheriff saying that he "[didn't] expect to concentrate on some guy in a truck with six illegals," preferring "to go after the professional smugglers who do this for money, the top people."[3] The Democratic governor at the time, Janet Napolitano, would make him change his mind.

In an effort to showcase her party's toughness on immigration, Napolitano reached out to ICE requesting that it grant 287(g) authority to her state. ICE granted the request and, by deputizing 160 MCSO officers, set a new national precedent.[4] Up to this moment, there had been only 200 officers deputized under 287(g) in the entire country. No local law enforcement agencies had immigration powers both on the streets and in jails. In late 2006, that changed, with ICE effectively giving the MCSO "the largest and most comprehensive 287(g) contract in the nation."[5]

Concomitantly, Arpaio's priorities changed. By 2007, MCSO deputies were arresting hundreds of undocumented immigrants.[6] By year's close, MCSO was regularly executing immigration raids in front of Pruitt's Home Furnishings.

Valerie, Bob, Alex, and others who would form the Arpaiositos began gathering every weekend, then *every day*, to face off with pro-immigrant activists at the furniture store. Johnny, another early member, recalled how the group's tactics evolved. At first, everyone just lofted signs and shouted. Then, they noticed that not only journalists, but also pro-immigrant activists were taking photos of the restrictionists. So, according to Johnny, the restrictionists returned the next day with cameras of their own. They took photos and videos of pro-immigrant activists, day laborers, and their potential employers, threatening to hand over the footage to ICE. Whether the Arpaiositos actually shared any of the footage with the authorities or not, this early tactic was in line with the restrictionists' notion that law enforcement *needed* citizens' help.

Further, the documentation effort gave the newly formed restrictionist group an immediate goal as well as the beginnings of a larger analysis about the state. The furniture store became a metaphor for the rest of Phoenix. A small business—embodying the very values that made America great—was being menaced by two apparently external threats: racialized foreigners and their Tucson-based supporters. Valerie and the others were even more upset that law enforcement's "hands were tied"; after all, it was the allegations of racial profiling that drove the cops to crack down on undocumented workers not in their official capacity, but as moonlighting security guards. Open policing around immigration resumed when the federal government granted 287(g) powers to MCSO, but the sheriff's immigration raids were nonetheless met with public objection.

A clear niche seemed to have opened: the Arpaiositos were going to be MCSO's civilian partner and public advocate.

Supporting MCSO as Civilian Deputies

The introduction of the 287(g) program thus created the conditions for collective action at the grassroots level. Long before the protests in front of Pruitt's Home Furnishings officially wound down, the Arpaiositos had begun talking about how they could continue to "protect" Phoenix. It spurred a number of early Arpaiositos to join the Maricopa County Sheriff's Office "volunteer posse."

Johnny recalled that, for a period, some determined activists "protested half the time [and] rode with Joe [Arpaio's deputies] the rest of the time." In his estimation, posse volunteers were no longer just "mall cops" (although posse volunteers did serve this function). Under Arpaio's leadership, the volunteer posse was a far more formidable force. From what I gathered, the transformation Johnny was describing did, at least partially, take place. Since Arpaio first took office in 1993, the volunteer posse had grown into a complex organization with multiple, semi-autonomous branches. Volunteers participated in search and rescue, served as radio operators, and engaged in all kinds of policing practices neatly titled "security" work. Posse members, I learned, could even accompany deputies on traffic stops and designated immigration sweeps. (The latter practice stirred some controversy, but did not stop Arpaio from creating an

illegal immigration operations posse in the winter of 2010). Posse volunteers looked remarkably like actual deputies, wearing uniforms and riding
in vehicles with official-looking insignia. Some, after going through the
department's Qualified Armed Posse Academy, could carry expandable
batons and even guns. The MCSO was a very attractive option for mobilized Arpaiositos in 2007.

By 2010, only one group member—Mark—still participated. Mark was
a gregarious, middle-aged white man who had been volunteering with the
"jeep posse" for a number of years. Born and raised in the Jacksonville
Beach area of Florida, Mark had moved to Arizona when he turned eighteen. He couldn't wait to get away from his "overbearing" parents, and had
a distant cousin living in Phoenix, working in the restaurant business.
Mark worked with his cousin for many years. "I did everything—back of
the house, front of the house, everything," he boasted. He took some night
classes, hoping to move into a different line of work, but eventually, he
gave up that pursuit. At the time that I spoke with him, Mark was unem-
ployed. He lived with his girlfriend and her teenage son. Mark had gotten
acquainted with the Arpaiositos during the furniture store protests, and
now, he said, most of his friends were restrictionists.

Riding with deputies in their cars was enjoyable and meaningful for
Mark. Often, these ride-alongs took place when deputies were doing traffic
control. Several times, he said, the deputies stopped vehicles that turned
out to have undocumented drivers and passengers. Mark proudly described
his support role on one such occasion: He and a deputy had pulled over an
old Toyota with a broken taillight in a residential neighborhood. It was
nighttime. The driver—who "appeared Mexican," according to Mark—
could not produce a driver's license or registration. Nor was he forthcoming with his responses to the deputy's questions.

The deputy, Mark explained, was suspicious of the driver's legal status.
As the deputy interrogated the man, a group of people gathered nearby.
Two of the bystanders started video-recording the scene on their cell
phones. Mark walked over to the group and asked them to put their cameras away, because it was "an ongoing investigation." A bystander challenged the request, asking why the driver had been pulled over. Mark said
he politely explained that the car had a broken taillight and the driver had
no driver's license. The driver was eventually arrested. Afterward, Mark

recalled, the deputy expressed gratitude for having his backup. The episode typified the experience of MCSO deputies for Mark: a simple traffic stop of an (assumed) "illegal alien" could easily turn into a tense situation. Mere bystanders could get confrontational. This was how he understood the posse's larger role as peacekeepers: to create a situation in which deputies could perform their duties.

Although he enjoyed fraternizing with deputies and still believed the posse provided an invaluable service to MCSO, Mark did not, by the time I met him, volunteer as much as he once had. Like other Arpaiositos, Mark had grown weary of some of the fellow posse volunteers. Increasingly, it seemed, posse members were acting "unprofessionally." Mark and another Arpaiosito filed a complaint with MCSO about one particularly problematic posse member, who they claimed had driven recklessly on patrol, worn his uniform while off-duty (i.e., when he was not accompanied by a deputy), and disrupted deputies' operations. The Arpaiositos believed that this kind of amateurish behavior could create more bad publicity for the sheriff and his deputies and threaten MCSO's ability to enforce immigration laws. They wondered what, beyond the posse, they could do to support the MCSO. It became obvious as more public controversy came down on the agency.

Public Advocates of MCSO

As MCSO practices attracted increasing public outcry, eventually making the department the focus of a grassroots campaign, the Arpaiositos turned themselves into its public advocates. As the start of this chapter described, a group called Citizens for a Better Arizona successfully recalled Arizona State Senator Russell Pearce. With Pearce out of office, CBA was getting ready to launch a similar campaign targeting Arpaio. The Arpaiositos made disrupting this recall effort their collective goal; their first opportunity presented itself at a press conference.

The press conference was slated to take place in front of the state capitol building in Phoenix, with an Arizona state senator announcing that he was sponsoring a bill to repeal SB1070. Opposing legislators convened on the other side of the lawn, where restrictionists gathered to watch their animated speeches. I stood on the lawn with Valerie, Mark, Johnny, and

Alex as we listened to the SB1070's legislative champions. Valerie and Mark held signs reading, "We support Joe Arpaio," while Johnny's read, "We are a nation of laws / Sheriff Joe Arpaio = law enforcer." Alex walked off, blending into the anti-SB1070 side of the lawn. Moments later, as I asked Valerie where Alex had gone, we heard a siren blare. Alex had triggered the piercing sound on his bullhorn megaphone, successfully disrupting the pro-immigrant legislators' speeches. The speakers urged the crowd to ignore him.

As Alex walked around with the bullhorn, Johnny scanned the crowd's perimeter. He nudged Valerie and nodded in the direction of "anti-Arpaio people" manning a table at the lawn's edge. Valerie nodded, and the pair sauntered over to the recall petition table. Valerie later told me that they had "politely" inquired about the recall effort. Johnny jotted down his contact information on a CBA clipboard. He wanted to get on the group's email listserv so that he would be notified of upcoming meetings.

After the press conference, the Arpaiositos began systematically monitoring CBA. Alex, who usually opted for more bare-knuckled, bullhorn-blaring tactics, reported that he and his wife, Alana, went undercover as CBA members. In a listserv email Johnny received, the group learned of an upcoming meeting, and Alex and Alana attended. After the meeting, Alana took fliers for all of CBA's upcoming events. Alex stealthily took photos of the other attendees, planning to post them on the Arpaiositos' website so that fellow activists could recognize CBA members on sight. Alex and Alana uploaded scans of the fliers to the Arpaiosito website and emailed them to local Tea Party and restrictionist groups, encouraging like-minded citizens to help frustrate CBA events. Meanwhile, other Arpaiositos closely monitored the CBA Facebook site. The disruption campaign was in full swing.

The Ambiguous Border, the Weak-State Effect, and the Arpaiositos

All these tactics—the Arpaiositos' involvement in the furniture store counter-protests, the sheriff's volunteer posse, and later, the struggle to thwart an anti-Arpaio campaign—were animated by the belief that the state needed to be bolstered. The Arpaiositos strove to create more avenues for local institutions—in this case, the sheriff's department—to assist the flagging state. If the MCSO was responsible for ICE's effectiveness in

Maricopa County, it made no sense to curtail 287(g), so activists sought out ways to support the sheriff's office in maintaining a system of localized immigration control.

Often, it felt like the battle was being waged on two fronts. While criticism and investigatory probes rained down on the sheriff from the federal level, the "Tucson" approach to immigration seemed to be gaining ground at the local level. Although they were not specifically aware of the Advocates' efforts, the Arpaiositos were nonetheless cognizant of the political field in which they were operating. Though Tucson was far more politically fractured about sanctuary than the Arpaiositos imagined, their overall analysis of a Phoenix-Tucson divide had some merit. As the Arpaiositos strove to protect the relationship between local law enforcement and immigration control, the Tucson-based Advocates tried to *sever* those ties. Such dynamics are indicative of the ambiguous border. The jurisdiction of immigration control had grown fuzzy. After the introduction of 287(g) powers in Arizona, it was no longer clear who the rightful gatekeepers of immigration enforcement were. The Arpaiositos' niche had opened.

As activists like Valerie, Mary, and Mark tried to boost local institutional support for the state, two hundred miles to their south, the Soldiers and Engineers worked to directly *extend the state's reach.* Civilianization and privatization of border control were becoming two more outlets for nativist activism.

THE SOLDIERS AND ENGINEERS: EXPANDING THE STATE

The Soldiers: Protecting Families on the Frontier

Laura Bauer was a farmgirl from the Midwest.[7] She first moved to Arizona in the 1970s, with a fresh degree in nursing. She had no plans to marry back into farm life; however, soon after arriving in Arizona, she met Jerry who ran a fifty-five-thousand-acre cattle ranch that sat on state and federal land approximately thirty miles north of the border. By Arizona standards, the ranch was "moderate" in size, Laura explained. It had been in Jerry's family for well over a century, the kind of family operation that required the grit and hard work of the entire household (and all their employees). Jerry and Laura would raise their children on the ranch. "[Jerry's] very committed to it. We all are. It's a beautiful place," she said, gesturing toward the mountainous vista.

Jerry and Laura were now in their sixties, but Laura could not imagine slowing down. There was too much to do. The work had compounded in size, she explained, because of the increased flow of immigrants. After crossing the Arizona-Sonora boundary, border crossers sometimes traversed the Bauers' ranch. Laura welcomed the Soldiers' presence, likening them to the civilian defense of the mid-twentieth century:

> In the Second World War, my aunt stood at night and watched the skies for planes, and she had this chart on her wall that identified all these different planes that could be approaching, and Jerry's mother, same thing. . . . That was civil defense. [Additionally], they had men who had vision problems or flat feet or hearing problems [so they could not enlist], and they worked here in the U.S. At night, [these men] would patrol power plants and things that were vulnerable to enemy attack. That's what the Soldiers are.

For Laura, the Soldiers' practices were comforting and historically familiar. Just as her aunt had scanned the night skies, just as men who could not fight volunteered to patrol power plants at home, the Soldiers volunteered to help the nation defend itself against its enemies.

Since the late 1990s, the border had felt like a war for the Bauers. The "enemies" were furtive and ubiquitous: they crossed through the ranch land, day and night, cutting fences, damaging water pipes, scaring cattle, and leaving behind refuse. Each cut fence required costly mending and compelled time-consuming searches for cattle that had wandered away. Each severed water pipe required replacement and led to many hours of manually hauling water to cattle. Over time, the Bauers grew to think about these occurrences not as the desperate efforts of crossers trying to survive, but as malicious acts of vandalism.

Laura told me the ranch also began to feel physically unsafe. She forbade her teenage daughter from riding around by herself. Several years later, husband and wife decided that the ranch house could *never* be left alone, in case someone tried to break in. Holidays became complicated affairs: Jerry and Laura went to a relative's home to celebrate Christmas Eve, while their son and daughter-in-law stayed at the ranch; then they switched on Christmas Day. By 2010, Laura and Jerry would not let their grandchildren play outside without adult supervision. When the Soldiers volunteered to patrol their land, supplementing what seemed like the limited presence of the Border Patrol, the Bauers were overjoyed.

In early 2017, the Soldiers reached out to Ron and Carol Griffin. The Griffins, like their friends the Bauers, also maintained a moderate-sized cattle ranch, which Ron's father had first acquired in the late 1980s. Like Jerry Bauer, Ron's family history with ranching stretched back to the late 1800s, when his ancestors arrived in the area, nearly a quarter century before Arizona was admitted to the Union. The Griffins' ranch abutted the U.S.-Mexico boundary. The first time I accompanied Ron to the southernmost edge of his ranch, it was 2011. We drove down, Ron's rifle close at hand. He was reluctant to let me get out of the vehicle to have a better look at the international boundary. Later, Ron explained the nightmare scenario for him and his wife: "Our biggest worry is riding in the back country along the trail and look up and there's a guy with an AK-47 and guys behind him with marijuana on their backs. We would feel uncomfortable even reporting it to the Border Patrol. That's how our friend Rob [Krentz] got killed."

Rob Krentz, also a cattle rancher, died from gunshot wounds on his ranch in southeast Arizona in 2010. His death attracted national attention. Conservative state legislators in favor of SB1070 leveraged the rancher's death to push their "papers, please" bill. Krentz's murder occurred a day after federal agents had arrested eight suspected drug smugglers and seized 250 pounds of marijuana on his ranch. To date, the crime has remained unsolved. Although investigators identified thirty people of interest in both Mexico and the United States (including an American permanent resident), many, including Krentz's widow, believed that the perpetrator was a Mexican drug cartel scout who had entered the country without permission.[8] The Griffins thought the lesson was clear: Drug cartel operatives would retaliate against ranchers they believed were communicating with the Border Patrol. It was why the Griffins liked the idea of using the Soldiers as intermediaries. They encouraged the Soldiers to install cameras on their ranch and share footage of any suspicious activity with Border Patrol. They gave the Soldiers permission to conduct occasional musters on their property.

For restrictionist activists, the ranchers, like the furniture store's owner in Phoenix, served as "representative characters" in a racialized and gendered allegory about the nation's fraught relationship with immigration. A representative character is a "public image that helps define . . . just what kinds of personality traits it is good to and legitimate to develop . . . [and] provides an ideal, a point of reference and focus."[9] "The entrepreneur" or small business owner, typed as male, thus embodies the values of individualism and self-reliance. The rancher or "cowboy" is another mainstay in American culture.[10] While both of these representative characters are imbued with whiteness and masculinity, the cowboy, in particular, has served as an enduring model of American "manhood."[11] For restrictionist activists, the Pruitts in Phoenix and rancher families like the Bauers, Griffins, and Krentzes in Southern Arizona were living embodiments of admired American cultural heroes. That racialized, foreign others threatened to emasculate these totems of Americanness was a galvanizing idea for my conservative respondents. They too, were part of a deeply *clarifying* allegory about how immigration was endangering "true" Americans.

For the Soldiers, especially, the daily trials rancher families faced were tangible examples of the consequences of unauthorized migration. On a number of occasions, I heard the Soldiers repeating stories Laura had told me, such as the time she and her husband had to borrow a water tanker from a neighbor because a water pipe had been cut and they had to manually fill their cattle troughs. Similarly, the fears that the Griffins expressed became the backbone of the Soldiers' internal and public-facing discourse about the legitimacy of their group's mobilization. Border ranchers' tales of their safe homes turned into places "overrun with armed intruders" offered the Soldiers actionable evidence of the dangers of the southern border.

When I interviewed him, Sam, a Soldier, deeply commiserated with Jerry and Laura. He was not a rancher, but lived on a property that intersected a migrant route:

> It's just not right, the lack of respect—being stolen from, hearing noises under my house, being woken up, somebody's trying to crawl under my house to sleep to stay warm. . . . I couldn't even have chickens, they killed them all for food. So that got me kind of riled, and that's why I joined the Soldiers.

At least, Sam conceded, he was not trying to live off of his chickens; the Bauers' livelihoods were being directly impacted by migration. For Sam, as for other Soldiers, the ranchers' stories of hardship and danger, provided concrete ways to conceptualize how migration was terrorizing Americans—even *cowboys*.

The Soldiers pegged the problem of insecurity to the border's barrenness, its lack of physical presence and protection. The local Border Patrol station was not equipped with the manpower or the resources to effectively police the area. Under these circumstances and despite the best intentions of individual agents, the agency failed to protect ranching families, so the group took it upon themselves to provide the Bauers and the Griffins with a modicum of protection. The Soldiers hoped that by their presence they could help deter, apprehend, or redirect unauthorized crossers.

Becoming the Border Patrol's Civilian Extension

The Soldiers grew out of a local chapter of the Minuteman Civil Defense Corps (MCDC) formed in 2005. They became a formal organization in their own right when MCDC disbanded between late 2008 and early 2009. The evolution meant evolving from an organization primarily serving as a media spectacle to publicize an "out-of-control" border to a far more media-shy group that tasked itself with helping local Border Patrol agents. To that end, the Soldiers had made their standard operating procedures (SOP) more proactive and focused on gathering intelligence. While the original Minutemen's goal was to be the agency's extra eyes and ears, several Soldiers characterized their predecessor's approach as "lawn chair vigilantism": activists, sitting in their "lawn chairs," often unarmed, simply waited for border crossers to come to them.

The Soldiers, by contrast, were better armed and carried out organized patrols. Members sometimes opted to carry two assault rifles at a time on reconnaissance tours. Whether or not the organization was sufficiently proactive remained a subject of internal conflict, however, and by 2017, the group splintered along this seam. This organizational split was important (and its consequences are explained in more detail below), yet the argument over tactics grew out of a shared aspiration to strengthen the state.

Both before and after the organizational split, the Soldiers continuously tried to work out what it meant to be a serious civilian extension of the Border Patrol. Primarily, this meant developing an SOP—the "rules" for how to look and act as a civilian force patrolling an area they deemed unsafe. Like the Arpaiositos, who came to physically resemble MCSO deputies when they volunteered with the posse, the Soldiers looked remarkably similar to Border Patrol agents. They wore militaristic uniforms adorned with the group's logo. They wore combat boots. Despite the scorching heat, a Soldier told me in 2012 that he always wore a pair of thick woolen socks left over from his days in the Air Force; the socks helped protect his skin against small cactus thorns. The Soldiers carried backpacks filled with food, ammunition, and occasionally first aid kits. The patrolling groups also carried radios and GPS devices, and one member always had a satellite phone. Participants strapped handguns to their belts and often carried assault rifles. On one patrol, Russell, the "mission commander," opted to bring his assault rifle but leave his water bottle behind; sternly, he told me that we were more likely to die from enemy gunfire than from dehydration.

The Soldiers straddled the boundary between civilian and soldier by continually reworking how to equip their bodies. For example, Rudy, a Vietnam veteran, had acquired an expensive bulletproof vest. He wore it underneath his uniform until he realized how much he suffered from carrying around its immense weight. Other members—including Russell, who anticipated gun battles in the desert—discouraged Rudy from wearing this heavy body armor, arguing that Border Patrol agents rarely wore vests because they interfered with quick movement. Rudy shed the vest. In a separate instance, at a monthly meeting, those present laughingly recalled a former member who used to wear a Kevlar helmet on patrols. While they agreed on the sensibility of bearing arms, wearing a ballistic combat helmet was considered ridiculous. Figuring out what members should wear was not only an important process by which the group readied itself for the uncertainties of the border, but also a communal activity that allowed members to carve out their identities as civilian soldiers.

Besides dress and equipment, the Soldiers also sought to acquire a soldier's disposition. In 2017, Rick, the leader of the more proactive faction of the Soldiers, explained to me that one of the skills he wanted participants to cultivate was "noise and body discipline." During forty-eight-hour stakeouts, two-person teams were instructed to sit silently and observe at their posts. These posts overlooked active migrant trails. Any activity was reported to the Border Patrol. As the opening vignette with Dougie suggests, however, participants did not always know what to do if they actually observed migrants. Moreover, the task of staying put in one place in the desert for forty-eight hours was excruciatingly difficult.

Nathan, a thirty-five-year-old participant, broached this topic when I asked him about the best and worst part of being a Soldier. He enjoyed the camaraderie but dreaded the monotony of stakeouts. Nathan had taken to listening to audiobooks, the volume so low in his headphones that he could barely make out the words. The modulation of the narrator's voice was enough to keep him awake. Still, it was clear that Nathan did not want Rick to know about this audiobook trick of his. Nathan believed (correctly, I later learned) that Rick would regard this habit as counterproductive to maintaining appropriate noise discipline. Much to Rick's annoyance, Nathan had once repeatedly asked permission to cut a stakeout nearly thirty-six hours short when it began to rain one evening. At first, Rick refused to grant permission for the men to return to camp from their observation post. But when Nathan radioed in that they had not brought any waterproof cover with them to the observation post and that their clothes and sleeping bags had been completely soaked, Rick yielded. When Nathan returned, I could see Rick watching him, a mild look of disapproval on his face. In Rick's view, enduring the rain was precisely the kind of bodily discipline that was necessary if the group wanted to seriously partner with the Border Patrol.

Maintaining a Good Relationship with the Border Patrol

In 2011 and 2012, when the Soldiers solicited donations—at meetings, at their booths in public events, and online—it was often for the repair and replacement of their cameras. This practice continued after the organizational split. I quickly learned that the cameras occupied a central place in the group's practices and ultimately provided the Soldiers with a major raison d'être. Specifically, the devices served three main purposes. First, they presented occasions to fashion oneself into a civilian soldier—an endeavor the Soldiers approached with great seriousness. Second, the cameras were important for documenting and publicizing the group's understanding of the border, and with it, why their mobilization was needed. Third, by documenting crossers, the Soldiers proudly cultivated a working partnership with the Border Patrol. As chapter 5 illustrated, this relationship allowed the group to distance themselves from charges of racism and assert the legitimacy of their activism.

In 2011, a team of Soldiers went on camera check patrols on the Bauers' ranch once or twice a week. Armed and clad in heavy military gear, they navigated the rough desert terrain in order to locate the cameras that they had hidden in crevices. Once the cameras were found, the group replaced their batteries, downloaded the previous week's footage, and repositioned them to overlook a well-traveled migrant path. Through trial and error, the Soldiers developed methods to keep the cameras from being detected and yanked out—like using black tape to cover any lights the cameras emitted and chaining the machines to surrounding rocks. If a camera was no longer recording crossers, the Soldiers moved it to a place where activity might be more likely.

On one camera patrol in which I participated, we wandered aimlessly for several hours searching for the cameras. The temperature range of the desert was unforgiving: we had started in the numbing cold of the predawn hours, but we were soon subjected to the blazing heat of midday. Though the previous week's camera handler had taken down the G.P.S. coordinates, some of the cameras' locations had gotten lost in the shuffle. Russell, leading the patrol that day, patiently listened to the vague and static-ridden verbal directions that the previous camera handler provided over the phone. We found one machine only after circling the same area for the third time. Another was sitting at the bottom of a steep wash. There was some discussion about whether it was safe for me to wait, alone and unarmed, at the top of the wash. Despite my protestations that I would be fine, Russell had one of the men stay behind with me. The rest of the team awkwardly balanced their assault rifles and other heavy gear as they clambered down a slippery path, with only prickly ocotillo shoots and mesquite tree branches for support. When we were finally done for the day, Russell grinned with satisfaction. He had completed the patrol successfully, in defiance of arduous conditions, relying almost solely on memory and observation.

Finding all six of the cameras turned out to be a time-consuming and fatiguing task. I had assumed that this outing was unusual, given that we had little information to go on. But actually, it was typical: the cameras' locations were haphazardly recorded, if at all. In fact, Ben, the software developer who was most familiar with the cameras, was unsure whether the Soldiers had six or seven machines. The day that I joined them, Russell and his team had to orient themselves in a vast open space, with few artificial markers, in order to find the camera equivalents of six needles in a haystack. In addition, the day's obstacles required endurance, persistence, and strength. There was even an opportunity to demonstrate masculine protectiveness over me, the only woman in the group. Even if the lack of proper recordkeeping meant the occasional lost camera, from a positive standpoint, it justified frequent forays out into the ranch and occasions for soldiering.

In addition to providing opportunities for soldiering and helping publicize how "out of control" the border had become, the cameras helped the Soldiers cultivate their working partnership with the Border Patrol. From what I had gleaned, the Soldiers had encountered crossers very infrequently before the organizational split. Although my respondents in 2011 and 2012 were ready with stories of *other* members' encounters, no one I spoke with had directly come across a migrant during a patrol. The same was true of the Soldiers' predecessors, the Minutemen.[12]

Nonetheless, the Soldiers believed they were of great service to the Border Patrol, unlike morally suspect "vigilante" border-watch groups. Every Monday, Ben handed over the camera footage, as well as the times and locations it was taken, to his local Border Patrol contact. Ben was sure the agency benefited from this "intel." Another Soldier, Michael, detailed the Soldiers' SOP vis-à-vis the agency: before a patrol, the group always informed the Border Patrol of their location, and they immediately notified the agency if they encountered any sign of "suspicious" activity.

At a monthly general meeting in 2012, Vic, a white man who appeared to be in his sixties, announced that he had been corresponding with a member of a Phoenix-based border-watch group. Interrupting, Sarah flatly stated that the Soldiers would no longer "engage" with that group, because their Phoenix counterparts could not stop "fighting among themselves long enough to develop an SOP." Not having a proper organizational structure or an SOP, she maintained, invited the wrong kind of participants—namely, "skinheads." "You can go on your own," she said firmly to Vic. "We can't tell you not to participate with them. But the problem is that there are a lot of rogues who don't follow the rules." If Vic participated with the Phoenix group, as a representative of the Soldiers, and something bad happened, then the Soldiers' reputation with the Border Patrol could get tarnished. Vic was visibly dissatisfied and would not let up. The Bauers' ranch seemed "under control," he insisted. Couldn't the Soldiers consider patrolling other places? Sarah chuckled. "I can't tell you the number of times we thought that the ranch was under control and then it turned out not to be true," she said.

Trying to change topics, Sarah asked if there were any more comments about the previous camera mission. It had been very quiet, one person commented—both in terms of encounters and activity on camera footage. Sensing that this could be more fodder for Vic's request to change their patrol sites, Sarah exhorted the group to not be disappointed when they didn't see "illegals." Relative quiet meant that the Soldiers were effective in a double sense: they were deterring migrants, thanks to their physical presence on the ranch, *and* providing the Border Patrol with important "intel" about which migrant routes were in use. "That's good!" she concluded.

It was this ongoing concern with how to be a valuable partner to the Border Patrol that ultimately fractured the group. The faction that went on to become its own organization under Rick's leadership was motivated by the idea that the Soldiers needed to evolve, adopting more "proactive" tactics of "reconnaissance" to help agents in the field. In this spirit, Rick began organizing bimonthly, weeklong operations. These ops no longer took place on the Bauers' ranch (which continued to be the sole base of operations for the other faction, under Sarah's and Ben's leadership). Instead, with Rick at the helm, ops were organized in a variety of regions often just a mile or two from the U.S.-Mexico boundary. Slowly, sometimes begrudgingly, participants became accustomed to manning observation posts for long periods. As if to match the group's concern with being more proactive, Rick's faction also began attracting younger, more physically fit volunteers from around the country.

Between 2005, when the Minutemen first brought their lawn chairs and binoculars to the border, and 2017, the Soldiers' appearance and tactics changed. The organization grew more militarized, both in appearance and in action. Meanwhile, labels like "militia" and "vigilante" gained currency, particularly on the political left. However, despite what these terms suggest, the Soldiers' underlying strategy remained unchanged. Theirs was always an effort to work *with* the state, to expand its reach. Indeed, the group's identity—the way in which they morally distinguished themselves from the universe of border groups—was based on this understanding. Of course, extending the state's scope did not necessitate a partnership with the Border Patrol.

The Engineers: The Border Security Consultants

"We had a lot of fun!" Chris enthused. We were standing in a dimly lit room. Wall-to-wall tables held several dusty computers. Chris gestured toward the door with his cigarette pack, and we walked through another workroom before stepping outside. We stood quietly, squinting to adjust to the abrupt transition from the dark computer lab to the bright Arizona outdoors. I looked beyond the terrain of wild grass in front of us, at the steel and rebar posts that marked the border some five hundred feet away. Looking westward, I spotted the olive-green uniform of a U.S. Border Patrol agent, slowly riding an all-terrain vehicle (ATV) along the fence.

In the early 2000s, Phil, the founder of the Engineers, had acquired the ranch that Chris and I stood on. When I first met him in 2011, Phil was in his early seventies. Soon after he acquired the ranch, Phil hung up framed copies of the Treaty of Guadalupe Hidalgo and the Gadsden Purchase Agreement at the entryway of one of the buildings. "It's a reminder that we're a nation of laws," he said solemnly. These mid-nineteenth-century treaties had delineated the modern edges of the United States, creating Arizona out of what had long been Mexico. He saw himself and the Engineers as continuing the work of these treaties.

Chris lit his cigarette. He was a thin, white man in his mid-forties, with a gaunt face that made him look far older. Chris had been with the Engineers for several years and worked odd jobs in construction and home repair to make ends meet. "We had a lot of fun," he repeated, smiling. He explained how one of the first tasks that the newly formed Engineers had undertaken in the early 2000s was aerial surveillance of the Border Patrol. They had acquired a small airplane.

Because, what we were doing [was] we had scanners, and we would listen to the [Border Patrol's] radio frequencies, which were open at that time— they were broadcasting in the clear. We would launch the airplane; we had the scanner aboard. We'd listen to their traffic and say, "Ok, we've got a target." We knew where they were going, because of the landmarks they were using. So what we did was we would document how the Border Patrol worked. When they'd hit some action, we'd go over and we'd videotape it. We learned a lot that way.

Studying the Border Patrol was in keeping with the Engineers' larger raison d'être, which was to figure out what was "wrong" with border security and develop a more effective alternative. To that end, the ranch had been converted into a veritable test site. Within eyesight of the border fence, the Engineers had built a large workroom and stocked it with expensive surveillance instruments. The adjoining room, where Chris and I had chatted, was empty, save for several computers that monitored ground sensors across the ranch. An old bus had been moved to a clearing on one side of the ranch buildings so that it forked the possible paths of anyone walking away from Mexico; by manipulating movement, the Engineers had, for the purposes of a previous surveillance project, ensured that potential crossers came within signal range. A thermal camera, mounted on the roof of a building, was also a remnant of an earlier project. Operated remotely by an Engineer living in Texas, the camera had once produced footage broadcast over the internet in real time.

The Engineers were mindful that scrutinizing the Border Patrol's practices was a risky enterprise. They worried that any criticism about the agency could cost the Engineers support in politically conservative circles. I became aware of this tense relationship between the Engineers and the agency on my first visit to the ranch in 2011. While I was speaking with him, Phil received a phone call inviting him to present at a national security conference being held in Phoenix the following month. Over the years, Phoenix had become a hub for such gatherings, where representatives of law enforcement mingled with technology contractors and strategists.[13] At this particular conference, the keynote speaker would be the producer of the National Geographic show, *Border Wars*.

Phil agreed to present. He was familiar with these kinds of conferences, having attended a similar border security event in California a few weeks earlier. But when he got off the phone, Phil wondered whether the organizers would disinvite him once they researched his work further. *Border Wars* had glorified the Border Patrol. For Phil, the television show was "a puff piece": "It's not analytical. [. . .] It raises more questions than it answers. I happen to know a lot about the Border Patrol and how it works, and it's just dumb." Phil attended the conference, but deliberately skipped the keynote address. As he'd predicted, it lionized the agency and earned the television producer a standing ovation from the dozens of uniformed DHS officials in the audience.

At the beginning of his own session, Phil took pains to clarify that he was critical of the *agency*, not of individual agents. Then he discussed how the Engineers offered a more systematic approach to "border control."

The Engineers shared the Soldiers' goal of expanding the state's reach. However, they perceived the Border Patrol not as a prospective partner, but as an object of study and criticism. They studied existing border enforcement structures, motivated by the prospect of developing technological alternatives. They hoped to eventually win a DHS contract to improve the way the state conducted border surveillance. The group joined the ranks of other "white-collar boundary builders"[14] attending conferences about border security. As they did so, the Engineers began to think of themselves as "border experts" and "techies" who could advise the state on matters of border security.

Techies on the Border

To be "techies" rather than "activists" was a self-understanding made apparent in two interrelated ways. First, this self-image was evident in individual Engineers' narratives about their participation in the group. For instance, Connor, whose story was recounted in chapter 3, compared his participation to working with Lockheed Martin, a defense company: "It was the freedom and possibility of developing something really, really cool, like we have now," he told me. "I mean, you go work for Lockheed— it's going to be twenty years before you're in charge of anything." To Connor's mind, everyday participation with the Engineers was rather like the work being done in security companies, minus the hierarchical organization. Activism gave him an opportunity to be a techie in a way that was not easily available elsewhere.

His deep ideological commitment to restrictionism notwithstanding, Phil, too, saw himself more as a techie than a political activist. When he introduced himself at border security conferences, spoke with journalists, or sat for interviews with me, Phil presented his work with the Engineers as the logical conclusion of a long career in systems engineering. The son of a musician, Phil had strayed far from the family trade. After earning a degree in math, then studying operations research, he was recruited by a think tank to help develop complex computer simulation models for guided missile destroyers. His expertise in the total systems approach—conceptualizing an entity, like a ship, as a whole system, rather than focusing on its individual parts—landed him jobs in natural resource development. At one point, his job was to troubleshoot failing companies. Throughout his career, he eagerly assumed the role of engineer-cum-consultant. Whether a ship or a troubled company, Phil's passion was figuring out how to make systems function in more integrated ways. The U.S. Border Patrol was just another complex system that was failing. The agency needed to be reworked, and Engineers had the technical knowledge to do just that.

Despite having no background in engineering or any related field, Dale, another young member, also grew to see himself as a techie. An accident had left him deaf in one ear, so he could not join law enforcement. Instead, he was a "jack of all trades." He began to get involved with the Engineers by doing odd jobs around the ranch, alongside Chris. Before long, Dale was actively involved in the operation and testing of technologies— whether it was manning infrared cameras or participating in aerial surveillance of the Border Patrol. As the chapter's opening narrated, Dale also had an important part to play during live simulations when he would pretend to be a border crosser. He seemed particularly excited by these "cool" sensors, but I realized this was his standard, enthusiastic response to each new technological venture. The techie identity was a mainstay in Dale's self-understanding, just as it was in Connor's and Phil's.

This style of self-presentation dovetailed with how the Engineers, as a group, distinguished themselves from other border-watch organizations.

When I happened to mention the Soldiers, for instance, Dale shook his head. How could a bunch of guys "playing dress-up on the border" be fighting immigration? Chris had drawn on a similar distinction. "I'm sure many of them, their hearts are in the right place," he began diplomatically. "But you can't compare them, with their military fatigues and their guns, to this." He gestured at the Engineers' workroom and its adjoining computer lab. Once again, the technical aspects of the Engineers' activities served as important boundary-making mechanisms. For Chris and Dale, the techie identity suggested that their organization was more serious than others.

As chapter 5 noted, such distinctions could also become the basis of how restrictionist activists came to understand what was and was not "racist." Connor, for example, also harbored serious doubts about the Soldiers. He did not think that the Soldiers had put in the effort to cultivate a working relationship with the Border Patrol. Without the steadying hand of the agency, it was more likely a group would undertake risky endeavors, and, one fateful day, have an encounter with a migrant that drew public scorn. It seemed that the Engineers drew a spectrum between the tactical and potentially unlawful, approach to restrictionism and the technical and more serious method of mobilizing. The Engineers situated themselves squarely on the technical end. "That's why it's cool doing the technical side," Connor explained, "because we can stand up and look and watch and detect instead of being right on top of these people [border crossers]."

Phil, the group's founder, was slightly more conciliatory in his assessment of the Soldiers; nonetheless, he, too, drew on a set of bright boundaries. "They're doing something important, [which is] to point out the problem," he said. By disseminating footage of migrant trails and showing how border crossing had not lessened over time, the Soldiers were constantly reminding the public of the "problem." "But they have no solutions," Phil continued matter-of-factly. "I do. I have a solution. Big difference." When one considered it in a more detached and less political manner, as a systems engineer would, the problem's true nature became evident. "The issue is operational control of the border," Phil explained. "What is that defined as? The prevention of all unlawful entries. [. . .] And that's what we're working towards."

I found out later that the Engineers and the Soldiers had, in fact, tried to collaborate on a number of occasions. But these efforts had been futile. In one such instance, the Soldiers had invited the Engineers to the Bauer ranch to test their sensors and fly a surveillance drone. The sensor had not worked, and the conditions had been too windy to fly the drone. From the Soldiers' perspective, the failure of the technologies stemmed from the Engineers' comparably limited experience in the desert. The frustrated Engineers saw the occasion as a minor technical setback and an important learning experience. The next day, they began customizing the drone so that it would be more weatherproof. Ultimately, the Engineers believed that their technological savvy made their efforts far more effective than those undertaken by the Soldiers.

As they distanced themselves from groups like the Soldiers, the Engineers increasingly associated themselves with the more "serious" border security industry. The group saw security and defense contractors as both partners and competitors. One day, I was chatting with Dale and Connor in front of the workroom when Phil drove up. By way of greeting, Phil joked that Dale and Connor should be careful not to divulge too much information about what the group was working on—I might be a spy for General Dynamics, a defense firm.

The Engineers' main way of associating with other techies concerned with border management was by attending border security conferences. In them, "white-collar boundary builders" peddled their wares and discussed border enforcement matters. In these settings, the Engineers rubbed shoulders with defense contractors, law enforcement agencies, and other stakeholders. As they did so, the Engineers began marketing their latest product, the sensor-based system of surveillance.

At one conference session, Phil, presenting himself as a "border expert," explained the problem with border enforcement, then how his group's sensors could address this problem. The DHS, he said, assesses border security using one set of numbers—apprehensions at a given time. Phil argued that that number should constitute only the numerator of the correct measure of apprehension; what DHS needed was the denominator, or the actual number of people making unauthorized entry. Without this crucial number, he insisted that it was impossible for the federal government to make any accurate claims about "operational control." In addition to making the border apprehension rate more calculable, he argued that the Engineers' sensor-based system could provide real-time information about where unauthorized entries took place, so that enforcement resources could be mobilized in more targeted ways. At another conference, the Engineers exhibited their system and claimed that it provided the only way to have "seamless coverage of the entire border."

Becoming DHS's Border Security Consultants

Although the Engineers were also interested in extending the reach of the state, the group believed that the agency's methods of detection had to be completely revamped. For this reason, the Engineers turned to creating a new, more technologically comprehensive surveillance boundary. As one Engineer put it, the question that drove their work was, "How do we know *everything* that's coming across the border?" To answer this question, the Engineers embarked on a process of dismantling, reassembling, and testing technologies that they hoped would let them acquire comprehensive information about the border region. By developing this new system, the Engineers hoped to become a contractor and consultant for the DHS.

In their very first project, the Engineers mounted a satellite internet video onto an ATV, hoping that it would enable "mobile coverage" of a local piece of the border. Even if the coverage was only of a small area, they reasoned, it could still have a significant impact when streamed, real-time over the internet. Multiple computer users—including those far from the U.S.-Mexico border—could install a software program that the Engineers had developed. This program would run in the background of their computers, and if the mobile system detected anything out of the ordinary, an alert would appear on the taskbar. It would be sufficient for just one user then to pick up the phone and contact immigration authorities in Arizona in order to initiate action. The system would thus allow concerned citizens to monitor the border from the comfort of their homes, wherever they might be.

The mobile system frequently broke down, however. The harsh weather conditions and rough terrain were formidable obstacles. When, in 2003, the Engineers reembarked on the quest for mobile surveillance, they acquired an unmanned aerial vehicle and mounted it with a system to send live video feed over cable networks. By the following year, they had made their drone night-vision capable as well. They gave up on the venture when the Federal Aviation Administration forced them to ground their drone, yet they hailed the experiment as a success, claiming that it was through their efforts that the DHS had finally been "shamed" into using drones at the border.

The technology approach always served as the backbone of the Engineers' work, but the group was not content to use sophisticated devices simply to apprehend unauthorized crossers. They sought systematicity, which required developing technologies that could be used to count, measure, and classify. In 2009, the Engineers embarked on an effort far grander than the lightweight manned aircraft surveillance of local Border Patrol practices; this time, a crew flew over all nine of the Border Patrol sectors that spanned the U.S.-Mexico border. They noted where fences were located and what types they were. After assembling the information on maps, the group concluded the DHS was claiming the border was much more fortified than it actually was.

At the time of my fieldwork, the Engineers were trying to work out other ways to assess the government's efforts at border enforcement. Attempting to determine, for a given area of the border, how many people crossed on a given day, they fashioned an infrared camera, fitted with a special lens, into a detector. This camera had a range of a few hundred feet; the Engineers envisioned an array of detectors eventually being installed along the entire length of the border. Its serious drawback was that the slightest movement—human or nonhuman—would set it off. Phil recalled the group's first decision to find an alternative:

> We were sitting there a little frustrated. Connor was saying, "That darned [infrared detector]. It's the ground sensors that make more sense." So, I contacted a seismic exploration company in Texas. [Afterward] we decided to install a half-mile of seismic equipment on the ranch here. . . . We put these together with all our electronics, and it was picking people up regularly at six hundred feet. . . . We installed that, and began testing it.

The new sensor system would hopefully produce real-time, intelligible information. It consisted of ground sensors connected to solar-powered seismographs that digitized signals for computers; the computers, in turn, were supposed to help distinguish between "threatening" and "nonthreat-ening" movement. Then, depending on what had triggered the signal, drones would be dispatched to film the area in question. The bottleneck was in developing the software to analyze the signals in real time.

> At six hundred feet, it takes over two minutes to walk up to the line [bound-ary]; so we can grab data thirty seconds at a time, which gives us the time to analyze it and see [whether] this is a person [or a] horse, or whatever. One of the problems with the little sensor at thirty feet is that you don't have very much time to analyze the signal. [What is giving off the signal] is here and then it's gone.

The group contacted a firm for software enabling live access to data col-lected from sensors. The Engineers also began developing additional soft-ware that could recognize what was being detected. They created an algo-rithm based on the contrast between how people and animals walk: while animals place their feet down, humans drop their weight onto their feet. While a group of humans walking together would multiply the frequency of the signal and therefore muddy it, the data would nonetheless create a unique signature and raise red flags.

After installing the new sensor system on the ranch, the Engineers con-ducted "live demonstrations" to publicize their work. The opening of this chapter described how Dale simulated a crosser by walking through the Engineers' ranch. As he did so, the sensor system was activated and Dale's location was immediately recorded. In Phoenix, meanwhile, another Engineer projected a map onto the screen in the Arizona State Legislature showing Dale's location and the direction he was moving. In another dem-onstration, the Engineers invited a state senator, prominent ranchers, sev-eral restrictionists, and journalists to their ranch. Along with Connor, this event's hosts included experts in seismic data. An Engineer flew an ultra-light aircraft over the border, triggering the sensors and sounding a loud alarm. Later, a group of volunteers, as mock "illegal aliens," walked north-ward on the ranch. When the sensors detected their footsteps, another alarm sounded and the Engineers' drone prototype automatically flew over the area, feeding live footage back to a computer. This live demon-stration, the Engineers hoped, would help spread the word about the effi-cacy of their alternative border surveillance system.

While they engaged in nativist activism differently than the Arpaiositos or the Soldiers, the Engineers were clearly involved in a state-building endeavor. Rather than partnering with the Border Patrol or the Sheriff's Office to defend a local site, as the Soldiers and the Arpaiositos did, the Engineers wanted to revamp the agency's enforcement methods along the entire border. To work out a better "solution" to the "border problem" the Engineers studied the agency, devised new systems of surveillance by drawing on interdisciplinary fields of knowledge, and tested out the new technologies that they developed. The group's point of entry to the state was through the growing "border security industrial complex."[15] The Engineers exhibited their work at border security conferences, reinforcing their identification as techies and border experts. All the while, they hoped to convince the state to use systems developed by a civilian organization.

CONCLUSION

Taking their cues from leftist public discourse, sociologists have adopted terms like *militia*, *extremist*, and *hysteria* in describing popular nativist mobilization. These terms, perhaps initially intended as shorthand for something that journalists and observers could not quite fully understand, have unfortunately taken on a life of their own. To the extent that Arizona-based nativist groups were thought to have any connection to larger movements or political phenomena, they became "the Tea Partiers."

Whether "vigilante" or "Tea Partier," these labels are misleading. The "vigilante" end of the discursive spectrum suggests that grassroots nativist organizations exist in a separate universe altogether, that they are so marginalized they lack any identifiable ties to recognizable institutions. The implication that this mobilization is simply a form of "hysteria" suggests that there are no nativist *organizations*, but only temporary assemblages of irrational people, who, if the public sufficiently ignores and censures them, will give up their madness and go home.

That groups like the Soldiers, Engineers, and Arpaiositos are "Tea Partiers" is equally misleading. Certainly, restrictionist respondents subscribed to Tea Party politics. The Engineers invited local Tea Party groups from around Arizona to come to the border and watch live demonstrations of their technologies. The Soldiers frequently set up booths alongside other conservative organizations at Tea Party "tax day" protests in Tucson. Meanwhile, the Arpaiositos tried to recruit from Phoenix-based Tea Party groups to fill their ranks, and for a time, even used the Tea Party's online forums to recruit new members. Despite these ties to the conservative movement, however, the restrictionist mobilization that I studied was always *separate* from the Tea Party. The "comfortably middle-class"[16] men and women who convened in public libraries to study the U.S. constitution were decidedly *not* my white-but-working-class respondents.[17]

If they represent neither passing hysteria, nor society's peripheries, nor the largest conservative social movement that the U.S. has seen in decades, how do we make sense of the Soldiers, Engineers, and Arpaiositos? That each group's day-to-day practices and immediate goals are so different further compounds the question. This chapter has shown, however, that the state-effect framework not only ties together restrictionist tactics, it also helps bring restrictionist mobilization back into *this* universe. Simply, these groups acted on the conviction that the state was a weak policing entity. Just as they felt like they no longer had charge over their own lives, they believed that the state was losing control over its dominion. In response, each group hoped to improve the state's ability to "see"— to expand and deepen its reach—and thereby strengthen it.[18]

The Arpaiositos wanted to ensure that the state could depend on local groups and social institutions for immigration control. Meanwhile, the Soldiers and the Engineers worked on extending the state's reach at the border itself. That all three groups were tolerated and even welcomed by numerous state actors suggests that state-building rather than vigilantism more accurately characterized the nature of their activism.

To understand such grassroots nativism as a state-strengthening endeavor requires us to recognize that these organizations were not operating in a political void. *Each group took advantage of the "niche-openings" created by the state.*[19] The Arpaiositos were unnerved that the federal government was trying to reverse localized immigration control—an arrangement that federal authorities had initiated. Similarly, the Engineers saw an opening for their work as the mushrooming border security industry fostered opportunities for public-private partnerships. The Soldiers boasted of their ties with Border Patrol agents, who continued to answer their calls and showed up when the group asked them to. This niche-filling nature is precisely why contemporary restrictionism in the United States exemplifies the "now you see it, now you don't" variety of racism.[20] The weak-state effect motivated a type of collective action that took place in the legitimate center rather than on the margins. It was dedicated to institution building.

Furthermore, by illustrating how grassroots restrictionism's forms served as direct foils to pro-immigrant activism, this chapter again illustrates the fruitfulness of a field approach to immigration politics. Like the Advocates, the Arpaiositos trained their focus on institutions in civil society—specifically, local authorities. The question of where to draw the boundary between civil society and the state motivated their competing activism.

Meanwhile, the Humanitarians fought with the Soldiers and the Engineers over the reach of the state. On the surface, both the Humanitarians and the Soldiers hiked deep into the desert in search of migrant routes. Both groups often referred to their work as "search and rescue." But the meanings ascribed to these practices contrasted sharply, depending on whether the group experienced the strong-state or the weak-state effect. The Humanitarians looked for migrants in order to mitigate the Border Patrol's presence. The Soldiers searched for migrants in order to reinforce the agency.

Similarly, the Humanitarians and the Engineers both scrutinized the Border Patrol's methods, but to very different ends. Seeing the Border Patrol as an oppressive force, the Humanitarians observed the agency to report on the abusive consequences of state power. The Engineers, meanwhile, studied the Border Patrol to determine its structural failings and help make the agency more potent.

Conclusion

GOING BEYOND THE WALL

Six years after Arizona Senate Bill 1070 was first introduced, Republican presidential candidate Donald Trump promised an audience of supporters in Phoenix that on the very first day of his presidency, his administration would "begin working on an impenetrable, physical, tall, powerful, beautiful southern border wall."[1] At that speech and many others, "build the wall" became a familiar chant. Trump understood the wall's mobilizing power, confiding to the *New York Times*, "You know, if it gets a little boring, if I see people starting to sort of, maybe thinking about leaving [the rally], . . . I just say, 'We will build the wall!' and they go nuts."[2]

Other Americans, particularly Democrats, adamantly oppose the construction of such a wall.[3] Many described it as preposterous.[4] Political opponents said it was racist.[5] One commentator deemed it "tantamount to giving the world the middle finger."[6]

The wall is an especially divisive issue among white Americans. As Trump was inaugurated in 2017, the Pew Research Center reported that most Black and Hispanic respondents opposed the wall, while their white counterparts split nearly evenly: 46 percent supported and 52 percent opposed its construction.[7] These racial patterns would continue into his presidency.[8]

Why did the prospect of the same wall spur both delighted approval and horrified condemnation? Why did funding for this wall cause two government shutdowns? More precisely, why did (white) Americans— many of whom lived in places both geographically and socially distant from the U.S.-Mexico borderlands—*care so much* about "the wall," one way or another?

Further confounding this puzzle is the fact that Americans, on both sides of the aisle, have little faith that a wall would stop *or even slow down* the immigrant flow into the country. In that same 2017 Pew Research survey, a mere 29 percent of respondents believed the wall would reduce unauthorized entry, while 68 percent believed that the wall would either have a minor impact (25 percent) or no impact at all (43 percent). Just 3 percent claimed they were unsure how the wall would affect immigration.[9] Still, it has continued to be a powerful rallying cry.

Long before Trump first declared that the southern border needed a wall (in 2015),[10] ordinary Americans, despite not having been directly impacted by immigration policy, were mobilizing in Arizona. It was not clear to me—or to them—whether their actions would yield sustainable, long-term solutions. My respondents doubted, like those asked about a prospective wall, that their collective mobilization would make much difference.

Gail, for instance, was certain that no matter how many new migrant trails Humanitarian volunteers discovered in the borderlands and how much the group tried to flood the desert with water, it would never be enough. Border crossers would continue to die. The Humanitarians would continue to discover their remains.

On the other side of the political spectrum, Rick believed that even if more Border Patrol agents agreed to work with his group, there was only so much of the border the Soldiers could guard. Even the Engineers, the organization in this study with the most measurable goal (winning a DHS contract), understood that nothing was definite. Technologies could fail. Even when they didn't, it was not certain that the people in power would take notice of the Engineers' work.

Doubts persisted among activists operating in urban centers, too. Despite the Advocates' myriad efforts to train noncitizens on how to avoid the state, Renee knew that the city was still made up of sites that could trigger deportation and family separation. Despite the support the Arpaiositos mustered for Sheriff Joe, Mary mobilized with the understanding that restrictionist police probably did little to deter noncitizens from living in her city.

With activists of all stripes viscerally aware that their organizations could never achieve what they hoped to achieve, why did they mobilize?

STUDYING SOCIAL MOVEMENTS AS POLITICAL STRUGGLES

To unpack these puzzles, this book has empirically attended to the *political* (rather than simply strategic) nature of social movements. That is, it tends away from the proclivity of social movement scholarship to focus on the *means* of mobilization while disregarding its *ends*. This means-focused approach has been particularly attractive in the study of contentious topics embroiled in so-called culture wars. By attending to the more objective aspects of a movement (like its tactics) and intentionally ignoring the subjective parts (in particular, people's worldviews and their political orientations), this body of scholarship about social movements and civic engagement contends that it can avoid rehashing hackneyed political debates.

This focus on a movement's means and discounting of its ends has colonized many subfields. In U.S.-based studies of immigration politics, more and more studies treat the political content of pro-immigrant and restrictionist positions—as well as the backgrounds and motivations of participants—as either self-evident or irrelevant. In lieu of pursuing "why" and "who" inquiries (*why* do people mobilize, *who* are these people in relation to social structures?), studies of immigration politics have become far more concerned with "how" questions (*how* do groups mobilize?).

What I learned in Arizona, however, was that these questions cannot be separated, nor could I make assumptions about the "why." If I assumed that people joined the Soldiers because they were taken in by the "hysteria" of "fringe," anti-immigrant sentiment (the "why") and mobilized to "take the law into their own hands" to seal the border (the "how"), I would be quickly proven wrong. Neither hysteric nor fringe, the average Soldier resembled many other working-class Americans grappling with downward social mobility and social isolation. They articulated these experiences through a language of racial resentment—again, not unlike many Americans.[11] That they were *proud* of collaborating with Border Patrol agents further derails the idea that they were compelled by vigilantism or a desire to replace the state. Participants experienced self-empowerment as they empowered the state at the border.

Although scholarship about pro-immigrant mobilization in the United States has been more empirical and analytically nuanced than research on restrictionism, it too has been guided by the narrow research agenda of conventional social movement frameworks. Again, following only the tactical repertoires, we would overlook, for example, many aspects of the Humanitarians' mobilization, including that they were almost entirely well-to-do white participants who had nothing obvious to gain from pursuing pro-immigrant policies. We would also have a harder time explaining the organizing logic of their strategic repertoire. That is, the "how" question might motivate a researcher to enumerate all the tactics in the Humanitarians' organizational toolbox, but this would not explain the relationship between individual tactics. Why, for instance, did the Humanitarians regularly rely on both seemingly instrumental *and* ostensibly non-instrumental, secular *and* religious ones? Moreover, the Humanitarians often knowingly preferred *less* strategic tactics to more effective ones. I soon realized that the "usual" way of studying collective mobilization was not going to be adequate.

I took a different approach. I put aside my assumptions and investigated both the why and how of mobilization across these five groups. To get at questions of why, I tried to elicit the relationship between group members' lived experiences and their ideas about the world. This is not, to be sure, a *new* approach: life history interviews have always been a key tool for social scientists. So has attending to people's beliefs about the social world—what Kristin Luker calls "worldviews" and Arlie Hochschild dubs "deep stories."[12] And as I listened to both my left-wing and right-wing respondents, as I observed how they mobilized, I realized that two diametrically opposed conceptualizations of American state power were operating.

"STATE EFFECTS" AS WORLDVIEWS

To pro-immigrant respondents, the state was an oppressive behemoth. Its victim was the third-world migrant, ruthlessly lobbed back and forth across the country's southern border. Americans, particularly white, middle-class Americans, had the power to intervene. In fact, having personally benefited from inequality, it was their *moral duty* to weaken the state and mitigate the cruelty migrants endured.

To restrictionist respondents, the state was enfeebled and uncoordinated, barely able to withstand the scourge of migration and cross-border drug trafficking. Concomitantly, the third-world migrant was imagined as a masculine perpetrator of violence rather than its victim. Restrictionists believed that porous borders invited the problems of the global South into American communities. By banding together, restrictionists saw themselves as concerned citizens trying to prop up the state against untold threats.

Thus, my research showed that the Arizona-Sonora frontier was an *ambiguous border*, a place where some saw the Border Patrol agent as an emasculated, fumbling state actor, and others saw him as a formidable, violent presence. Pro-immigrant activists experienced what I have called the *strong-state effect*. Their restrictionist counterparts were under the *weak-state effect*.

Each effect, I have argued, is more than a static impression of the state—it functions as an assemblage of beliefs and ideas about how the social world works. That the state effects operated as robust worldviews became particularly apparent when I asked each side about the allegation that seemed to threaten them the most.

For pro-immigrant activists, it was the topic of cartel workers, who, like "regular" migrants, risked the dangers of the desert. The strong-state effect framework offered a useful heuristic—a binary of the powerless crosser and the powerful state—that allowed activists to sidestep an alternative, enticing, but problematic binary between deserving and undeserving recipients of humanitarian rescue. The deserving/undeserving binary implied that Americans were entitled to adjudicate the third-world migrant's merit—an idea that many of my left-wing respondents desperately wished to avoid.

The powerless crosser/powerful state binary, however, suggested that *all* racialized border crossers, regardless of who they were, were ultimately subject to forces beyond their control, and for this reason, blameless. Differentiating between a "'bad" cartel member and a "good" economic migrant was not only inappropriate, but it also unwittingly pardoned the real culprit—the American state. There were social costs for activists who refused to conform to this narrative. Those who held the border-crossing "Others" accountable for their actions came to feel alienated from their peers. This underscored the strong-state effect's firmness and influence as a collective worldview.

Likewise, the weak-state effect offered restrictionists an interpretive schema to understand how the border came to be. It also gave them a way to dispute the most threatening allegation made about them—that theirs was a movement motivated by racism. Restrictionist activists combined their concern about the state's feebleness with mainstream conceptions of racism as an extremist, fringe phenomenon. Again, a binary was at play. In this case, the binary separated the "bad" activists (the "real racists") from the "good" activists (restrictionists). The determining factor was the extent to which one's actions helped state actors do immigration enforcement work.

My right-wing respondents argued that "real racists" were socially marginalized individuals, not organizations. They did not aim to reinforce the state, but derailed the efforts of the Border Patrol and other state actors. They were prone to taking dangerous risks, thereby damaging the already fragile reputation of restrictionist organizations. Restrictionists, on the other hand, pointed to their collaborative efforts with state actors to justify both the necessity and legitimacy of their own mobilization.

As a worldview, each effect also served as the organizing logic of mobilization strategies; it linked the "why" and "how" of collective action.

The strong-state effect compelled pro-immigrant organizations to weaken the state in hopes of bringing relief to the oppressed third-world migrant. Whether religious rituals or secular strategies, the organizations' tactics reflected this goal. The Humanitarians concentrated on restricting the state's reach in the desert. In addition to claiming the borderlands as a region necessitating humanitarian intervention, the group effectively fashioned itself into a human rights watchdog of the Border Patrol. The Advocates, meanwhile, tried to erect protective buffers against the state's deportation apparatus. They trained immigrants on how to manage encounters with state authorities and struggled to pull more of civil society into adopting sanctuary policies. Over time, the Humanitarians and the Advocates organically shifted toward collaboration on state-weakening projects.

Meanwhile, the weak-state effect prescribed the restrictionists' methods. The three restrictionist organizations' methods were foils against the efforts of the Humanitarians and the Advocates. As the Humanitarians tried to limit the state's reach, the Soldiers and Engineers tried to extend it. The Soldiers carefully molded themselves into the Border Patrol's civilian extension and the Engineers sought to become a trusted DHS contractor enhancing the Border Patrol's capacity. As the Advocates tried to shield noncitizens from encounters with the state by encouraging local institutions, including local law enforcement, to opt out of immigration enforcement, the Arpaiositos strove to empower groups—particularly the Maricopa County Sheriff's Office—to *assist* in immigration policing. In each of these endeavors, my right-wing respondents sought to work with state actors. In some cases, they were successful; Border Patrol agents, DHS officials, and MCSO deputies, at the very least, listened to and engaged with my right-wing respondents.

This book also illustrates how the distinct state effects experienced by each side articulated with distinct intersectional identities. Activists are raced, gendered, and classed actors. Their social positions and identities structure their politics and participation. In Arizona, I found that there were contrasting biographies across the ideological divide: pro-immigrant activists, overall, were socioeconomically better off than their more precariously positioned restrictionist opponents. Yet, all these activists grappled with what I call a *conflictual identity*, one that was embedded in structural inequality. Pro-immigrant activists struggled with being *progressive, but privileged*, and restrictionists with being *white, but working class*. Each of these conflictual identities sheds light on the book's core puzzle: why my interlocutors participated in immigration politics, a struggle that had no immediate bearing on them.

THE PROGRESSIVE-BUT-PRIVILEGED ACTIVIST
AND (HER) DESIRE FOR SELF-TRANSFORMATION

Across the board, all the pro-immigrant activists in this study felt uncomfortable with their personal privilege. To them, such privilege seemed at odds with their hopes for a more equitable world. Pro-immigrant activists were hyper-aware of the benefits that had accrued to them in their lifetimes. In most cases, leftist respondents had grown up in middle- and upper-middle-class homes, many in predominantly white neighborhoods. Nearly all the pro-immigrant activists that I interviewed were university educated. Many also had additional graduate and professional degrees. Some had been poised for or had embarked on high-status careers.

Considering their socioeconomic backgrounds, pro-immigrant activists' work came with a significant opportunity cost. Almost all had put the pursuit of education, career, status, and wealth on hold to pursue progressive endeavors. They listed the numerous causes they had joined with a readiness that demonstrated the agitation stemming from their identities as progressive-but-privileged people. Activism helped them manage this uncomfortable kind of self. The border was a place where my leftist respondents experienced "self-transformation" as they figured out how to be privileged *and* progressive.

Pro-immigrant activists projected their own sense of personal power onto the state. Just as they believed their own power was undeserved and unfair, so too, they argued, was that of the American state. In Arizona's borderlands, however, personal power no longer operated as an embarrassing impediment. Where the state seemed invincible, the privileges of class, citizenship, and often whiteness were refashioned into tools of resistance. Activists could navigate state-scrutinized spaces fearlessly. They could reach out to state institutions that would never be receptive to racialized noncitizens. For the first time, it seemed, power and status gave activists a clear and *necessary* role.

That this brand of pro-immigrant activism was particularly satisfying to those who identified as white is important. Consider Amanda's experience with the Humanitarians. Having grown so uncomfortable with the group's racial dynamics, Amanda eventually stopped participating. In many respects, Amanda's life history resembled those of her colleagues.

Like other leftists in this study, she too was the beneficiary of generational upward social mobility. She too was poised to move up the social hierarchy in her lifetime. She too had disrupted this upward trajectory to engage in various political causes. And she too justified this disruption by referring to the personally transformative nature of volunteering in the desert.

Yet, as one of the only participants of color, Amanda also reported feeling alienated and uncomfortable as she witnessed her predominantly white colleagues act like they were the saviors of "poor Mexicans." The powerful state/powerless crosser binary that had ideologically anchored other Humanitarians did not anchor her. While the image of the powerless crosser had helped her colleagues navigate the increasingly complex social landscape of the borderlands, the same image had felt like a demeaning, racist trope to Amanda. Feeling more and more out of place, she quit. Her experience illustrates how the pro-immigrant activism that I observed, was integrally about managing the anxieties of being an upwardly mobile *white* person in America.

THE WHITE-BUT-WORKING-CLASS ACTIVIST AND (HIS) DESIRE FOR SELF-EMPOWERMENT

The close interplay between identity management and state-directed mobilization was not unique to the left. While a sense of personal power overwhelmed respondents on the left, the feeling of powerlessness unmoored those on the right. This variation reflected the class differences across the two sides.

Most restrictionists came from humbler circumstances, describing childhoods in working-class and lower-middle-class households. Some had completed high school, others a few years of college. Few had four-year university credentials or graduate degrees. Most restrictionists had tacked together a series of short-lived jobs to make ends meet. Those who had embarked on *careers*, like David, usually found them in the military. Others, like Connor and Rick, had thought they were embarking on careers when they were rudely confronted with the devastation of job loss. Restrictionists also did not have the long records of volunteering, organizing, and activism their left-wing counterparts did. Indeed, much like other white, working-class Americans, few had taken part in civic engagement, let alone any form of communal life prior to joining restrictionist groups in Arizona.[13]

As white-but-working-class people, restrictionists reported an acute sense of deprivation. The common feeling was *powerlessness*. They described a dissonance between their in-group status as white men (or, in some cases, as white women or racialized American citizens) and a general sense of uncertainty that attended lifetimes of economic precarity, downward mobility, and increasing social isolation. A sense of demotion framed their life histories. What was once there—clarity about how the world worked and optimism about the future—had vanished. What they once felt—mastery and control over their destiny—was gone.

The sharpening of racial resentment became the apotheosis in this narrative of demotion. In various ways, right-wing respondents articulated animosity toward racialized people, particularly Latinos. In this worldview, the presence of "illegals" (shorthand for anyone racialized as Latino or Brown) caused an array of social problems for Americans. In this framework, the third-world migrant was not the *object* of outside forces; he *was* the outside force. To make matters worse, the U.S. government failed to protect against this threat. For restrictionists, the state was personified in the figure of the emasculated, solitary Border Patrol agent, standing in the middle of a vast, open desert, wondering how he could possibly stave off unauthorized migration on his own.

Like their pro-immigrant counterparts, restrictionist activists also projected their sense of self onto the state; concomitantly, *state*-directed mobilization was also simultaneously a *self*-directed mobilization. Much as it had for their opponents, working on the state offered restrictionists a chance to work on themselves. Unlike pro-immigrant respondents, however, restrictionists did not report that they were relinquishing upward mobility or making substantial sacrifices to participate in grassroots immigration politics.

Rather, for restrictionists, participation offered novel opportunities. In a few cases, it even offered a steady source of livelihood. For some, it presented a chance to assume meaningful leadership roles. For most, mobilization offered a rare sense of camaraderie. Most significantly, activism restored their sense of control.

Like my pro-immigrant interlocutors, the restrictionists in this study readily admitted that their groups oftentimes did not achieve the goals they set out to achieve. This realization, however, did not shake their belief in the importance of their mobilization. Right-wing respondents felt a singular sense of agency as they shored up the state. White-but-working-class respondents were carving out a role in a world that seemed keen to disenfranchise and emasculate them. The project of state empowerment was also a project of self-empowerment.

But this project of self-empowerment was specifically a project of whiteness. Just as pro-immigrant activism offered a way to "accomplish" white femininity, restrictionism offered a way to "accomplish" white masculinity. The experiences of Tommy, one of the few Mexican American restrictionists I met, is illustrative of this fact. He resembled other Soldiers in many respects. He was a man. He was also a veteran. He even worked in law enforcement. All of these attributes gave him gradations of racial privilege, of whiteness, that helped him find common ground with other Soldiers. And, like his working-class colleagues, Tommy also reported feeling powerless in different parts of his life.

Nonetheless, Tommy was also acutely aware of the racial dimension of his group's mobilization in a way that his white companions were not. When pressed, he admitted that he would not be a Soldier if there were no illicit drug trade and crossers were exclusively made up of "good" (women and children) migrants. However, by mentioning his own undocumented relatives as well as the economic pressures that cause anyone—including men—to migrate, Tommy also seemed to question the "dangerous brown man" trope that his fellow Soldiers used to justify their actions. Just as Amanda's more nuanced assessment of coyotes led her to challenge the prevailing pro-immigrant image of the third-world migrant (as victim), Tommy also questioned how restrictionists imagined the third-world migrant (as victimizer). Moreover, by explaining how he relied on "common sense'" to steer clear of white supremacist groups who were "obsessed with race"—groups that he could "name" if he had to—Tommy indicated that he was clearly mindful of the racial dimensions and racist proclivities of civilian border patrols.

Where Amanda's racial consciousness had led her to quit, however, Tommy ultimately downplayed his experiences of marginalization. Instead, he fastened himself even more securely to the justifications that the weak-state effect, as a worldview, proffered. Even so, Tommy and Amanda's shared unease is noteworthy. It demonstrates how the people for whom this state-directed mobilization felt particularly empowering and transformative were *white*.

IMMIGRATION ACTIVISM AT THE U.S.-MEXICO FRONTIER: A TERRAIN TO PLACATE (WHITE) ANXIETIES ABOUT INEQUALITY

When American citizens engage in immigration politics, it is not *only* because they want to change the rules of immigration. The activists in this book participated because they wanted to experience a change *in themselves*. The struggle around immigration has become a terrain on which Americans grapple with their personal positions in an increasingly unequal world. When my respondents tried to make sense of who belonged, they were simultaneously concerned about how (and whether) *they* belonged.

To think through this idea, I argue that Southern Arizona became a *frontier* for two groups of Americans grappling with their positionalities in a world of inequalities. It is a space of self-actualization. There, citizens seek respite from inequality, even finding ways to right the wrongs of power imbalances as they understand them.

That immigration politics can serve as a substitute for struggles around inequality, including class struggle, has been observed by other scholars. In a study of South Africa and the United States, Marcel Paret found that economic insecurity fostered both inclusionary and exclusionary immigration politics.[14] He argued that immigration is a particularly attractive terrain of struggle among precarious groups with otherwise limited avenues for collectively asserting their power, particularly vis-à-vis employers. Thus, pro-migrant and restrictionist mobilizations can allow effectively "invisible" groups to demand better working conditions from the state.

Like their counterparts in South Africa, immigration restrictionists in Arizona also experienced an overwhelming sense of deprivation. In some cases, white-but-working-class respondents articulated this deprivation in terms of grievances about how the state seemed to distribute resources unfairly. Connor, for example, bemoaned the squandering of medical resources on racialized bodies. He and his companions expressed (white) entitlement when they insisted that America belonged to them—and not to the third-world migrant.

Overall, however, Arizonan restrictionists were vague in drawing a link between their demands for exclusion and grievances related to resource distribution. Exclusionary politics was not part of a clear program to secure state-enabled livelihoods or any other instrumental goal. As far as the restrictionists in this study were concerned, in fact, the state was simply too *weak* to facilitate better livelihoods for Americans.

Nonetheless, restrictionists *did* use the politics of immigration and national belonging to form groups and to foster a sense of camaraderie among themselves. Moreover, like Paret, I also found that precariously positioned restrictionists utilized the immigration struggle to render themselves visible to the state. Rather than demanding that the state recognize them as deserving recipients of its services, they demanded that the state recognize them as *worthy civilian partners* in enforcement. As they mobilized, restrictionists felt like they were reclaiming a socially valuable role for themselves.

Immigration politics was not just about compensating those who lacked structural power, however. This book demonstrates how immigration politics was, at the same time, a struggle waged by those *with* structural power. This politics attracted privileged Americans, mostly white and middle class, and in many cases, women. They mobilized not to recuperate but to relinquish power—or, at least, to collectively harness their privilege to weaken the state and bring some relief to the suffering of the imagined third-world migrant.

What kept people engaged, oftentimes *despite* the proven ineffectiveness of their actions, was the conviction that their state-directed action was also helping them alter the (im)balance of power between themselves and the rest of society. In other words, immigration politics is not just a struggle over whether to include or exclude the racialized noncitizen Other. It is simultaneously a struggle to figure out one's own place, as a citizen and, oftentimes, also as a white person, in America.

This lens on immigration politics—wherein we consider the multiple meanings that different groups of Americans associate with this struggle—may also shed some light on the controversy around Trump's wall. At the same time that my respondents stayed engaged in immigration activism even though they harbored serious doubts about the effectiveness of their mobilization, Americans around the country, particularly those who identified as white, held strong convictions about the wall, while doubting it could actually halt undocumented immigration. The wall's import is clearly more symbolic than material. Thus, it may be more about managing white American identity than changing prevailing immigration patterns. The debate reflects Americans' anxieties around increasing inequality. It also reflects different ideas about how best to soothe these anxieties. The wall debate, like the local immigration struggles I observed in Arizona, may be an expression of a highly fraught politics of whiteness.

GOING BEYOND THE WALL

My research suggests that to make progress in the immigration debate, both in the United States and around the world, we need to think about and address growing social inequality. This inequality is fostering anomie, unease, and uncertainty across the socioeconomic spectrum, including among those who are ostensibly "secure" citizen-members. We need to be mindful of how staking a claim in immigration politics, then, might be a way to articulate other concerns. And we cannot address problems of inequality exclusively by altering immigration policy, much less by relying on the same kinds of narrow, conventional border policy changes that have been used in the past.[15]

My findings suggest that ordinary Americans are hungry for a kind of politics in which there is more room for local self-determination. Participants across the two sides rarely agreed on much, yet all the activists I spoke to in Arizona shared in their trepidation about the federal government's capacity to address local problems. I noted this shared attitude as early as 2011, when I realized that pro-immigrant interlocutors did not wholly subscribe to the Democratic Party, even under the charismatic leadership of Barack Obama. Similarly, restrictionist respondents were not all too certain about the national Tea Party movement.

These shared reservations became even more palpable in 2017. Both sides thought that building a U.S.-Mexico border wall was a bad idea. That leftists opposed such a proposal, of course, was not surprising. What *was* surprising was that they saw the wall—and Trump's election—not as deviations from the "civil" politics of the past, but as a logical extension of the policy frameworks set in motion by previous administrations. Even right-wing respondents remained concerned about the fate of immigration policy after the 2016 presidential election. Despite having voted for Trump, Mary the Arpaiosito told me that it was easy to make big promises during the campaigning season. "That's what politicians do: they tell you what you want to hear." Trump was no different. Meanwhile, Phil the Engineer referred to the wall as a "media fence"—a sexy idea that appealed to the public, but would not give the Border Patrol operational control over the borderlands. National politics was removed from the needs of ordinary Americans.

The polarization of immigration politics is a symptom of worsening inequality and the expression of local communities' desire to do something about that inequality. By titling my conclusion "Going Beyond the Wall," I am issuing a call to go beyond the conventional ways of politically managing migration. It is an invitation to transcend hackneyed debates around whether comprehensive immigration reform is or is not desirable. It is an invitation to transcend arguments about the merits of building more walls or tearing them all down. One way forward is earnest engagement in deep discussions about the underlying conditions of insecurity and inequality that *intensify* the significance of immigration politics for people across social strata. This would require us to ask completely different questions. The most crucial may be, *What would it to take to make people feel secure enough in their everyday lives and certain enough about their future prospects that the topic of who can and cannot immigrate is no longer even politically salient?*

APPENDIX 1 Methods

This appendix describes two problems that ethnographers face and how I grappled with them. The first is gaining access. I discuss how I navigated my outsider status among politically-conservative restrictionists, *and*, as it turned out, among leftist, pro-immigrant activists. The second problem arose once I sat down to talk to my respondents. I learned that, like other sociologists studying politically contentious issues before me, I had to figure out how to ask my respondents about their political behavior without inviting them to repeat hackneyed political arguments. I discuss the importance of combining life history interviews with participant observation when studying contentious topics.

GAINING ACCESS

My identity mattered, just as those of my respondents mattered. I am a middle-class, Turkish woman with black hair, brown eyes, and dark skin. I did not grow up in the United States, but I speak with an American accent, leading people in Arizona to often mistakenly code me as Latina. My common name (Fidan) was frequently heard and interpreted as "Fidel." I anticipated that it might be difficult gaining the trust of politically conservative activists—many of them older white men. Who would talk to Fidel, the racially ambiguous woman?

I knew that my institutional affiliation would also matter. When I first entered the field, I was a University of California, Berkeley graduate student in my late twenties; on my revisit, I was in my early thirties and an assistant professor at the University of Toronto in Canada. I was deeply concerned that my affiliation with a university would hinder my chances of building rapport with this group. Indeed, the dearth of empirical research on restrictionist activism and other right-wing mobilization owes, in no small part, to the problem (and often just the *anticipation* of the problem) of access. In conservative discourse, the university is thought of as a hotbed of liberal causes. By extension, academics are assumed to be unsympathetic to conservative political programs.[1] So, I worried: who would talk to a PhD student, especially one from UC Berkeley, the "home" of leftist causes?

Nonetheless, I dove in. In 2010, the group I call the Soldiers was among the most active in this part of Southern Arizona. Once a local chapter of the Minutemen movement, they had recently become their own entity. In addition to carrying out biweekly patrols, the organization's main preoccupation was capturing video footage of unauthorized migrants crossing the desert. I emailed the Soldiers to introduce myself, asking whether I could attend their next meeting. Ben agreed. As I had anticipated, my outsider status was palpable from the get-go. At one of the first meetings I attended with the Soldiers, I sat next to an older, white, bearded man who smiled and extended his hand to introduce himself. Then he asked if my husband was coming. I realized that a man—even one significantly younger than my interlocutor—belonged in that setting more than I did.

By early 2011, I had also gained access to two other restrictionist organizations, those I refer to as the Engineers and the Arpaiositos. I chose these organizations because they were both entangled in relations of conflict and (attempted) collaboration with the other groups in this study. Years before I met them, the Engineers had launched a campaign to expose what they believed were "treasonous" ideas that the Advocates espoused about the United States. The campaign entailed recurring posts on the Engineers' well-visited website disparaging a core leader of the Advocates. The head of the Engineers, Phil, also regularly reached out to news outlets to discuss the dangers his leftist opponent posed to America's well-being.

The Engineers were in embedded relationships of cooperation with like-minded restrictionists. Importantly, I learned that the Engineers had tried to collaborate with the Soldiers' predecessors, the Minutemen. That the collaboration had fizzled did not stop the Engineers from trying again when the Soldiers emerged as an independent organization under new leadership. Once I figured out how the Engineers were embedded players in the field of local immigration politics, I contacted the group's leader, Phil, over email. Almost immediately, he encouraged me to drive out to the group's ranch near the border. He was used to hosting journalists and other interested guests, and my timing was serendipitous: the Engineers were experiencing a bottleneck. As they waited on a piece of software to be delivered, they had nothing but time. I interviewed Phil. Then, with his permission, I was able to speak to other members of the Engineers at great length, particularly Connor and Dale.

Just like the Engineers, the Arpaiositos were entrenched in the field of conflict and collaboration that I wanted to study. They had actually cohered into a self-identifying group through direct conflict with pro-immigrant activists.[2] As chapter 7 and the section about Mary in chapter 3 explain, the pro-immigrant protests and restrictionist counterprotests in front of the furniture store in Phoenix had pulled future Arpaiositos into immigration enforcement politics and into each other's acquaintance. While the Arpaiositos never collaborated with the Engineers or the Soldiers, they were well aware of both groups.

Cold-calling had worked with the Soldiers and the Engineers, but I could not find a way to contact the Arpaiositos. I did learn through their website that a meeting was scheduled on the plaza in front of the state capitol building in Phoenix. When I came across a group of five people in the midst of a lively discussion, two wearing shirts emblazoned with the group's name and large "I support Arpaio" buttons, I knew I had found them. The Arpaiositos fell silent when I approached. As I started to introduce myself, a stern looking woman, Cheryl, cut me off.

She bombarded me with questions: Where was I from? What did I do for a living? How did I hear about them and their meeting today? As I began telling her that I was a student studying immigration politics and that I had learned about their meeting from their website, she moved on. What was my stance on the Tea Party? What did I think of RINOs (Republicans in Name Only, an acronym the Tea Party frequently used to designate Republican politicians and others who were not adequately conservative)? Was I a registered Republican? What did I think of Citizens for a Better Arizona (the organization that helped recall the state senator who had sponsored SB1070)?

My heart pounded as I stumbled over my replies. My personal views did not align with the Tea Party, I said, but as a student of politics, I wanted to learn more about them. I had not registered with any party, because I was not an American citizen. Just a graduate student on a visa. Believing that I had failed miserably to make a good first impression—that I had attracted *more* suspicion with my stuttering responses—I blurted that I wanted to be respectful of their time. If they wanted me to leave, I would. The impassive Cheryl suddenly cracked a smile. She had not intended to scare me off, she said. It was just that the group had to be careful of "moles." Then, she invited me to stay, saying, "Maybe you and your study can help us figure out what we should do." Later I learned that I reminded Cheryl of her son's girlfriend, of whom she was very fond.

I also learned that Cheryl's questions were less about me, and more about them—specifically, who they were as an organization and how they were positioning themselves vis-à-vis other political groups. I had caught the Arpaiositos at a moment of introspection. They were reexamining their mission. Specifically, the organization was coming to the realization that they no longer wanted to spend all their time participating in the Maricopa County Sheriff's Office volunteer posse. Instead, they wanted to develop new strategies to support Sheriff Joe.

One possibility was to devote their energy to undermining CBA, the group preparing to try to recall the controversial sheriff from office.[3] Growing increasingly distrustful of local right-wing leaders, the Arpaiositos were also reexamining their relationship to the Republican Party and the local Tea Party movement. My timing, thus, was also fortunate with the Arpaiositos. During this period of transition, the group wanted to deliberate and discuss. Who better to help them talk it out but an ethnographer of politics?

In general, my outsider status solicited three kinds of response from restrictionist activists: a refusal to engage, paternalistic engagement (as the young, female student), and suspicious engagement (as the unknown Other). In some cases, people adopted a blend of the latter two responses. First, some restrictionists simply did not want anything to do with me. This flat-out refusal to speak with me only happened with some Soldiers, however, and I surmised that it had a bit to do with the group's evolution out of the Minutemen, a group designed to create media spectacle. Indeed, when the world first met the Minutemen in April of 2005 in Tombstone, Arizona, the crowd of journalists outnumbered the participants.[4]

When the Soldiers became its own organization, the group also changed their standard operating procedures. As chapter 7 explained, the Soldiers sharply contrasted their more armed and proactive approach to their predecessors' lawn-chair-sitting and reactive strategy. This shift also entailed a change in how the group interacted with the media and others (like graduate students). The Soldiers strove to fashion their group into a more "professional" outfit, collaborating with the Border Patrol. The negative publicity surrounding the Minutemen mounted with the murders of Raul Flores Jr. and his nine-year-old daughter, Brisenia, by a group claiming affiliation with the Minutemen and the infighting and scandals reported among movement leaders. The Soldiers were distancing themselves, and it was no wonder some were reluctant to speak with me.

Many restrictionist activists, including Soldiers, *did* speak with me. Largely, it was masculine protectionism that facilitated this access. Restrictionist activists saw the state as failing to uphold its moral obligation to protect its citizenry from external threats. In response, the Soldiers would prop up the state by going into the desert and conducting reconnaissance on behalf of the Border Patrol. When I accompanied the Soldiers into the desert, I, oddly, became the stand-in for the vulnerable and feminine nation. My physical presence as a woman in an all-male space made it easier for the Soldiers to imagine the object of their protective function. This masculinist protectionism also informed how the other two restrictionist groups interacted with me. Frequently, I was likened to activists' daughters, granddaughters, or nieces, or in Cheryl's case, her son's girlfriend. Respondents felt they needed to take me under their wing to help me finish my "school project" and to set me straight about worldly affairs.

Third, some restrictionist activists were initially suspicious of my intentions, but engaged me out of intrigue. My field notes from a winter day in 2011 capture one such instance:

> Don, who upon finding out I am from UC Berkeley, says "never in [his] wildest imagination, did [he] picture a Berkeley student out on patrols with us." I feel uncomfortable and do not know what to say. At the same time, however, I can see that in his own way, Don is trying to accommodate my presence: "At the very least," he continues, "you'll find what we're doing interesting even if we can't agree on anything else." He then chats with me for another hour and eventually agrees to be interviewed.

Albeit awkward and uncomfortable, these sorts of interactions constituted valuable data. One common occurrence was when respondents interrogated me about whether I was a "mole." This question could be posed half-seriously, or sometimes, *very* seriously. Depending on our rapport, I would sometimes joke back. Other times, I would more soberly explain my project and my research intentions. I tried to exploit these moments to glean more information, hoping my interlocutors would verbalize their suspicions in more detail. These moments forced respondents to articulate their understandings of themselves and their perceived opponents. They gave me a clearer sense of who or what these activists believed were sources of insecurity in the world.

For instance, while Cheryl was peppering me with questions the first time I met the Arpaiositos, Alex, was shoving his camera in my face. He liked to take photos of his political foes and post them online. Valerie asked me if I was a spy for "the occupiers and the CBA," referring to the young, black-clad members of Occupy Phoenix, who were becoming visible at anti-Arpaio events. Although very uncomfortable, being at the center of this aggressive vetting process was revealing. It gave me a clearer picture of who the Arpaiositos saw as their primary opponents. The Engineers concocted a different theory about "Fidan the spy." The Engineers joked that I was conducting espionage on behalf of General Dynamics, a defense company. Although these interactions felt uneasy and I worried that my access to these groups was tenuous, these moments were also rich sources of data.

Gaining access was a delicate dance with pro-immigrant activists as well. Building rapport with this group proved to be challenging in ways that I had not anticipated. Just as with the Soldiers, I chose the Humanitarians because they were a highly active group and an obvious starting point for a study of immigration-related mobilization in this area of Arizona. Indeed, the Soldiers saw the Humanitarians as their primary political opponents in the desert, further indicating that the left-wing group was a key player in the local political field. Lori, the young woman I met in Mexico, facilitated my introduction to the Humanitarians.

However, preexisting tensions in the group initially interacted with my ability to build rapport with some members, particularly younger ones. The group understood their presence in the desert as directly confronting the state. Given this framework of conflict and defiance, every encounter with Border Patrol field agents felt highly significant to volunteers. They feared that a single wrong move by a volunteer could bring down the wrath of the state and jeopardize the organization's ability to maintain their domain of humanitarianism in the wilderness. The Humanitarians thus struggled among themselves to determine how best to interact with Border Patrol field agents and leaders.

Younger volunteers preferred a more adversarial relationship toward the agency than their older and often male counterparts. This approach made them feel vulnerable and at risk while doing humanitarian aid work in rural areas. By extension, older volunteers thought a friendly demeanor toward agents would serve to keep the Humanitarians safe from harassment and prosecution. This distinction in attitude also seemed to correspond to people's political ideologies. Younger participants who were openly suspicious (and afraid) of Border Patrol agents in the field also tended to subscribe to anarchist ideas (of varying levels of sophistication) as well as an anarchist subcultural style that held limited appeal for older volunteers. In 2011, when I first started studying the Humanitarians, this rift was a source of lively discussion and, sometimes, unconcealed resentment. Understandably, the stakes were high: how group members interacted with agents could make the difference between the organization's survival or demise.

I suspect that I inadvertently took a side in this high-stakes debate. First, despite my relative youth, my self-presentation—including my conventional hairstyle and style of dress—did not immediately mark me as anarchistic or politically radical. Second, as I became friendly with older volunteers, talking to them before and after meetings, it may have appeared that I agreed more with this group than with their younger colleagues. Third, it made sense that a group that felt uncomfortable about being too transparent to the state would also feel nervous about being around a researcher studying them. Fourth, the fact that I was also studying right-wing groups—which I revealed to left-wing respondents early on—raised suspicion among younger volunteers. For instance, when I tried to strike up a conversation with one, she angrily asked what I could learn from right-wing groups. They were, she told me, motivated by racism. What more did I need to know? Given the vulnerability that younger volunteers already felt vis-à-vis agents (and restrictionist groups), my presence, as someone who was studying them *and* their opponents, may have been unnerving.

Finally, though I could never be entirely sure, a part of me wondered whether there was also tacit racial tension around my presence in an organization that, at any given time, had only a handful of members who were people of color. As far as I could tell, the anarchist subgroup was exclusively white. Perhaps in combination with the factors listed above, racial tension may have contributed to my limited access. By 2017, the disagreement over how to interact with state actors remained, its contours still largely defined by age and, to some extent, gender. But the overt resentment that I had witnessed in earlier years seemed to have dissipated. Younger, anarchist-leaning members were much more open to talking to me. There had been a lot of turnover in membership, and some of the more bitter participants had left. Several Humanitarians independently reported to me that the group had done a lot of soul searching to figure out how to build trust between participants. They had reflected on being a predominantly white organization and were coming to terms with it by developing ways to support immigrant-led organizations.

Although I never gained access to every single Humanitarian (just as I never gained access to every single Soldier), the skill set I cultivated in graduate school—the capacity to research a complex topic and synthesize it quickly—facilitated my ability to build rapport with more pro-immigrant activists over time. Week after week and month after month, state legislators proposed new bills, think tanks churned out new policy proposals, and media outlets reported on the state of affairs at the U.S.-Mexico border. I kept track of all this information and took it upon myself to provide periodic updates to both the Humanitarians and the Advocates. I also became more directly involved on the research aspect of their projects. I wrote and edited press releases, worked on reports, and engaged in discussions about political developments. Being a "participant-researcher" helped me gain the trust of some pro-immigrant activists who were once wary of my presence.

Ultimately, I gained access to two pro-immigrant and three restrictionist organizations. From 2011 to 2012 and on my revisit in 2017, I participated in meetings, protests, conferences, and other events organized and attended by the members of these groups. I either wrote down my observations in the moment or memorized them in order to transcribe them immediately afterward. Often, I took audio-recorded notes on my drive home from events. I conducted eighty-six formal, semi-structured interviews of one to three hours, thirty-four with restrictionists, forty with pro-immigrant activists, and twelve with other stakeholders. I also benefited from countless informal interviews and conversations over the course of my research. All my data—from interview transcriptions to field notes—were carefully coded.

ASKING THE RIGHT QUESTIONS

In addition to the challenges of gaining access, I had to figure out how to ask my interlocutors the *right* questions. In particular, I had to steer my respondents away from repeating hackneyed political arguments and resorting to worn-out public discourse that shed little light on their beliefs and motives for mobilizing. People, even those who have gone the extra mile to mobilize for a cause, are quick to repeat prevailing ideas associated with their political positions. For instance, in a 2011 interview, I asked Sam, a longtime Soldier, why he patrolled the borderlands. His answer was a variation of standard restrictionist discourse about how contemporary immigrants are dangerous criminals: "Most of the people coming across now are of a criminal element. Not all, [but] most. They're on the run from wherever they're from. They're hauling drugs. They're smuggling humans. They're hiding from something."

"How do you know that there's a criminal element there?" I asked, hoping he would elaborate." But his response was unenlightening:

> You look at the Border Patrol blotters, and the percentage of the people that they are catching have past criminal histories. That's the easiest, paper-factual way of looking at it. Six years ago, 97 percent of who [Border Patrol agents] were catching were just certainly immigrants. Turn them around, send them back. Nowadays, they're having to detain 60 percent for other reasons, [like, there are] warrants out for their arrest from the last time they were in the country and all that kind of stuff. So, you know, and the drugs and all that. What the answer to all that is, is so complicated.

Sam's answer told me nothing about his personal motivations for mobilizing. Instead, I got a regurgitated trope about how unauthorized immigrants tended to be criminals and, therefore, dangerous.

When interlocutors resort to calcified rhetoric of this sort, some researchers opt to ignore activists' political discourse altogether. However, discounting the value of *all* political talk seemed too extreme and, indeed, inappropriate in a study about political conflict. In Sam's case, for example, the idea that immigrants were dangerous criminals was, in fact, an important aspect of his worldview, and I should not dismiss it. Yet it was incomplete in explaining why Sam took the additional step of mobilizing. Nor did it get at why he participated in a group like the Soldiers, which, as it turned out, was not very effective at deterring the third-world "criminal" from crossing the border.

Combining Interviews with Ethnography

Complementing formal interviews with ethnography helped in two important ways. First, participant observation helped me build rapport, which allowed me to arrange formal interviews later. Recall my interaction with Don, the Soldier who was simultaneously wary and genuinely surprised that a UC Berkeley student would be interested in his organization. We first met at the group's base camp. I had just returned with a group of men from a patrol, and I was red-faced and sweaty. A layer of dust covered my clothes. Like a true novice, I had worn sneakers instead of thick hiking boots, so burrs from desert flora clung to my shoes and burrowed into my socks. I limped gingerly when I walked and tried desperately, whenever I had the chance, to comb the burrs off. I looked rather pathetic and out-of-place. With Don, the fact that I had demonstrably made the effort to accompany the group on a patrol in order to learn more about them earned some points. Rather than just dismissing me, he engaged with my questions and eventually agreed to be interviewed. Similarly, ethnography also facilitated my access to pro-immigrant activists. As I noted earlier, my constant presence at their events and my involvement as a "participant-researcher" helped me gain access and build trust among people who were initially unsure.

Second, observing what activists actually *did* to mobilize, what kinds of challenges they faced, and how participants behaved in-situ, gave me insight into their ideas and motivations. I then used these observations to construct relevant questions for my formal interview sessions. For example, once I learned that a focal point for the Advocates was the organization of two annual pilgrimages, I could ask members why they found these seemingly non-instrumental and largely symbolic events so important. Pairing my own observations of what people *did* with what they *said* they did in interviews also revealed interesting gaps and contradictions. Indeed, this was how I realized that an organization's stated goals did not often match up with what members actually did. This realization—that the social movement organizations I was studying were not as instrumental as the sociology literature would lead us to believe—became one of the central puzzles guiding my study.

Life History Interviews

In addition to relying on ethnography to solicit more than hackneyed political discourse, I changed my interviews so that they focused on respondents' life histories before I asked about their motivations for activism and ideas about immigration policy. This approach allowed interlocutors to ease into the interview with biographical material that was familiar. It helped them grow acclimated to the process and to their role as interviewees. The respondent became the narrating guide and the expert. Within this framework, respondents were less likely to resort to cliché when I began to ask why they felt passionately about immigration politics. Even when clichéd political talk did surface, we had covered enough of their background that I could ask them to elaborate in more meaningful ways.

For instance, I managed to salvage the interview with Sam when I backtracked and asked him about his biography. When I revisited the question of why he felt it was important for *him* to patrol the border, Sam returned to the topic of immigrant criminality. Now I knew that he had wanted to pursue a degree in criminal justice but was forced to drop out of high school just shy of graduating because he could not afford staying enrolled without working full-time. I also knew that he had applied to a number of law enforcement jobs but never managed to get his foot in the door. He felt bitter about his job situation, the patchwork of short-term, low-income jobs he had to take. A persistent sense of loneliness and insecurity about the future framed his entire narrative. When we looped back to the topic of immigration, this time, he pinpointed the moment he grew interested in immigration: it had been six years earlier, when Sam had just moved into a modestly priced house in a rural area just west of Tucson. The property abutted state trust land where he could relax by quail hunting, and so things finally seemed to be looking up.

Soon, Sam realized his house was in a high-traffic area for unauthorized border crossers. He could not hunt quail for fear of inadvertently shooting someone ("these guys are running all over the place"). His neighbors complained that border crossers killed their dogs. The woman who later became Sam's wife felt so unsafe that she moved to Tucson, and Sam felt indignant that his property was not "respected."

> It's just not right, the lack of respect—being stolen from, hearing noises under my house, being woken up, somebody's trying to crawl under my house to sleep to stay warm. . . . I couldn't even have chickens, they killed them all, for food. So, that got me kind of riled and that's why I joined the Soldiers.

Sam acknowledged that the burglaries and trespassing were spurred by a need—seeking respite from the cold, satisfying hunger—yet they irritated him to no end. Just when he was gaining a foothold in life, everything seemed to be falling apart again. This time, the source of his misfortune was not vague, nameless forces but the "illegals." Sam began "detaining" people he caught near his house, commanding them to sit down on the ground, making sure that they saw he was armed and serious. Then he called the Border Patrol. Unexpectedly, Sam became the "law enforcement" figure he had always wanted to be. When he happened to find out about the Soldiers at a gun show, Sam knew he had found kindred souls. "So I thought to myself, that's something I could get involved with. Here's a problem where I actually can be proactive with." Before long, he struck up friendships with other members. He patrolled with the organization as often as he could. The context that the life history approach gave me was invaluable to understanding his discussion of the criminal third-world migrant. I also better understood the events that led up to his mobilization and how he grew obsessed with the topic of immigration.

POSSIBLE CRITIQUES

Scholars and other readers might offer two big critiques about this research. First, they might wonder how representative my study is. To what extent are my findings also true of the entire population of immigration activists in Arizona, or even the United States? To this critique, I have two responses.

First, even if I had wanted to focus on a representative sample or use random sampling in this research project, it would have been a difficult, if not impossible undertaking. Ideally, to have a representative sample, one first needs to have some idea of the entire population. However, in reality, it would be very challenging to determine the full universe of active organizations that engage in immigration politics, even just in Southern Arizona. Although we tend to think of social movement groups as relatively stable and cohesive organizations, in reality, they tend to be perpetually in flux. Members join and leave. Groups that were very active suddenly collapse. New leaders come along and suddenly resurrect long-defunct groups.

In fact, I observed this instability firsthand. On my ethnographic revisit, after five years, I learned that the Arpaiositos had fallen apart. The Advocates had managed to stay afloat, thanks in large part to the intervention of Humanitarian volunteers. The Soldiers had almost disbanded, but new leadership energized and grew the group. The head of the Engineers suffered from a heart condition, and once-active members were experiencing severe burnout. It was not clear whether the group would last much longer.

In addition to the intrinsic instability of social movement groups, what even constitutes a "group" can sometimes be notoriously unclear. Over the course of research, for instance, I became acquainted with a two-man operation (a retired DEA agent and a former Border Patrol agent) that conducted armed patrols in a small, unincorporated community eleven miles north of the U.S.-Mexico border. They were very active for a number of years, and community residents would call this duo when they encountered border crossers on their property, preferring to talk to a civilian liaison than directly to the Border Patrol. Should this two-man group be considered among the population of activist restrictionist organizations? Similarly, in Arizona, I realized that the internet had become an important vehicle for broadcasting political messages, particularly restrictionist ones. More than once, I encountered activist groups that only seemed to exist online. It was hard to determine how many members they had or whether they ever mobilized offline. Was it necessary to mobilize offline to be an effective group? Once again, it was unclear if these groups should be considered part of the universe of restrictionist organizations in Arizona.

Second, and more importantly, the goal of this study was not to assemble a representative sample or make generalizable claims. Rather, the intent was to explore, in a qualitatively deep manner, the motivations, beliefs, and mobilization strategies of two oppositional local movements. This study's unique contribution is as an in-depth empirical study of *both* pro-immigrant activists and immigration restrictionists. This approach is largely absent in immigration studies, but it is also unconventional for sociologists to empirically investigate any two oppositional groups, in *any* political domain. There are very good reasons for this lacuna, including the challenges I faced: access and asking the kinds of questions that can extract informative data on contentious, current issues. My hope is that this study can inspire others to investigate whether the themes that I have highlighted are relevant elsewhere.

A final critique might be that respondents may not have been completely truthful with me. I have no illusions about the fact that my outsider status affected the way people responded to me. I often wondered whether and how my data would be different if I had been a white American man. Perhaps some of my interlocutors, particularly the politically conservative ones, would have been more forthcoming or told me entirely different things. I am certain that some activists filtered what they said when I was present. There were times, for instance, when restrictionist activists cracked racist or sexist jokes, then turned to apologize to me, reflexively, even though I had said nothing. Had I been a white, middle-aged man, I doubt they would have apologized. They may have engaged in far *more* offensive banter that could have constituted an important data point. Similarly, there were times when I knew that my presence made some left-wing activists nervous. As I described earlier, under circumstances where the stakes felt high, the company of a researcher, especially one who was also engaging the opponents, may have caused people to hold back.

Unfortunately, some variation of this critique applies to *any* study. How can we, as researchers, be certain of the truthfulness of what our respondents are telling us? There are three reasons why I firmly believe that my findings accurately capture reality. First, my research took place over a long period of time. This meant that I had sustained contact with research subjects, making it harder for people to keep hidden their true beliefs and feelings. I was initially in the field from 2011 to 2012, then maintained contact with some people during the time I was away. My ethnographic revisit in 2017 also opened up an opportunity to reconnect with respondents and see how the field had changed.

Second, I relied not on one-time formal interviews but also informal re-interviews and participant observation. Combining ethnography with interviews is a form of triage, allowing the researcher to compare what people reveal in a calm and formal interview setting to what they do and say in other moments. As an ethnographer, I observed how activists mobilized on a day-to-day basis and participated as much as I could. I saw how activists interacted with fellow participants, allies, and movement outsiders. I witnessed how they dealt with conflict and setbacks. In many cases, I asked about these observations when I re-interviewed people a second or third time. Alternatively, if a follow-up interview was not possible, I used participant-observation as an opportunity for informal follow-up conversations. The more time I spent in the field, the more respondents opened up.

Third, to the extent that my outsider status affected what people said to me or to each other when I was around, this talk still constituted important data. For instance, when a restrictionist activist turned to me to apologize for a racist comment or joke, that action suggested that this group was concerned that outsiders might perceive of restrictionist activism as intrinsically racist. Similarly, I gleaned information from the fact that certain pro-immigrant activists were uncomfortable with my presence, while others were not, realizing, over time, that this divide matched up with a preexisting rift inside the organization. As drain-

APPENDIX 1   247

ing as it was to constantly worry about how much longer respondents would put up with an outsider like me, this status also gave me insights that I may have never had were I fully accepted into the field.

That said, I do hope that this study inspires other researchers, with different positionalities and lived experiences than mine, to take the baton and further develop the questions and the findings of this book. When I first began planning this study in 2010, I wondered whether I would be crafting the story of place and a topic that would exhaust the public's interest in a year's time. Arizona Senate Bill 1070, for a period, triggered a national discussion about the state of the U.S.-Mexico borderlands. It even motivated widespread civic engagement in the form of a boycott and a counter-boycott. But what would happen, I wondered, when the novelty of SB1070, along with the outrage and delight it had sparked among Americans, wore off?

Ten years later, questions around national gatekeeping are as controversial as before, if not more so. Recently, Americans experienced the longest government shutdown in their country's history, all because of immigration politics. This degree of contention around immigration is not unique to the United States. In other places, like my home country of Turkey, there are similarly passionate debates about newcomers, as the government completes the construction of a concrete barrier along four-fifths of its border with Syria. I hope that this historical moment encourages people to reflect on the underlying social conditions motivating this level of contentiousness. I hope, also, that our global community will have conversations about how to create societies in which people feel sure enough about their lives and futures that migration no longer fosters so much furor and controversy.

Interviewees

Table A2.1 Pro-immigrant Activists

Activist	Race	Age	Education[a]	Job at Time of Interview	Job History	Parents' Occupations	Prior Collective Action[b]
Gail	White	28	BA	Unemployed	Paralegal at immigrant advocacy nonprofit	Cartographer, salesperson	Immigrant and refugee advocacy
Lucas	White	36	BA	Part-time cabdriver	Schoolteacher, interpreter	Software designer, homemaker	Immigrant and refugee advocacy
Nina	White	32	MSW, MPA	Academic program coordinator	Volunteer coordinator at nonprofit, nutrition counselor	Professors	AmeriCorps, refugee advocacy
Gary	White	70	MDiv	Retired	Pastor	Civil engineer, homemaker	Sanctuary movement
Barbara	White	70	BA	Retired	Early childhood educator	Miner, secretary	Sanctuary movement
Scott	White	37	BA	Freelance editor	Tutor, research assistant	Navy sailor, homemaker	None
Emma	White	24	MA	Unemployed	Babysitter	Nurse, Army helicopter mechanic	None
Silvia	Latina	55	MD	Retired	Family physician	Community organizer, waitress	Community organizing
Justin	White	68	BA	Retired	Schoolteacher, school principal, counselor	Farmers	None
Robert	White	71	MDiv	Retired	Pastor	Pastor, schoolteacher	Sanctuary movement
Larry	White	66	BA	Retired	Marketing director at publishing company	Utility company employees	Worker union
Lori	White	22	Some college	Unemployed	Research assistant	Lawyer, lawyer	None
Alyssa	White	18	Some high school	Unemployed	Cashier	Small business owners	None

Sally	White	56	BA, RN license	Nurse	U.S. Customs employee	Schoolteacher, civil engineer	Central America solidarity movement, nurses union
Mariela	White/Latina	24	BA	Unemployed	Migrant farmworker organizer	IT salesman, teacher's assistant	Migrant farmworker organizing, maquila organizing
Annie	White	25	BA	Unemployed	Documentary editor, sculpture fabricator	Small business owners	Anarchist group
Shirley	White	78	PhD	Retired	Clinical psychologist	Miner/mechanic, homemaker	Latin America solidarity movement, worker union, sanctuary movement, antiwar movement
Guy	White	47	MA	Program coordinator at nonprofit	Research assistant	Engineer, homemaker	Immigrant advocacy
Ken	White	76	BA	Retired	Schoolteacher, local politician, business owner	Ranchers	None
Graham	White	33	BA	Freelance journalist	Tutor, social justice organization outreach coordinator	Storeowner, administrative assistant	Anarchist group
Kyle	White	26	MA	Unemployed	Assistant to medical examiner, research assistant	Manager at fiberglass company, retail floor manager	None
Nancy	White	70	MSW	Retired	Social worker, university lecturer	Farmers	Central America solidarity movement
Renee	Latina	35	MPA	Advocates' director	Migrant farmworker organizer	Air Force soldier, homemaker	Migrant farmworker union

(continued)

Table A2.1 (continued)

Activist	Race	Age	Education[a]	Job at Time of Interview	Job History	Parents' Occupations	Prior Collective Action[b]
Carolina	Latina	31	High school	Part-time Advocates staff	None	Police officer, maquila worker	Movimiento Estudiantil Chicanx de Aztlán (MEChA)
Chloe	White	27	MA	Part-time lecturer	University lecturer, PhD student	Car parts manufacturing employee, saleswoman	None
Camila	Latina	69	PhD	Retired	Professor	Copper miner/construction worker, homemaker	Antiwar movement, Chicano student movement, Central America solidarity movement
Kevin	White/Latino	34	BA	Documentary filmmaker	News station employee	Postal worker, Hospital administrator	None
Amanda	Latina	29	BA	Unemployed	Paralegal	Police officer, secretary	None
Liliana	White/Latina	26	BA	Unemployed	Program coordinator at nonprofit	Engineer, homemaker	Republican student club
Dan	White	70	BSc	Landscaping business owner	Army soldier, pool repairman	Mechanic, homemaker	Central America solidarity movement, antiwar movement, worker union, Veterans for Peace
Beatriz	White/Latina	47	BA	Part-time Advocates staff	Social justice organization staff	Chicken farm manager, quality control technician	Refugee advocacy

Magdala	Latina	50	BA	Part-time Advocates staff	None	Insurance company worker, homemaker	Parent-teacher organization
Gabriela	Latina	61	JD	Lawyer	Secretary of local Democratic Party	Copper miner / union steward, union secretary	Antiwar Movement, Chicano student movement, refugee and immigrant rights advocacy
Jerry	White	40	BA	Freelance writer	Freelance copyeditor	Army soldier, Army soldier	None
Peter	White	62	BA	Small business owner	Farmworker, Army Special Forces, unordained minister	Lineworker/gardener, domestic worker	Army
Dennis	White	60	BA	Social justice organization director	Freelance journalist	Pastor, homemaker	Antiwar movement
Betty	White	63	BA, RN license	Nurse	Nurse's assistant	School principal, schoolteacher	Civil rights movement
Tyler	White	30	MS	Freelance journalist	Tutor	Small business owners	Anti-sweatshop movement, anarchist group
Brianna	White	32	BA	Unemployed	Server, printing coop worker	Doctor, musician	Anarchist group
Frank	White	78	PhD	Retired	Psychologist	Engineer, homemaker	Latin America solidarity movement, sanctuary movement, antiwar movement

a. By 2017, Lori had acquired a BA and was applying to graduate programs. Mariela had become a lawyer, and Amanda had started attending law school.

b. In the last column, "Collective Action" refers to any form of endeavor undertaken by a group of people in pursuit of a common objective. Collective action includes, but is not limited to, political participation and civic engagement.

Table A2.2 Restrictionist Activists

Activist	Race	Age	Education	Job at Time of Interview	Job History	Parents' Occupations	Prior Collective Action
Rick	White	57	Some college	Unemployed	Construction crew manager, Marine Corps	Truck driver, homemaker	Marine Corps
Ben	White	35	BSc	Software developer	IT consultant	Engineer, homemaker	Gun rights group
Ned	White	48	High school	EMT	Marine Corps	Air Force soldier, homemaker	Marine Corps
Tommy	Latino	49	High school	Correctional officer	Marine Corps	Grocers	Marine Corps
Chris	White	46	Some college	Part-time repairman	Electrician's assistant	Mechanic, homemaker	None
Dougie	White	50s	High school	Retired	Marine Corps military police, sheriff's deputy	Marine Corps, doula	Marine Corps
James	White	45	High school	Unemployed	Mechanic, Marine Corps	Logger, homemaker	Marine Corps
David	White	73	High school	Retired	Air Force mechanic	Mechanic, homemaker	Air Force
Linda	White	59	Some college	Office temp worker	Retail worker	Miner, homemaker	None
Russell	White	68	High school	Retired	Air Force soldier, firing range employee	Electrician, homemaker	Air Force
Michael	White	64	High school	Jewelry repairman	None	Roofer, English-language learner teacher	None
Billy	White	30	BSc	Software engineer	None	Police officers	Gun rights group
Malcolm	White	65	High school	Retired	Coast Guard seaman	Air Force soldier, homemaker	Air Force
Connor	White	40	BSc	Paramedic	IT manager, Army soldier	Engineer, homemaker	Army
Phil	White	72	MA	Business owner	Systems engineer	Music composer, homemaker	Restrictionist group
Travis	White	mid–40s	High school	Unemployed	Construction worker	Glazier, homemaker	None
Ian	White	52	High school	Unemployed	HVAC technician	Air Force soldier, homemaker	Air Force
Dale	White	36	Some high school	Repairman	Construction worker	Army soldier, homemaker	Army

Name	Race	Age	Education				
Mary	White	59	Some college	Unemployed	Bartender, waitress, retail worker	Machinist, homemaker	None
Cheryl	Latina	45	Some college	Unemployed	Postal worker, Army soldier	Auto body shop worker, dental hygienist	Army
Rafael	Latino	43	Some high school	Landscaper	Fast food employee	Gardener, domestic worker	None
Bob	White	68	AA	Retired	Military surplus store employee	Cashier, homemaker	Restrictionist group
Valerie	White	58	High school	Unemployed	Retail worker	Waitress	None
Alex	Native	63	Some high school	Retired	Janitor	Subsistence farmers	None
Johnny	White	67	High school	Retired	Firefighter	Schoolteachers	None
Mark	White	59	High school	Unemployed	Cook, server	Construction worker, retail worker	None
Alana	Native	57	Middle school	Homemaker	Domestic worker	Subsistence farmers	None
Don	White	66	High school	Retired	Truck driver	Welder, homemaker	None
Sam	White	46	Some high school	Contractor	Repairman, gas station attendant, construction worker	Construction crew manager, homemaker	None
Brandon	White	63	High school	Retired	Plumber	Plumber, homemaker	None
Greg	White	65	High school	Retired	Car salesman	Deputy warden, homemaker	None
Aaron	White	62	AA	Medical equipment repair technician	Customer care representative	Carpenter, beautician	None
Tony	White	45	BA	Firefighter	Army soldier	Police officer, homemaker	Army
Curtis	White	mid-50s	BA	Ceramic tile contractor	General contractor	Contractor, homemaker	None

Table A2.3 Additional Interviewees

Interviewee	Position	Relationship to Main Activist Groups in Study
Laura	Cattle rancher	Invited Soldiers onto ranch
Ron	Cattle rancher	Invited Soldiers onto ranch
Carol	Cattle rancher	Invited Soldiers onto ranch
Daryl	Cattle rancher	Lived in area where Humanitarians and Soldiers operated
Maria	Cattle rancher	Lived in area where Humanitarians and Soldiers operated
Karen	Cattle rancher	Lived in area where Humanitarians and Soldiers operated
Albert	Cattle rancher	Lived in area where Humanitarians and Soldiers operated
Gerald	Former Border Patrol agent	Lives in area where Humanitarians and Soldiers operated
Randy	Director, Citizens for a Better Arizona	Target of Arpaiosito mobilization
Luis	Pro-immigrant activist, Recall Arpaio campaign	Target of Arpaiosito mobilization
Howard	Pro-immigrant activist	Occasional collaborator with Advocates and Humanitarians
Sergio	Director, immigrant-led rights group	Occasional collaborator with Advocates

Notes

1. Table 1 broadly catalogs how each group defines a "win." Organizational goals were elusive because activists wanted to see systemic change, which required more than small policy shifts. This book illustrates that rather than the prospect of success, what sustained participation was a relentless effort to either strengthen or weaken the state. This ongoing state-directed endeavor was meaningful because it helped participants manage the dilemmas of their intersectional subjectivities.

2. State of Arizona Senate, Senate Bill 1070, see https://www.azleg.gov /legtext/49leg/2r/bills/sb1070s.pdf.

3. An examination of the perspectives of frontline state actors is beyond the scope of this book. However, for fascinating studies of Border Patrol agents and other immigration enforcers, see Vega (2018) and Armenta (2017), respectively.

4. For excellent studies about immigration politics from the perspective of immigrants themselves, see Andrews (2018a) and Prieto (2018).

5. McCarthy and Zald (1977).

6. Myers (2008, 170).

7. The pro-immigrant movement in the U.S. is heterogeneous, composed also of immigrants who are directly impacted by immigration policy. However, the focus of this study is on a group of pro-immigrant activists who are "conscience constituents." It thus answers Myers's (2008) call for more research about the identity work of privileged allies.

8. Mohanty (1984).

9. Ibid., 338.

10. See the methodological appendix for a discussion of my positionality and how it shaped my research.

11. Bourdieu (1991, 172).

12. Bourdieu maintains that any given position in a field is meaningful only insofar as it is in relation to other positions "by virtue of the interplay of oppositions and distinctions" (1991, 186).

13. Ibid.

14. De Leon, Desai, and Tuğal (2015) argue that people form sociopolitical groups and movements *through* conflict.

15. By interviewing both pro-life and pro-choice activists, Luker (1984) found that underneath the abortion debate was a debate about what role women should occupy in society. Similarly, Ginsburg (1998) showed how the controversy was reinforced by differing resolutions to the tension women faced between domesticity and work life.

16. Braunstein (2017) showed how a local tea party group and a progressive faith-based organization valued "active" political engagement over passive citizenship and were propelled by "similar populist concerns" about the economic well-being of ordinary Americans (6). This similarity harkens back to an earlier study comparing "two wings of the same [1960s] generation": the conservative Young Americans for Freedom and the progressive Students for a Democratic Society (Klatch 1999, 9). Despite profound ideological differences, both student groups had a "populist thrust" in their political programs (33). As to differences, Braunstein (2017) argues how more so than their policy goals, it is the day-to-day organizational practices that culturally vary across the conservative and liberal groups that she studies.

17. Bernstein (1997) shows how a movement's identity strategy is shaped by the interaction between the social movement, state actors, and the opposition. Meyer and Staggenborg (1996) also discuss how, given that countermovements (i.e., right-wing movements) affect political opportunity structures, social movement theory must heed movement-countermovement dynamics.

18. In an extraordinary study, Matthew Hughey (2012) uses the comparison of white national and white antiracist activists to get at the shared ideals of white identity in the United States. Analyzing the two ends of the political spectrum allows him to discern the "hegemonic whiteness" norms that shape *all* white racial identity formation.

19. Zepeda-Millán's (2017) detailed analysis of Latino-led mass protests in spring 2006 is arguably an exception, in that he discusses how the interplay between two sides of a conflict explains collective action. He shows how nativist policy threats triggered a shared racial consciousness among undocumented

immigrants as well as naturalized and U.S.-born citizens. He argues that it was this racial consciousness that made a historic mobilization possible.

20. Voss and Bloemraad (2011); Hondagneu-Sotelo (2007, 2008); Nicholls (2013); Hondagneu-Sotelo and Salas (2008); Yukich (2013); Félix, González, and Ramírez (2008); Ramírez (2011); Martinez (2008); Getrich (2008); Cordero-Guzman et al. (2008); Kotin, Dyrness, and Irazábal (2011).

21. Massey and Sanchez R. (2010); Romero (2011); Kil, Menjívar, and Doty (2009); Navarro (2008); Nevins (2002); De Genova (2004); Massey, Durand, and Malone (2002). Robin Dale Jacobson's (2008) interview-based study about the supporters of Proposition 187 in California and Harel Shapira's (2013a) ethnography of the Minutemen in Arizona are both important exceptions. Jacobson's book meticulously explicates the "new nativism" among activists who supported the voter initiative to restrict social services to undocumented residents. However, her study does not discuss activists' biographies and lived experiences, making it unclear how their support for Prop 187 articulated with their backgrounds. (I discuss the limitations of Shapira's study in more detail later in this chapter.)

22. See in particular the articles in the influential volume edited by Voss and Bloemraad (2011). See also Zepeda-Millán (2017).

23. Hondagneu-Sotelo 2007; Hondagneu-Sotelo 2008; Kotin et al. 2011.

24. Walder (2009, 393).

25. See in particular Massey and Sanchez R. (2010). Scholarship of this variety also emphasizes the symbolic effects of laws on people (Calavita 1996; Cacho 2000; Ngai 2003; De Genova 2004; Bosniak 2008; Newton 2008).

26. Such studies (Calavita 1996; Cacho 2000; Ngai 2003; De Genova 2004; Bosniak 2008; Newton 2008) imply that rather than having their own ideas, their nativist ideas are completely derived from restrictionist laws and policies (Elcioglu 2015).

27. Massey and Sanchez R. (2010, 70–71); Navarro (2008). I include Doty (2009, 2001) among these authors even though she suggests restrictionist border groups should not be dismissed as "ridiculous, disgruntled fringe elements" (2009, 6), but analyzed as a form of "statecraft from below" necessary to "the more familiar acts of statecraft by government officials" (2001, 528). Nonetheless, her (2009) book repeatedly refers to them as "vigilante" groups, defined as "*extralegal* groups" (15, my italics). Relatedly, the mechanisms by which these organizations engage in "statecraft"—beyond just their anti-immigrant rhetoric—also remain empirically unclear.

28. Shapira (2013a) writes that "political ideology—whether right or left—has no coherency, and to search for it is to get the Minutemen fundamentally wrong. To understand these folks ideologically is to understand them poorly" (17). See endnote 47 in this introduction for a longer discussion of the empirical merits and theoretical limitations of his study.

29. See, for instance, Paige's (1975) study of the relationship between various rural political movements' ideologies and different modes of agricultural production.

30. For a detailed discussion of this shift in political sociology, see Walder (2009).

31. Shapira (2013a, 2013b); Braunstein (2017). His criticism of Kristin Luker's (1984) study of abortion politics and the significance she places on ideology arguably puts Ziad Munson (2009) in this camp. For Munson, ideology cannot explain activists' motivations to join the pro-life movement, given that their beliefs about abortion only cohered *after* mobilization. Thus, he suggests the importance of personal networks and the specific timing of individual contact with a movement. Likewise, I find that activists' worldviews—in this case, the strong-state effect and weak-state effect—became more internally coherent through mobilization and sustained group socialization. However, the wholesale dismissal of ideological inclinations yields a partial picture of contentious political struggles, which are at their very core, *ideological* struggles. Instead of a piecemeal focus on one aspect of mobilization, I take all the pieces of the puzzle seriously: the form of mobilization and its political content, the participants' backgrounds before joining and their actions after joining.

32. Shapira (2013a, 4).

33. Shapira (2013b).

34. Braunstein (2017, 7).

35. I am certainly not the first sociologist to make this critique. Mayer Zald (2000) and Sharon Nepstad (2004) among others, have all discussed how the social movement paradigm problematically dismisses the relevance of ideology and participants' life histories. "[I]f your goal is to describe and analyze specific movements or families of movements," Zald writes, "then it is highly likely that you must take into account the ideological diagnoses and prognoses that shape movement adherents' world view and programs of action" (5). As "ideologically structured action," social movements are *constrained* by participants' worldviews, including beliefs about what is a feasible course of action (5). Moreover, to understand their ideological commitments, one cannot treat participants as "already-socialized" individuals. Rather, one must analyze "life processes" to understand how "sympathetic bystanders become sympathetic" (7).

Nepstad (2004) similarly discusses the "neglected human component" of social movement paradigms: "To understand why people act, we must place humans at the center of our analysis and focus on the meaning of protest, not merely the mechanisms. . . . We must explore activists' beliefs, values, and meaning systems. . . . We ought to study the biographical and socialization experiences that shape activists' moral vision, purpose, and commitment" (7). Worldviews are particularly germane to understanding activism that has questionable "efficacy" (12). Elsewhere, Nepstad (2007) emphasizes the *particular* importance of ideology in mobilizing conscience constituents. This idea also surfaces in Daniel Myers's (2008) discussion of straight "allies" in the gay rights movement as well as Doug McAdam's (1986) classic study of white students' participation in Freedom Summer. According to Nepstad, ideology, or "oppositional consciousness," allows potential conscience constituents to overcome the barriers that their privilege poses. Socialized into the dominant culture and lacking personal experience with being oppressed, conscience constituents lack the basic building blocks of an "insurgent mindset" (2007, 665). Ideology effectively "break[s] through their shield of privilege," making them "aware of injustice" and "encourag[ing] identification with oppressed groups" (685). McAdam similarly finds that ideological commitment to a cause is a necessary precondition for participation in "high-risk/cost activism." Moreover, his finding that prior experience with activism and preexisting relationships with other activists were what "pulled" people into Freedom Summer, suggests the importance of activists' biographies. In analyzing participants' class and race positions, I am also heeding Marxist critiques of social movement scholarship; these critiques emphasize the importance of social structure in shaping mobilization (Paret 2018; Hetland and Goodwin 2013).

36. Here, I am heeding the call of Goodwin and Jasper (1999) and others to integrate two distinct paradigms in social movement theory, namely, the political opportunity structures framework and the identity politics approach. The former defines social movements as challenges to state authorities (see Tilly 1984, for example). The latter emphasizes how "new social movements" are concerned with identity creation, and therefore target civil society and everyday life rather than the state (see Melucci 1989). Building on the work of Tuğal (2009) and Taylor and Whittier (1995), I also question the distinction between state-directed and civil society–directed mobilization. Like them, I find that organized collective struggle can challenge *both* state and society simultaneously. In my research, scaling back state power was also a way for pro-immigrant activists to manage the discord they felt between their progressive politics and their own social power. On the right, restrictionists mobilized to intensify state power; doing so, helped them cope with the tension they felt between their in-group status as white men and their economic precarity.

37. Pierre Bourdieu noted a similar "tension between expectations and opportunities, aspirations and resources, dispositions and positions" in his research of various groups (Burawoy 2009, 176). Bourdieu's discussion of the down-classing that students and lecturers experienced when more teachers were hired to accommodate a growing student population in 1968 is particularly pertinent. Although these enrollment and hiring decisions were meant to make education more accessible, they decreased the value of diplomas for students and promotion for teachers, creating a common feeling of dispossession. In *Distinction*, Bourdieu again describes this "structural mismatch between aspirations and real probabilities" ([1979] 1984, 144). The significance of these disjunctures is

that, if steered correctly, they have the potential to be politically disruptive (Burawoy 2019, chapter 9). In this study, I find that both upwardly mobile pro-immigrant activists as well as restrictionist activists with declining opportunities experienced tension between their respective dispositions and positions. Their expectations for themselves did not match the objective possibilities available to them—until they began mobilizing in Southern Arizona.

38. I define *privilege* in terms of both racial (white) and, importantly, class (middle-class) privilege.

39. Arguably, a few restrictionists were more lower-middle class than working class. Nonetheless, I use *working-class* to signal this group's comparatively limited life opportunities against their pro-immigrant opponents. Restrictionist activists tended to have less formal education; experience downward mobility; and, by and large, *did not have a lot of choice* in whether they were employed or about the nature of their employment. By contrast, pro-immigrant activists were more educated and upwardly mobile. In most cases, I found that pro-immigrant participants would forgo opportunities for career advancement in order to become full-time activists in Arizona; they would acquire low-wage jobs with flexible schedules to accommodate their activism, so whatever (precarious) job they had was the result of a *deliberate choice* rather than the foreclosed opportunity dictating the restrictionists' labor participation.

40. Gest (2016), Carlson (2015), Hochschild (2016), and Cramer (2016) have all discussed, to varying degrees, how a sense of white entitlement paired with the experience of downward mobility, particularly among working-class and lower-middle-class people, can engender confusion, anxiety, and racial resentment. In a study about two cities that have experienced severe economic decline, Gest explains how working-class whites emerged as a "new minority," overwhelmed with a feeling of "[demotion] from the center of their country's consciousness to its fringe" (2016, 15). Some of these scholars have also documented the relationship between a sense of deprivation and understandings of the state. Gest detected a "perception of the state's weakness" among residents of Youngstown, Ohio (2016, 118), while Carlson shows how gun carrying in Detroit, Michigan, can function as a "critique of the state's ability to secure social order" (2015, 9).

The literature also cues us into another conflictual selfhood, at the other end of the class spectrum. Heron's (2007) discussion of the 'desire for development' among white middle-class Canadian women is relevant here. An enduring legacy of the nineteenth century, Heron writes, was the incomplete formation of bourgeois identities and the unique pressures that they exerted on women: "To be really middle-class was to be white and male, and to demonstrate approved cultural competencies, including appropriate moral behavior" (91). White middle-class women were and continue to be "subjects but not-subjects" because "to fully be 'somebody,' in all the ways that count still remains the domain of white middle-class men" (92). Demonstrating "moral behavior" or performing 'goodness' became a key way women could be 'counted' in society.

This "ambiguous" positioning of white women is still relevant and is part of a bourgeois white subjectivity that desires *other* people's development. The development workers that Heron interviews, report "an obligation to intervene for the 'betterment' of the Other wherever he or she resides" (7). For example, to explain why she became a development worker, one of Heron's interlocutors describes wanting to "make myself feel better by doing something for someone somewhere" (47). Thus, 'bettering' the circumstances of the Other feels personally rewarding because it provides an avenue to constitute a moral self. Moreover, there is evidence that encounters with a particular kind of Other—the migrant—present increasingly important opportunities for this kind of "self-making" among racially-privileged, middle-class women (Choo 2017, 498). Though not white, middle-class South Korean women nonetheless occupy a position of racial privilege vis-à-vis migrants in South Korea. Choo shows how this group, like Heron's development workers, experience "self-transformation" when they volunteer at an immigrant integration program (504). That is, their "racialized maternal guardianship of migrant women" allows volunteers to feel 'counted' as they carve out a role for themselves in a society rigidly stratified along lines of gender, class, and race (511).

Together, these studies suggest two premises important to the study at hand: First, tensions closely related to white (or racially privileged) subjectivity, or sense of self, become more acute with upward or downward mobility. Second, these fraught subjectivities can drive action intended as critiques of the state. As such, what can be at stake in a mobilization is not just an instrumental end, like changing policy, but the integrity of one's selfhood.

41. Myers (2008) discusses the uncomfortable "insider-outsider" status of allies: despite being "members of the activist community" (i.e., progressive), they are also simultaneously "part of the enemy" (i.e., privileged) (168). Consequently, an ally's commitment is always suspect, making it harder for them to use their activism to "verify" their sense of self as a good person (176–177). Russo (2018) also documents how troubling it can be for activists "who discover that their own unearned privilege is predicated on others' disadvantages" (132). This distressing self-knowledge can drive people to embrace ascetic, high-risk activism involving extreme physical discomfort (see 129–138).

42. McDermott (2006 chapter 2); Wray (2006); Heron (2007).

43. Shapira (2013a) also found that identity and self-actualization drove mobilization among the restrictionist activists he studied. He writes how, for the Minutemen, "personal identity is connected to national identity, and the emasculation of America is experienced as a personal emasculation" (36). I build on and depart from this insight in two important ways. First, I show how although identity management (and doing gender) sustain mobilization, so does the *political*,

state-directed nature of their activism. That is, restrictionist activism feels empowering and masculinizing to them precisely *because* it targets the state. Second, I show how in addition to gender, *class and race* are key to understanding the dynamics of this mobilization—across both sides of the struggle. Restrictionism is not just a way to do masculinity; it is a way to do white middle-class masculinity, just as pro-immigrant activism is a way to do white middle-class femininity.

44. Mahrouse (2014, 95).

45. Frankenburg (1993, 169).

46. Heron (2007) provides an excellent discussion of the role of the "helping imperative" within white middle-class femininity in the global North. See, in particular, chapters 1 and 2 of her book.

47. That the U.S.-Mexico border serves as a unique space for fostering meaningful actions and relationships among a group of Americans is also suggested by Shapira (2013a), who, in a beautifully written ethnography, concludes that the Minutemen used the border as a "resource for restoring conditions of life that they have struggled to maintain: soldiering, securing the nation, protecting family members, and establishing masculine camaraderie" (152). Casting the Minutemen as "Robert Putnam's ideal democratic actors" (18) against a background of declining associational life is compelling—and continues to be relevant for the right-wing activists that I also studied. However, it dangerously minimizes the political content of the Minutemen's actions.

Indeed, as Shapira's own data clearly illustrate, the Minutemen's practices felt meaningful *precisely because* the men were trying to cultivate a particular relationship with the state and thereby change the configuration of power in the borderlands. During an encounter between left-wing and right-wing activists in the desert, Shapira chronicled how Fred, a Minuteman, told a group of pro-immigrant volunteers that his organization also gave migrants food and water. Fred explained, "What we do . . . is we give the illegals food and water and then we call the Border Patrol." In response, Heather, a pro-immigrant activist replied, "Well, what *we* do is give them food and water and ask them if they want us to call the Border Patrol" (129). Following this vignette, Shapira asked his readers whether "the difference between asking . . . to call the Border Patrol or simply calling the Border Patrol" was "a big or small difference" (132). Avoiding a direct answer to this question, he states, "That there are differences between the two [groups] is certain, but what is also certain is that they, and many of us, imagine this difference as much larger than it is" (132). Shapira reads the two groups' actions as simply two forms of volunteering, each of which was linked to a distinct "project of the self" (22) and "a way of living" (23). One should not be distracted by the groups' ideological differences, Shapira maintains. What matters is how this activism fostered a sense of community and made members' "ideas . . . about themselves, make sense."

However, this encounter in the desert can be read differently. That it was a government agency—the Border Patrol—against which Heather and Fred defined their respective groups, is significant. Much like Renee, whom we met earlier, Heather strove to curtail the state's reach. Heather's organization cast the border as a site where American civilians could mitigate and limit the state's impact through the provision of humanitarian aid. Moreover, it is significant that Heather and her colleagues gave migrants an opportunity to avoid encounters with the state altogether. If a migrant did not want to be "rescued" by the Border Patrol, they could drink the water that Heather's group provided, and continue on their way.

The Minutemen cultivated a different kind of relationship with the state. Fred's organizational protocol was to call the Border Patrol no matter the circumstances. As Shapira's own data show, the Minutemen stayed in touch with the agency at all times, trying to get the Border Patrol to recognize their group as a helpful civilian partner (62–69). Like Dale and his group, Shapira's Minutemen acted with the understanding that the state needed outside help. Thus, by capturing contrasting interactions each group had with the state, Shapira's data suggest a far more *political* story. To ignore the oppositional nature of this civic engagement is to miss a central element of why people get involved in this kind of endeavor.

Divided by the Wall builds on Shapira's findings about the importance of self-transformation, but does so without losing sight of the activists' political dispositions and their organizations' political programs. This is where the concept of the "state effect" is useful, as the next section shows.

48. Evans, Rueschemeyer, and Skocpol (1985) famously urged scholars to "bring the state back in[to]" the study of politics. Critics of this call included Mitchell (1988, 2006). For a fuller discussion of how the state effect framework emerged, see Brissette (2016).

49. Mitchell (2006, 84).

50. Ibid., 90.

51. Gupta (1995); Yang (2005); Brissette (2016).

52. Brissette (2016, 1166).

53. Mitchell (1991, 94).

54. Andreas (2000); Brown (2010).

55. Unlike Mitchell, I am less interested in the actual nature of state practices. Rather, I develop his concept to get at the various ways that statecraft can be *perceived* across society.

56. West and Fenstermaker (1995, 23).

57. Ibid.

58. Ibid.

59. West and Zimmerman (1987).

60. In a fascinating study set in deindustrialized Michigan, Jennifer Carlson (2015) showed how carrying a gun allowed white working-class men to fashion themselves into "citizen-protectors." By subscribing to this model of citizenship, predicated on protecting oneself and others, Carlson's respondents made claims to being "good men, respectable husbands, and responsible fathers" in a context

where other ways of doing (white) masculinity, (such as being the family's sole breadwinner), were no longer possible (166). Also see Kimmel (2013).

61. See Heron (2007) as well as endnote 40 above for a summary of her argument. Syed and Ali (2011) also trace the "white woman's burden" from colonialism to the postcolonial development context.

62. Here, I build on scholarship about how activism, particularly among conscience constituents, can provide participants with an avenue for self-affirmation (Jasper 1997; Nepstad 2004; Myers 2008; Russo 2018). My work extends this finding by showing how the self-fulfilling potential of activism (a) extends to the arena of immigration politics, (b) is experienced by activists on the left *and* the right, (c) articulates with specific intersectional identities, and (d) fits with particular perceptions of the state.

63. Lichterman (1998, 411).

64. Baiocchi and Connor (2008, 139).

65. Auyero and Joseph (2007, 5–6).

PART 1. USING IMMIGRATION POLITICS TO REMAKE ONESELF

1. Tuğal (2009).

CHAPTER 1. ARIZONA AND THE MAKING OF AN AMBIGUOUS BORDER

1. Banks (2010).
2. Padgett (2010).
3. Miller (2014).
4. Cornelius (2005); Nevins (2007).
5. Coleman (2012).
6. Massey, Durand, and Malone (2002, 107).
7. Nevins (2002).
8. Dunn (2010).
9. Cornelius (2001, 663); Nevins (2002, 90–92).
10. Dunn (2010, 61).
11. Nevins (2002).
12. Andreas (2000); Nevins (2002); Cornelius (2005).
13. De León (2015, 66).
14. Macías-Rojas (2016, 35–36).
15. U.S. Border Patrol (2017a).
16. De León (2015, 35–36).
17. Martínez et al (2013).

18. Andreas (2000) Cornelius (2001, 666).

19. Slack (2019).

20. Dunn (1997); Nevins (2002); Miller (2014).

21. Ewing (2014, 200).

22. Meissner et al. (2013).

23. Miller (2014, 27); U.S. Border Patrol (2017b).

24. Krogstad, Passel, and Cohn (2019).

25. Armenta (2017, 25).

26. HoSang (2010, 161).

27. Armenta (2017, 29).

28. Michaud (2010, 1085).

29. Abrego et al. (2017, 702).

30. Ibid., 1094–1095.

31. Shahani and Greene (2009, 23–29); Macías-Rojas (2016, 38).

32. Romero (2006).

33. Armenta (2017, 26–29).

34. U.S. Immigration and Customs Enforcement (2010).

35. Michaud (2010).

36. U.S. Department of Justice (2010).

37. Howe (2012a, 2012b); U.S. Supreme Court (2012, 9–11).

38. Abrego et al. (2017).

39. Scholars consider the prevention-through-deterrence policy and the 287(g) program to be interrelated initiatives that ushered in the criminalization of immigration of the mid-1990s (Nevins 2002, 118; Abrego et al. 2017; Macías-Rojas 2016). The passage of IIRIRA, in particular, marked the rhetorical and legislative merging of an area of civil law (immigration enforcement) with criminal law. Consequently, the goal of immigration control shifted from the *regulation* of migration to the *punishment*, imprisonment, and criminal prosecution of noncitizens, including legal permanent residents (Macías-Rojas 2016).

40. Weber (1946).

41. Kimmel (2013); Slotkin (1992).

42. Kimmel (2013, 20).

43. Slotkin (1992, 13).

44. *Angry White Men* is the title and topic of Kimmel's (2013) book.

CHAPTER 2. BEING PROGRESSIVE, BUT PRIVILEGED

1. Menjívar 2007; Hondagneu-Sotelo 2008.

2. When I discuss the downward and upward mobility of activists in this study, unless noted otherwise, I am referring to both their perceptions of themselves and their objective experiences.

3. Religious overtones infuse pro-immigrant mobilization in ways that they do not restrictionist activism. For instance, this narrative of a turning point is reminiscent of a religious conversion, and pro-immigrant respondents often relied on biblical references to explain the imperative to help. My data reinforce and extend the scholarship that has noted the importance of religion in pro-immigrant mobilization, most notably Hondagneu-Sotelo (2008). I show, however, that religion is used by activists as part of a larger effort to weaken the state.

4. As later chapters show, this conception of migrant agency sharply contrasted with that of right-wing restrictionist activists. Nonetheless, it is important to note that both the left and the right discursively relied on homogenized knowledge about migrants, thereby rendering them objects for intervention.

5. Others have also found that academia and travel abroad can promote "compassion for oppressed peoples" (Eddy 2011, 223) and a willingness to critically examine U.S. foreign policy (Nepstad 2004, 90–92).

6. Others have also documented how this sudden awareness of one's privilege can "become a constant, clamoring call to action" (Kraemer 2007, 27). See also Russo (2018)'s discussion of her respondent, Maya (132–133), and sociologist Nepstad's (2004) narration of her own decision to change career plans to join an international peace group (6).

7. One draw of activism is the "pleasure of protest" (Jasper 1997, 217). In anarchist subcultures, the "pleasures of direct action and resisting the state" can be particularly compelling to participants (Eddy 2011, 228). One study found that having a "direct action tactical identity" could serve as a pathway to high-risk activism (227). Building on these studies, I find that what makes direct action pleasurable is it allows respondents like Gail to confront and exploit their privilege.

8. GAO (2016).

9. Youakim (2013).

10. GAO (2016, 28)

11. Frankenburg (1993, 49–50).

12. Ibid., 49.

13. Basler (2008, 139).

14. Basler (2008).

15. Now known as the Western Hemisphere Institute for Security Cooperation, the School of the Americas is a military academy in Fort Benning, Georgia, that has trained thousands of Latin American military personnel. Its alumni include numerous former Latin American dictators.

16. Frankenburg (1993).

17. Frankenburg (1993) also finds that the progressive white women in her sample discussed their growing awareness of racism as a discrete turning point framed by before-and-after narratives (160). So, too, did Frankenburg's respon-

dents experience inner turmoil: "[R]ace cognizance . . . generated a range of political and existential questions about white complicity with racism, and these women sought to grapple with such questions in individual and collective ways"; for some, the inner conflict led to activism (160). Frankenburg explains that the turning point or awakening narrative reflects the "marginality or non-normativeness of race cognizance, among white Americans and in public discourse" (158). In other words, the rareness of this way of thinking about difference—particularly among white Americans—is why her subjects' geneses were "marked" occasions.

18. This kind of buffering work was not the only tactic in the Advocates' strategic repertoire. Chapter 6 explains in more detail how the Advocates trained noncitizens to protect *themselves* from the state and urged entities with ambiguous relations to immigration policing apparatus to not cooperate in immigration enforcement. All these tactics are motivated by left-wing activists' concerns about growing state strength.

19. Chapter 6 describes the migrant pilgrimage in more detail, including how it fits with the strong-state framework.

20. Frankenburg (1993, 160); Eddy (2011, 223–224).

CHAPTER 3. BEING WHITE, BUT WORKING CLASS

1. This feeling of losing control has also been documented among white, downwardly mobile men in Michigan by Carlson (2015). Her respondents tried to empower themselves by carrying guns and refashioning themselves into purposeful "citizen-protectors."

2. Gest (2016, 15).

3. In 2011, Arizona ranked tenth for highest unemployment rate. Economic recovery was slow and many people, particularly in construction, were forced into nonstandard employment after the recession. For more, see Rex (2014).

4. Durkheim ([1897] 2006, 276).

5. Ibid., 282.

6. Roediger (1991).

7. Harel Shapira (2013a, 2013b) also found that many of his respondents were not deeply engaged in political matters. This does not mean, however, that restrictionists did not have analyses of the state. In fact, their perceptions of the state were an integral part of explaining how and why they mobilized.

8. Frankenburg (1993, 147).

9. Committee on Oversight and Government Reform (2012).

10. This section of the book draws on Jennifer Sherman's discussion of moral capital in poor communities and is inspired by her book, *Those Who Work, Those Who Don't* (2009).

11. Dupnik (2010).

12. This idea is further elaborated in chapter 5, in relation to restrictionists' understandings of racism.

13. Although ICE uses state prisons for immigration detention purposes, Tommy's workplace was not such a facility.

14. Dyer ([1997] 2017, 70).

CHAPTER 4. THE "OTHER" BORDER CROSSER

1. Slack (2019) also critically notes the prevalence of this kind of totalizing narrative about immigrants in the United States. In an excellent study about cartel violence against deportees and migrants in the Mexican borderlands, Slack explains how just as the right's wholesale demonization of immigrants is problematic, so is the left's "'pure' victim narrative" (18). Both sides, essentially, insist on a "cartel member / noncartel member binary" (59), belying the messy reality his ethnographic study reveals: that it is increasingly difficult to cross the border without getting directly or indirectly, voluntarily or involuntarily, entangled, and sometimes "stuck" (51), in drug trafficking organizations. Slack finds that academics and activists have largely ignored these entanglements, despite the fact that "there is significant crossover between the death toll of migration and the death toll of the drug war" (29). I would argue that the popularity of certain representations—and specifically, the "third-world migrant" construct—are partly to blame for this lacuna. To help begin filling this gap, this chapter illustrates how one group of pro-immigrant activists struggled to understand and articulate this "crossover."

2. The principles of humanitarianism are discussed in more detail in chapter 6.

3. Sanchez (2015) found that smugglers were of all ages.

4. Sanchez and Natividad (2017).

5. How humanitarianism served as a critique is explained in chapter 6.

6. As the next chapter illustrates, restrictionist activists had a very different take on border crossers' bodies, describing them as robust and dangerous. These physical characterizations of the third-world migrant reflect the strong- and weak-state effects: In the pro-immigrant worldview, the third-world migrant is figuratively "small" and feminized compared to the immense physical presence of the U.S. Border Patrol. By contrast, the restrictionist worldview is anchored in the idea that the federal agency has been rendered impotent by the growing (masculine) presence of border crossers.

7. See Yukich (2013). This binary has even gained prominence in some undocumented immigrant communities in the United States (Andrews 2018b).

CHAPTER 5. "WE WORK WITH BORDER PATROL"

1. Shapira (2013a) also observed that for the Minutemen, "the sense that the Border Patrol respects them is critical for their own sense of respect" (67). In this chapter, I extend the political significance of this observation. I discuss how the "respect" they garner from Border Patrol and the collaborative efforts they pursue with the agency, allow restrictionists to, as Taylor and Bernstein (2019) put it, "neutralize charges of racism."

2. Frankenburg (1993).

3. Riccardi (2011).

4. Drawing attention to activists of color ("Tommy is Mexican" and "We have another guy who was out here, he's Native American. We've had some Asian guys out here"), is a common strategy for disputing the charge of racism. Taylor and Bernstein (2019) refer to this strategy of tokenism as "distraction." It is premised on the idea that if one's organization was truly racist, then one would not have participants of color.

5. Vega (2014, 1775).

6. In particular, the racist myth of the Black male's propensity for animalistic, sexual violence has been used to justify systematic violence against Black people, including post-Reconstruction extralegal lynchings in the American South. See Davis (1981). The restrictionist version of the third-world migrant construct similarly depicts the border crosser as a hyper-masculine figure that preys upon women. This gendered moral code was not broached with the same intensity by the Arpaiositos or the Engineers.

7. See, for instance, Fernandez 2019. The perpetrators of this sexual violence are varied, though: in addition to smugglers, they have included U.S. Customs and Border Protections personnel.

8. Spivak (1988); Davis (1981).

9. Nagel (1998, 253). See also Enloe (1990).

10. Dorr, Elcioglu, and Gaydos (2014).

11. Young (2003); Nagel (1998, 257).

12. Rick spoke of "the humanitarians" in a generic sense, rather than as an organizational designation. In addition to the group that I call the Humanitarians, at least two other organizations regularly put water out in the desert.

13. Vega (2014).

14. As a pejorative, this term is much more commonly used by explicitly white supremacist groups to shame white people thought to betray the well-being of whites as a racial group.

15. Frankenburg (1993, 155).

16. Ibid., 156.

17. Taylor and Bernstein (2019).

18. Massey and Sanchez R. (2010); Navarro (2008).

19. Hughey (2012) also finds this to be true *even* among far-right organizations that advocate for white separatism.

20. Frankenburg (1993, 137–147).

21. Bonilla-Silva (2010).

22. Gest (2016a) argues that group solidarity among white working-class individuals in both the United States and the United Kingdom is rare. Unlike other working-class groups, whites in these countries lack a "defined identity around which they may mobilize" (136). Similarly, Shapira (2013a) found that few opportunities for communal life were available to the aging, white veterans who composed the Minutemen movement at the time. Mobilization at the border thus served as a valuable opportunity for the men to build community and cultivate social capital.

CHAPTER 6. WEAKENING THE STATE

1. Hondagneu-Sotelo (2007, 2008); Menjívar (2007).

2. See Russo (2018) for a detailed and thoughtful analysis of this event.

3. This chapter and the next one are based on Elcioglu (2017).

4. For an excellent discussion of how this event uses embodied experience and emotion to "break the shield of privilege" and help conscience constituents form a collective identity among themselves and with movement beneficiaries, see Russo (2014).

5. While she does not describe it as a state-weakening tactic in the way that I do, Russo (2018) also finds that, like other protest campaigns that "bear witness," this pilgrimage provides privileged allies an opportunity to challenge what they regard as the U.S. security state. This event renders state violence visible, experientially knowable, and morally objectionable to participants. Consequently, "those who are generally thought to enjoy certain privileges along with a socially structured ignorance—white, middle-class social groups from the Global North—refuse to ignore or offer consent to" the state's conduct (5). Moreover, the physically demanding and "sacrificial" (106) nature of this kind of protest allows participants to temporarily "divest from their privilege" (101)—which, I find, is particularly attractive to progressive-but-privileged activists.

6. See Inter-American Court of Human Rights (2003).

7. The popular border-crossing regions in Arizona are parklands, under the jurisdiction of federal agencies like U.S. Department of Fish and Wildlife Services; nonprofit organizations like Friends of the Park are not uncommon in these areas.

8. International Federation of Red Cross and Red Crescent Societies and International Committee of the Red Cross (2004, 3).

9. Ibid., 5.

10. Ibid., 5–6.

11. After a protracted legal battle, this part of the initiative was ruled invalid by the U.S. Supreme Court in 2013.

12. Introduced in 2001, the Development, Relief and Education for Alien Minors (Dream) Act would have offered a pathway to citizenship to undocumented immigrants who had arrived in the United States as children. Although the DREAM Act failed to pass, undocumented youth who identified as DREAMers became a potent political force in the years that followed. See Nicholls (2013).

13. Arizona et al. v. United States 2012; see also Howe (2012a, 2012b).

CHAPTER 7. STRENGTHENING THE STATE

1. In October 2009, ICE showed ambivalence about Arpaio's request to renew 287(g) agreements with MCSO. ICE eventually renewed Maricopa County's jail agreement, but not its street authority (Archibold 2009). Arpaio retorted that he would continue enforcement under an Arizona state law that allowed undocumented immigrants to be charged as "co-conspirators of human trafficking" (Teo 2010). By December 2011, ICE finally ceased all 287(g) agreements with MCSO (DHS 2011). This termination by no means ended collaboration between local law enforcement and immigration authorities, in Phoenix or elsewhere in the United States.

2. Valerie was partially correct: In interviews, a member of the Humanitarian and two members of the Advocates separately confirmed that they had carpooled to Phoenix and joined local pro-immigrant activists rallying in front of the furniture store. But the sentiment that it was unlikely that pro-immigrant activists in Phoenix were homegrown is suggestive of how Valerie understands the relationship between the two cities.

3. Gabrielson and Gibline (2008).

4. Greene (2013, 27–28); Shahani and Greene (2009, 37).

5. Greene (2013, 38).

6. Gabrielson and Gibline (2008).

7. With the exception of Rob Krentz, names of ranchers have been changed.

8. Duara (2017).

9. Bellah et al. (1985, 39).

10. Ibid., 144–45.

11. Kimmel (1987).

12. Shapira (2013a, 160).

13. Miller (2014).

14. Ibid., 58.

15. Ibid., 27.

16. Skocpol and Williamson (2012, 23).

17. Just as the who, why, and how of mobilization are closely interrelated in the groups I studied, the same is likely to be true among committed Tea Partiers. In addition to being predominantly white, they are "better-off economically and better-educated than most Americans" (ibid., 23). This social position, combined with a very conservative outlook, may help explain the group's overriding concern with tax hikes above everything else, including immigration, and particularly a boots-on-the-ground style of restrictionism. Indeed, during my fieldwork, I was struck by how *rarely* immigration was discussed at the Tea Party gatherings that I attended in Phoenix and Tucson. This absence was even true at the national Tea Party Patriots Convention in February 2011: despite the fact that organizers held it in Phoenix in order to *counter* the anti-SB1070 boycott of Arizona, only two short sessions, out of the three full days of the conference, were about immigration.

18. Scott (1998).

19. Nicholls (2014).

20. Bonilla-Silva (2010).

CONCLUSION

1. Trump (2016).

2. New York Times Editorial Board (2016).

3. Pew Research Center (2017).

4. Chicago Tribune Editorial Board (2017).

5. Walsh (2017).

6. Meadors (2016).

7. Pew Research Center (2017).

8. Pew Research Center (2018).

9. Pew Research Center (2017).

10. Joshi (2017).

11. See, in particular, Gest (2016), Cramer (2016), Bonilla-Silva (2010) and Eliasoph (1999).

12. Luker (1984); Hochschild (2016).

13. See Sander and Putnam (2010), particularly pp. 13–15, and Gest (2016). See also Shapira's (2013a) discussion in chapter 1 on how the Minutemen, as an organization, filled a particular interactional and institutional void in participants' lives.

14. Paret (2018).

15. Korteweg (2017) makes a similar point in her critique of immigrant integration as a focal point for policy. "The focus on immigrant integration separates 'immigrants' from those who become the 'real' population of the nation, which in

turn leads to a failure to attend to various political troubles of 'host' societies, both those that are and those that are not related to the increased presence of those labelled as 'immigrant'" (429).

APPENDIX 1. METHODS

1. Binder and Wood 2013.

2. This fact is an illustration of de Leon, Desai, and Tuğal's (2015) argument that political groups are not historically inevitable, but that they emerge through conflict. It is my contention that the Arpaiositos would not have formed were it not for the conflict between day laborers and law enforcement, and eventually, between pro-immigrant protesters and restrictionist counterprotesters. The saga of this conflict is elaborated in chapter 7.

3. Chapter 7 explains the transition in more detail.

4. Cooper (2005); Kelly (2005).

References

Abrego, Leisy, Mat Coleman, Daniel Martínez, Cecilia Menjívar, and Jeremy Slack. 2017. "Making Immigrants into Criminals: Legal Processes of Criminalization in the Post-IIRIRA Era." *Journal of Migration and Human Security* 5(3): 694–715.

Andreas, Peter. 2000. *Border Games: Policing the U.S.-Mexico Divide.* Ithaca, NY: Cornell University Press.

Andrews, Abigail. 2018a. *Undocumented Politics: Place, Gender, and the Pathways of Mexican Migrants.* Oakland: University of California Press.

———. 2018b. "Moralizing Regulation: The Implications of Policing 'Good' versus 'Bad' Immigrants." *Ethnic and Racial Studies* 41(14): 2485–2503.

Archibold, Randal. 2009. "Immigration Hard-Liner Has Its Wings Clipped." *New York Times,* October 6. Accessed April 8, 2016. http://www.nytimes .com/2009/10/07/us/07arizona.html?_r=0.

Arizona et al. v. United States. 2012. 11-182 (Supreme Court).

Armenta, Amada. 2017. *Protect, Serve, and Deport: The Rise of Policing as Immigration Enforcement.* Oakland: University of California Press.

Auyero, Javier, and Lauren Joseph. 2007. "Introduction: Politics under the Ethnographic Microscope." In *New Perspectives in Political Ethnography,* edited by Javier Auyero and Lauren Joseph, 1–13. New York: Springer.

Baiocchi, Gianpaolo, and Brian Connor. 2008. "The Ethnos in the Polis: Political Ethnography as a Mode of Inquiry." *Sociology Compass* 2(1): 139–155.

Banks, Leo. 2010. "Our Lawless Mexican Border." *Wall Street Journal*, April 9. Accessed June 23, 2018. https://www.wsj.com/articles/SB100014240527023 0341160457516857150847796 4.

Basler, Carleen. 2008. "White Dreams and Red Votes: Mexican Americans and the Lure of Inclusion in the Republican Party." *Ethnic and Racial Studies* 31(1): 123–166.

Bellah, Robert, Richard Madsen, William Sullivan, Ann Swidler, and Steven Tipton. 1985. *Habits of the Heart: Individualism and Commitment in American Life*. New York: Harper & Row Publishers.

Bernstein, Mary. 1997. "Celebration and Suppression: The Strategic Uses of Identity by the Lesbian and Gay Movement." *American Journal of Sociology* 103(3): 531–565.

Binder, Amy, and Kate Wood. 2013. *Becoming Right: How Campuses Shape Young Conservatives*. Princeton, NJ: Princeton University Press.

Bonilla-Silva, Eduardo. 2010. *Racism without Racists: Color-Blind Racism and Racial Inequality in Contemporary America*. 3rd edition. Lanham, MD: Rowman and Littlefield Publishers.

Bosniak, Linda. 2008. *The Citizen and the Alien: Dilemmas of Contemporary Membership*. Princeton, NJ: Princeton University Press.

Bourdieu, Pierre. [1979] 1984. *Distinction: A Social Critique of the Judgment of Taste*. Cambridge, MA: Harvard University Press.

———. 1991. *Language and Symbolic Power*. Cambridge, MA: Harvard University Press.

Braunstein, Ruth. 2017. *Prophets and Patriots: Faith in Democracy across the Political Divide*. Oakland: University of California Press.

Brissette, Emily. 2016. "From Complicit Citizens to Potential Prey: State Imaginaries and Subjectivities in U.S. War Resistance." *Critical Sociology* 42(7–8): 1163–1177.

Brown, Wendy. 2010. *Walled States, Waning Sovereignty*. Brooklyn, NY: Zone Books.

Burawoy, Michael. 2019. *Symbolic Violence: Conversations with Bourdieu*. Durham, NC: Duke University Press.

Cacho, Lisa Marie. 2000. "'The People of California Are Suffering': The Ideology of White Injury in Discourses of Immigration." *Cultural Values* 4(4): 389–418.

Calavita, Kitty. 1996. "The New Politics of Immigration: Balanced-Budget Conservatism and the Symbolism of Proposition 187." *Social Problems* 43(3): 284–305.

Carlson, Jennifer. 2015. *Citizen-Protectors: The Everyday Politics of Guns in an Age of Decline*. New York: Oxford University Press.

Chicago Tribune Editorial Board. 2017. "Editorial: Mr. President, Don't Build That Wall." *Chicago Tribune*, January 26. Accessed December 5, 2018.

http://www.chicagotribune.com/news/opinion/editorials/ct-trump-mexico
-wall-immigration-edit-0127-jm-20170126-story.html.

Choo, Hae Yeon. 2017. "Maternal Guardians: Intimate Labor and the Pursuit of
Gendered Citizenship among South Korean Volunteers for Migrant Women."
Sexualities 20(4): 497–514.

Coleman, Mathew. 2012. "The 'Local' Migration State: The Site-Specific
Devolution of Immigration Enforcement in the U.S. South." *Law & Policy*
34(2): 159–190.

Committee on Oversight and Government Reform. 2012. *Fatally Flawed: Five
Years of Gunwalking in Arizona.* Washington, DC: U.S. House of Representatives, Report of the Minority Staff. Accessed October 29, 2019. https://
oversight.house.gov/sites/democrats.oversight.house.gov/files/documents
/Fast%20and%20Furious.Minority%20Report.pdf.

Cooper, Marc. 2005. "The 15-Second Men." *Los Angeles Times*, May 1. Accessed
December 21, 2018. http://www.latimes.com/opinion/la-op-minutemen1may
01-story.html.

Cordero-Guzmán, Hector, Nina Martin, Victoria Quiroz-Becerra, and Nik
Theodore. 2008. "Voting with Their Feet: Nonprofit Organizations and
Immigrant Mobilization." *American Behavioral Scientist* 52(4): 598–617.

Cornelius, Wayne. 2001. "Death at the Border: Efficacy and Unintended
Consequences of U.S. Immigration Control Policy." *Population & Development Review* 27(4): 661–685.

———. 2005. "Controlling 'Unwanted' Immigration: Lessons from the United
States, 1993–2004. *Journal of Ethnic and Migration Studies* 31(4): 775–794.

Cramer, Katherine. 2016. *The Politics of Resentment: Rural Consciousness in
Wisconsin and the Rise of Scott Walker.* Chicago: University of Chicago
Press.

Davis, Angela. 1981. "Rape, Racism and the Myth of the Black Rapist." In
Women, Race, and Class. New York: Random House.

De Genova, Nicholas. 2004. "The Legal Production of Mexican/Migrant
'Illegality.'" *Latino Studies* 2(2): 160–185.

De León, Jason. 2015. *The Land of Open Graves: Living and Dying on the
Migrant Trail.* Oakland: University of California Press.

De Leon, Cedric, Manali Desai, and Cihan Tuğal. 2015. *Building Blocs: How
Parties Organize Society.* Stanford, CA: Stanford University Press.

Dorr, Noam, Emine Fidan Elcioglu, and Lindsey Gaydos. 2014. "Welcome to the
Border": National Geographic's *Border Wars* and the Naturalization of
Border Militarization." *Working USA* 17(1): 45–60.

Doty, Roxanne Lynn. 2001. "Desert Tracts: Statecraft in Remote Places."
Alternatives: Global, Local, Political 26(4): 523–543.

———. 2009. *The Law into Their Own Hands: Immigration and the Politics of
Exceptionalism.* Tucson: University of Arizona Press.

Duara, Nigel. 2017. "Death on the Border: Arizona Used Rancher's Killing to Justify Harsh Immigration Laws, but the Truth of the Case Is Unclear." *Los Angeles Times*, June 23. Accessed December 5, 2018. http://www.latimes .com/nation/la-na-arizona-krentz-20170623-story.html.

Dunn, Timothy. 1997. *The Militarization of the U.S.-Mexico Border, 1978–1992: Low-Intensity Conflict Doctrine Comes Home*. Austin: University of Texas Press.

———. 2010. *Blockading the Border and Human Rights: The El Paso Operation That Remade Immigration Enforcement*. Austin: University of Texas Press.

Dupnik, Clarence W. 2010. "Arizona's Immigration Mistake." *Wall Street Journal*, May 5. Accessed December 15, 2017. https://www.wsj.com/articles /SB10001424052748704342604575222420517514084.

Durkheim, Émile. (1897) 2006. *On Suicide*. London: Penguin Books.

Dyer, Richard. (1997) 2017. *White: Essays on Race and Culture*. London: Routledge.

Eddy, Matthew. 2011. "Freedom Summer Abroad: Biographical Pathways and Cosmopolitanism among International Human Rights Workers." *Research in Social Movements, Conflict and Change* 31: 209–258.

Elcioglu, Emine Fidan. 2015. "Popular Sovereignty on the Border: Nativist Activism among Two Border Watch Groups in Southern Arizona." *Ethnography* 16(4): 439–462.

———. 2017. "The State Effect: Theorizing Immigration Politics in Arizona." *Social Problems* 64(2): 239–255.

Eliasoph, Nina. 1999. "'Everyday Racism' in a Culture of Political Avoidance: Civil Society, Speech, and Taboo." *Social Problems* 46(4): 479–502.

Enloe, Cynthia. 1990. *Bananas, Beaches, and Bases: Making Feminist Sense of International Politics*. Berkeley: University of California Press.

Evans, Peter, Dietrich Rueschemeyer, and Theda Skocpol. 1985. *Bringing the State Back In*. Cambridge: Cambridge University Press.

Ewing, Walter. 2014. "'Enemy Territory': Immigration Enforcement in the U.S.-Mexico Borderlands." *Journal on Migration and Human Security* 2(3): 198–222.

Félix, Adrián, Carmen González, and Ricardo Ramírez. "Political Protest, Ethnic Media, and Latino Naturalization." *American Behavioral Scientist* 52(4): 618–634.

Fernandez, Manny. 2019. "'You Have to Pay with Your Body': The Hidden Nightmare of Sexual Violence on the Border." *New York Times*, March 3. Accessed September 11, 2019. https://www.nytimes.com/2019/03/03/us /border-rapes-migrant-women.html.

Frankenburg, Ruth. 1993. *White Women, Race Matters: The Social Construction of Whiteness*. Minneapolis: University of Minnesota Press.

Gabrielson, Ryan, and Paul Gibline. 2008. "Reasonable Doubt." *East Valley Tribune*, July 8. Accessed October 29, 2019. http://www.eastvalleytribune.com/page/reasonable_doubt.

GAO. 2016. *Unaccompanied Children: HHS Should Improve Monitoring and Information Sharing Policies to Enhance Child Advocate Program Effectiveness*. Washington, DC: U.S. Government Accountability Office, 2016. Accessed March 9, 2018. https://www.gao.gov/assets/680/676687.pdf.

Gest, Justin. 2016. *The New Minority: White Working Class Politics in an Age of Immigration and Inequality*. New York: Oxford University Press.

Getrich, Christina. 2008. "Negotiating Boundaries of Social Belonging: Second-Generation Mexican Youth and the Immigrant Rights Protests of 2006." *American Behavioral Scientist* 52(4): 533–556.

Ginsburg, Faye. 1998. *Contested Lives: The Abortion Debate in an American Community*. Berkeley: University of California Press.

Goodwin, Jeff, and James Jasper. 1999. "Caught in a Winding, Snarling Vine: The Structural Bias of Political Process Theory." *Sociological Forum* 14: 27–54.

Greene, Judith. 2013. "Local Democracy on ICE: The Arizona Laboratory." In David Brotherton, Daniel Stageman, and Shirley Leyro, eds. *Outside Justice: Immigration and the Criminalizing Impact of Changing Policy and Practice*. New York: Springer.

Gupta, Akhil. 1995. "Blurred Boundaries: The Discourse of Corruption, the Culture of Politics, and the Imagined State." *American Ethnologist* 22(2): 375–402.

Heron, Barbara. 2007. *Desire for Development: Whiteness, Gender, and the Helping Imperative*. Waterloo, ON: Wilfred University Press.

Hetland, Gabriel, and Jeff Goodwin. 2013. "The Strange Disappearance of Capitalism from Social Movement Studies." In *Marxism and Social Movements*, edited by Colin Barker, Laurence Cox, John Krinsky and Alf Gunvald Nilsen, 83–102. Leiden, Netherlands: Brill.

Hochschild, Arlie. 2016. *Strangers in Their Own Land: Anger and Mourning on the American Right*. New York: The New Press.

Hondagneu-Sotelo, Pierrette. 2007. *Religion and Social Justice for Immigrants*. New Brunswick, NJ: Rutgers University Press.

———. 2008. *God's Heart Has No Borders: How Religious Activists are Working for Immigrant Rights*. Berkeley: University of California Press.

Hondagneu-Sotelo, Pierrette, and Angelica Salas. 2008. "What Explains the Immigrant Rights Marches of 2006? Xenophobia and Organization with Democracy Technology." In *Immigrant Rights in the Shadows of Citizenship*, edited by Rachel Ida Bluff, 209–225. New York: New York University Press.

HoSang, Daniel. 2010. *Racial Propositions: Ballot Initiatives and the Making of Postwar California*. Berkeley: University of California Press.

Howe, Amy. 2012a. "Win, Lose, or Draw? The Arizona v. United States Argument in Plain English." *SCOTUSblog*, April 27. Accessed October 29, 2019. http://www.scotusblog.com/2012/04/win-lose-or-draw-the-arizona -v-united-states-argument-in-plain-english-with-argument-audio-links/.
———. 2012b. "S.B. 1070: In Plain English." *SCOTUSblog*, June 25. Accessed October 29, 2019. http://www.scotusblog. com/2012/06/s-b-1070-in-plain-english/.
Hughey, Matthew. 2012. *White Bound: Nationalists, Antiracists, and the Shared Meanings of Race*. Stanford, CA: Stanford University Press.
Inter-American Court of Human Rights. 2003. "Advisory Opinion OC-18/03 of September 17, 2003, Requested by the United Mexican States: Juridical Condition and Rights of Undocumented Migrants." Accessed May 6, 2018. http://www.corteidh.or.cr/docs/opiniones/seriea_18 _ing.pdf.
International Federation of Red Cross and Red Crescent Societies (IFRC) and International Committee of the Red Cross (ICRC). 2004. "Code of Conduct for the International Red Cross and Red Crescent Movement and Non-Governmental Organizations (NGOs) in Disaster Relief." Accessed May 3, 2018. https://www.icrc.org/eng/assets/files/publications/icrc-002-1067.pdf.
Jacobson, Robin Dale. 2008. *The New Nativism: Proposition 187 and the Debate over Immigration*. Minneapolis: University of Minnesota Press.
Jasper, James. 1997. *The Art of Moral Protest: Culture, Biography, and Creativity in Social Movements*. Chicago: University of Chicago Press.
Joshi, Anu. 2017. "Donald Trump's Border Wall—An Annotated Timeline." *Huffington Post*, February 28. Accessed December 5, 2018. https://www .huffingtonpost.com/entry/donald-trumps-border-wall-an-annotated -timeline_us_58b5f363e4b02f3f81e44d7b.
Kelly, David. 2005. "Minutemen Prepare to Lay Down the Law." *Los Angeles Times*, April 2. Accessed December 21, 2018. http://articles.latimes.com/2005 /apr/02/nation/na-minute2.
Kil, Sang, Cecilia Menjívar, and Roxanne Lynn Doty. 2009. "Securing Borders: Patriotism, Vigilantism and the Brutalization of the U.S. American Public." *Sociology of Crime, Law and Deviance* 13: 297–312.
Kimmel, Michael. 1987. "The Cult of Masculinity: American Social Character and the Legacy of the Cowboy," in *Beyond Patriarchy: Essays by Men on Pleasure, Power, and Change*, edited by M. Kaufman, 235–249. New York: Oxford University Press.
———. 2013. *Angry White Men: American Masculinity at the End of an Era*. New York: Nation Books.
Klatch, Rebecca. 1999. *A Generation Divided: The New Left, the New Right, and the 1960s*. Berkeley: University of California Press.

Korteweg, Anna. 2017. "The Failures of 'Immigrant Integration': The Gendered Racialized Production of Non-Belonging." *Migration Studies* 5(3): 428–444.

Kotin, Stephanie, Grace R. Dyrness, and Clara Irazábal. 2011. "Immigration and Integration: Religious and Political Activism for/with Immigrants in Los Angeles." *Progress in Development Studies* 11(4): 263–284.

Kraemer, Kelly. 2007. "Solidarity in Action: Exploring the Work of Allies in Social Movements." *Peace & Change* 32(1): 20–38.

Krogstad, Jens, Jeffrey Passel, and D'Vera Cohn. 2019. "5 Facts about Illegal Immigration in the U.S." *Pew Research Center*, June 12. Accessed August 24, 2019. https://www.pewresearch.org/fact-tank/2019/06/12/5-facts-about -illegal-immigration-in-the-u-s/.

Lichterman, Paul. 1998. "What Do Movements Mean? The Value of Participant Observation." *Qualitative Sociology* 21(4): 401–418.

Luker, Kristin. 1984. *Abortion and the Politics of Motherhood*. Berkeley: University of California Press.

Macías-Rojas, Patrisia. 2016. *From Deportation to Prison: The Politics of Immigration Enforcement in Post-Civil Rights America*. New York: New York University Press.

Mahrouse, Gada. 2014. *Conflicted Commitments: Race, Privilege, and Power in Solidarity Activism*. Montreal, QC: McGill-Queen's University Press.

Martínez, Daniel, Robin Reineke, Raquel Rubio-Goldsmith, Bruce E. Anderson, Gregory L. Hess, and Bruce O. Parks. 2013. *A Continued Humanitarian Crisis at the Border: Undocumented Border Crosser Deaths Recorded by the Pima County Office of the Medical Examiner, 1990–2012*. Tucson: Binational Migration Institute, University of Arizona.

Martinez, Lisa. 2008. "Flowers from the Same Soil": Latino Ethnic Solidarity in the Wake of the 2006 Immigrant Mobilizations. *American Behavioral Scientist* 52(4): 557–579.

Massey, Douglas, Jorge Durand, and Nolan Malone. 2002. *Beyond Smoke and Mirrors: Mexican Immigration in an Era of Economic Integration*. New York: Russell Sage Foundation.

Massey, Douglas, and Magaly Sánchez R. 2010. *Brokered Boundaries: Creating Immigrant Identity in Anti-Immigrant Times*. New York: Russell Sage Foundation.

McAdam, Doug. 1986. "Recruitment to High-Risk Activism: The Case of Freedom Summer." *American Journal of Sociology* 92(1): 64–90.

McCarthy, John, and Mayer Zald. 1977. "Resource Mobilization and Social Movements: A Partial Theory." *American Journal of Sociology* 82(6): 1212–1244.

McDermott, Monica. 2006. *Working-Class White: The Making and Unmaking of Race Relations*. Berkeley: University of California Press.

Meadors, Marvin. 2016. "Trump's Wall Is Nothing but the World's Biggest Phallic Symbol." *Huffington Post*, September 3. Accessed December 5, 2018. https://www.huffingtonpost.com/entry/trumps-wall-is-nothing-but-the -worlds-biggest-phallic_us_57cb960fe4b0b9c5b738f8c5.

Meissner, Doris, Donald Kerwin, Muzaffar Chisti, and Claire Bergeron. 2013. "Immigration Enforcement in the United States: The Rise of a Formidable Machinery." *Migration Policy Institute*, January. Accessed June 20, 2018. http://www.migrationpolicy.org/pubs/enforcementpillars.pdf.

Melucci, Alberto. 1989. *Nomads of the Present: Social Movements and Individual Needs in Contemporary Society.* Philadelphia: Temple University Press.

Menjívar, Cecilia. 2007. "Serving Christ in the Borderlands: Faith Workers Respond to Border Violence." In *Religion and Social Justice for Immigrants*, edited by Pierrette Hondagneu-Sotelo, 104–121. New Brunswick, NJ: Rutgers University Press.

Meyer, David, and Suzanne Staggenborg. 1996. "Movements, Countermovements, and the Structure of Political Opportunity." *American Journal of Sociology* 101(6): 1628–1660.

Michaud, Nicholas D. 2010. "From 287(g) to SB1070: The Decline of the Federal Immigration Partnership and the Rise of State-Level Immigration Enforcement." *Arizona Law Review* 52: 1083–1134.

Miller, Todd. 2014. *Border Patrol Nation: Dispatches from the Front Lines of Homeland Security.* San Francisco: City Lights Publishers.

Mitchell, Timothy. 1988. *Colonising Egypt.* Cambridge: Cambridge University Press.

———. 2006. "Society, Economy, and the State Effect." In *The Anthropology of the State: A Reader*, edited by Aradhana Sharma and Akhil Gupta, 169–186. Malden, MA: Blackwell Publishing.

Mohanty, Chandra Talpade. 1984. "Under Western Eyes: Feminist Scholarship and Colonial Discourses." *Boundary* 2(12–13): 333–358.

Munson, Ziad. 2009. *Making of Pro-Life Activists: How Social Movement Mobilization Works.* Chicago: University of Chicago Press.

Myers, Daniel. 2008. "Ally Identity: The Politically Gay." In *Identity Work in Social Movements*, edited by Jo Regel, Daniel Myers, and Rachel Einwohner, 167–187. Minneapolis: University of Minnesota Press.

Nagel, Joanne. 1998. "Masculinity and Nationalism: Gender and Sexuality in the Making of Nations." *Ethnic and Racial Studies* 21(2): 242–269.

Navarro, Armando. 2008. *The Immigration Crisis: Nativism, Armed Vigilantism, and the Rise of a Countervailing Movement.* Lanham, MD: Altamira Press.

Nepstad, Sharon. 2004. *Convictions of the Soul: Religion, Culture, and Agency in the Central America Solidarity Movement.* New York: Oxford University Press.

———. 2007. "Oppositional Consciousness among the Privileged: Remaking Religion in the Central America Solidarity Movement." *Critical Sociology* 33: 661–688.

Nevins, Joseph. 2002. *Operation Gatekeeper and Beyond*. New York: Routledge.

———. 2007. "Dying for a Cup of Coffee? Migrant Deaths in the U.S.-Mexico Border Region in a Neoliberal Age." *Geopolitics* 12: 228–247.

New York Times Editorial Board. 2016. "A Chance to Reset the Republican Race." *New York Times*, January 30. Accessed December 5, 2018. https://www.nytimes.com/2016/01/31/opinion/sunday/a-chance-to-reset-the-republican-race.html?smid=tw-nytopinion&smtyp=cur.

Newton, Lina. 2008. *Illegal, Alien, or Immigrant: the Politics of Immigration Reform*. New York: New York University Press.

Ngai, Mae. 2003. "The Strange Career of the Illegal Alien: Immigration Restriction and Deportation Policy in the United States, 1921–1965." *Law and History Review* 21(1): 69–108.

Nicholls, Walter. 2013. *The DREAMERS: How the Undocumented Youth Movement Transformed the Immigrant Rights Debate*. Stanford, CA: Stanford University Press.

———. 2014. "From Political Opportunities to Niche-Openings: The Dilemmas of Mobilizing for Immigrant Rights in Inhospitable Environments." *Theory and Society* 43(1): 23–49.

Padgett, Tim. 2010. "The Dangerous Border: Actually One of America's Safest Places." *Time*, July 30. Accessed June 23, 2018. http://content.time.com/time/nation/article/0,8599,2007474,00.html.

Paige, Jeffrey. 1975. *Agrarian Revolution: Social Movements and Export Agriculture in the Underdeveloped Word*. Berkeley: University of California Press.

Paret, Marcel. 2018. "Migration Politics: Mobilizing against Economic Insecurity in the United States and South Africa." *International Journal of Comparative Sociology* 58(1): 3–24.

Pew Research Center. 2017. "Most Americans Continue to Oppose U.S. Border Wall, Doubt Mexico Would Pay for It." *Pew Research Center*, February 24. Accessed December 5, 2018. http://www.pewresearch.org/fact-tank/2017/02/24/most-americans-continue-to-oppose-u-s-border-wall-doubt-mexico-would-pay-for-it/ft_17-02-24_borderwall_demographic/.

———. 2018. "Whites Divided on Expanding Border Wall; Hispanics, Blacks Widely Opposed." *Pew Research Center*, June 18. Accessed September 8, 2019. https://www.pewresearch.org/fact-tank/2018/06/18/americans-broadly-support-legal-status-for-immigrants-brought-to-the-u-s-illegally-as-children/ft_18-06-18_immigrationviews_whites-divided-wall/.

Prieto, Greg. 2018. *Immigrants under Threat: Risk and Resistance in Deportation Nation*. New York: New York University Press.

Rex, Tom. 2014. "Economic Recovery in Arizona Remains below Historical Norm." *Indicator Insight* 4(4): May. http://arizonaindicators.org/sites /default/files/content/publications/Indicator-Insight-vol4-issue4.pdf.

Riccardi, Nicholas. 2011. "Mother Describes Border Vigilante Killings in Arizona." *Los Angeles Times*, January 25. Accessed June 29, 2018. http://articles .latimes.com/2011/jan/25/nation/la-na-minutemen-murder-20110126.

Roediger, David. 1991. *The Wages of Whiteness: Race and the Making of the American Working Class.* London: Verso.

Romero, Mary. 2006. "Racial Profiling and Immigration Law Enforcement: Rounding Up of Usual Suspects in the Latino Community." *Critical Sociology* 32(2): 447–473.

———. 2011. "Constructing Mexican Immigrant Women as a Threat to American Families." *International Journal of Sociology of the Family* 37(1): 49–68.

Russo, Chandra. 2014. "Allies Forging Collective Identity: Embodiment and Emotions on the Migrant Trail." *Mobilization: An International Quarterly* 19(1): 67–82.

———. 2018. *Solidarity in Practice: Moral Protest and the U.S. Security State.* Cambridge: Cambridge University Press.

Sanchez, Gabriella. 2015. *Human Smuggling and Border Crossings.* London: Routledge.

Sanchez, Gabriella, and Nicholas Natividad. 2017. "Reframing Migrant Smuggling as a Form of Knowledge: A View from the U.S.-Mexico Border." In *Border Politics*, edited by Cengiz Gunay and Nina Witjes, 67–83. Cham, Switzerland: Springer.

Sander, Thomas H., and Robert D. Putnam. 2010. "Still Bowling Alone? The Post-9/11 Split." *Journal of Democracy* 21(1): 9–16.

Scott, James. 1998. *Seeing Like a State: How Certain Schemes to Improve the Human Condition Have Failed.* New Haven, CT: Yale University Press.

Shahani, Aarti, and Judith Greene. 2009. "Local Democracy on ICE: Why State and Local Governments Have No Business in Federal Immigration Enforcement." *Justice Strategies Report*, February. Accessed November 11, 2019. https://justicestrategies.org/sites/default/files/publications/JS-Democracy -On-Ice.pdf.

Shapira, Harel. 2013a. *Waiting for José: The Minutemen's Pursuit of America.* Princeton, NJ: Princeton University Press.

———. 2013b. "From the Nativist's Point of View." *The Sociological Quarterly* 54(1): 35–50.

Sherman, Jennifer. 2009. *Those Who Work, Those Who Don't: Poverty, Morality, and Family in Rural America.* Minneapolis: University of Minnesota Press.

Skocpol, Theda, and Vanessa Williamson. 2012. *The Tea Party and the Remaking of Republican Conservatism.* New York: Oxford University Press.

Slack, Jeremy. 2019. *Deported to Death: How Drug Violence is Changing Migration on the U.S.-Mexico Border.* Oakland: University of California Press.

Slotkin, Richard. 1992. Gunfighter Nation: The Myth of the Frontier in Twentieth-Century America. New York: HarperCollins Publishers.

Spivak, Gayatri Chakravorty. 1988. "Can the Subaltern Speak?" In *Can the Subaltern Speak? Reflections on the History of an Idea*, edited by Rosalind Morris, 21–78. New York: Columbia University Press.

Syed, Jawad, and Faiza Ali. 2011. "The White Woman's Burden: From Colonial Civilization to Third World Development." *Third World Quarterly* 32(2): 349–365.

Taylor, Malaena, and Mary Bernstein. 2019. "Denial, Deflection, and Distraction: Neutralizing Charges of Racism by the Tea Party Movement." *Mobilization* 24(2): 137–156.

Taylor, Verta, and Nancy Whittier. 1995. "Analytical Approaches to Social Movement Culture: The Culture of the Women's Movement." In *Social Movements and Culture*, edited by Hank Johnston and Bert Klandermans, 163–187. Minneapolis: University of Minnesota Press.

Teo, Dawn. 2010. "'Toughest Sheriff in America' Stripped of ICE Agent Status." *Huffington Post*, March 18. Accessed April 21, 2016. http://www.huffington-post.com/dawn-teo/toughest-sheriff-in-ameri_b_310314.html.

Tilly, Charles. 1984. "Social Movements and National Politics." In *State Making and Social Movements: Essays in History and Theory*, edited by Charles Bright and Susan Harding, 297–317. Ann Arbor: University of Michigan Press.

Tuğal, Cihan. 2009. "Transforming Everyday Life: Islamism and Social Movement Theory. *Theory and Society* 38(5): 423–458.

Trump, Donald. 2016. "Transcript of Donald Trump's Immigration Speech." *New York Times*, September 1. Accessed December 6, 2018. https://www.nytimes.com/2016/09/02/us/politics/transcript-trump-immigration-speech.html.

U.S. Border Patrol. 2017a. "United States Border Patrol Southwest Border Sectors: Total Illegal Alien Apprehensions by Fiscal Year (Oct.1 through Sept. 30)." Accessed June 21, 2018. https://www.cbp.gov/sites/default/files/assets/documents/2017-Dec/BP%20Southwest%20Border%20Sector%20Apps%20FY1960%20-%20FY2017.pdf.

U.S. Border Patrol. 2017b. "United States Border Patrol: Sector Profile—Fiscal Year 2017 (Oct. 1 Through Sept. 30)." Accessed June 20, 2018. https://www.cbp.gov/sites/default/files/assets/documents/2017-Dec/USBP%20Stats%20FY2017%20sector%20profile.pdf.

U.S. Department of Homeland Security. 2011. "Statement by Secretary Napolitano on DOJ's Findings of Discriminatory Policing in Maricopa County." Press release, December 15. Accessed February 7, 2020. https://www.dhs.gov/news/2011/12/15/secretary-napolitano-dojs-findings-discriminatory-policing-maricopa-county.

U.S. Department of Justice. 2010. "For Immediate Release: Citing Conflict with Federal Law, Department of Justice Challenges Arizona Immigration Law." *Justice News*, July 6. Accessed June 23, 2019. http://www.justice.gov /opa/pr/citing-conflict-federal-law-department-justice-challenges-arizona -immigration-law.

U.S. Immigration and Customs Enforcement. 2010. "287(g)-Identified Aliens for Removal." Accessed June 21, 2018. https://www.ice.gov/doclib/foia /reports/287g-masterstats2010oct31.pdf.

U.S. Supreme Court. 2012. Arizona et al. v. United States. No. 11-182. Accessed June 23, 2018. http://www.supremecourt.gov/opinions/11pdf/11-182.pdf.

Vega, Irene. 2014. "Conservative Rationales, Racial Boundaries: A Case Study of Restrictionist Mexican Americans." *American Behavioral Scientist* 58(13): 1764–1783.

———. 2018. "Empathy, Morality, and Criminality: The Legitimation Narratives of U.S. Border Patrol Agents." *Journal of Ethnic and Migration Studies* 44(15): 2544–2561.

Voss, Kim, and Irene Bloemraad, eds. 2011. *Rallying for Immigrant Rights: The Fight for Inclusion in 21st Century America*. Berkeley: University of California Press.

Walder, Andrew. 2009. "Political Sociology and Social Movements." *Annual Review of Sociology* 35: 393–412.

Walsh, Sean Collins. 2017. "Congressman Beto O'Rourke: Trump's Wall Is 'Racist.'" *Statesman*, January 27. Accessed December 5, 2018. https://www .statesman.com/news/20170127/congressman-beto-orourke-trumps-wall-is -racist.

Weber, Max. 1946. "Politics as a Vocation." In *From Max Weber: Essays in Sociology*, edited by H. H. Gerth and C. Wright Mills, 77–128. New York: Oxford University Press.

West, Candace, and Sarah Fenstermaker. 1995. "Doing Difference." *Gender & Society* 9(1): 8–37.

West, Candace, and Don Zimmerman. 1987. "Doing Gender." *Gender & Society* 1(2): 125–151.

Wray, Matt. 2006. *Not Quite White: White Trash and the Boundaries of Whiteness*. Durham, NC: Duke University Press.

Yang, Shu-Yuan. 2005. "Imagining the State: An Ethnographic Study." *Ethnography* 6(4): 487–516.

Youakim, Elizabeth. 2013. "Spotlight on: The Young Center for Immigrant Children's Rights." *Children's Legal Rights Journal* 33(1): 223–227.

Young, Iris Marion. 2003. "The Logic of Masculinist Protection: Reflections on the Current Security State." *Signs: Journal of Women in Culture and Society* 29(11): 1–25.

Yukich, Grace. 2013. "Constructing the Model Immigrant: Movement Strategy and Immigrant Deservingness in the New Sanctuary Movement. *Social Problems* 60(3): 302–320.

Zald, Mayer. 2000. "Ideologically Structured Action: An Enlarged Agenda for Social Movement Research." *Mobilization* 5(1): 1–16.

Zepeda-Millán, Chris. 2017. *Latino Mass Mobilization: Immigration, Racialization, and Activism.* Cambridge: Cambridge University Press.

Index

ACLU (American Civil Liberties Union),
180–81
activists: as conscience constituents, 6; costs
and benefits of activism, 8; demographics
of study participants, 8; gender and,
16–17, 20; ideology's impact on tactics,
14–16, 17*fig*; motivations for, 268n3,
268n5, 268n6; organizations, overview of,
18–19*tab*; previous scholarship on, 8–12;
study methods and data collection,
20–22; worldview and, 260–61n35.
See also pro-immigrant activists;
restrictionist activists
Advocates: Camila, 41, 68, 252; Chloe, 62–66,
109–10, 181–82, 252; citizenship fairs,
174–75; discourse about drug trafficking,
105; ideology and tactics of, 14–15, 17*fig*;
know-your-rights training, 171–74;
Magdala, 171–74, 253; memorial for
Carlos, 1–2; moral mandate for action,
41–44; 264n46; organizations, overview
of, 18*tab*, 21; prepare yourself workshops,
174–76; pro-immigrant advocates, overview of, 67–69; protection networks,
175–76; Renee, 1–2, 4, 35, 57–62, 67, 105,
109, 174, 175–76, 180, 181, 221, 251; state
effects and worldview, 225; strategies,
overview of, 155–57, 183–84; third party

alliances, 176–82; work with Humanitarians, 182. *See also* pro-immigrant activists
Agreements of Cooperation in Communities
to Enhance Safety and Security (ICE
ACCESS), 36, 37. *See also* Immigration
and Customs Enforcement (ICE)
Alana (Arpaiositos), 195, 255
Alex (Arpaiositos), 185–86, 189–90, 195, 255
Alyssa (Humanitarians), 157–58, 159, 160,
161–63, 250
Amanda (Humanitarians), 122–25, 226–27,
252
American Civil Liberties Union (ACLU),
180–81
ambiguous border: defined, 14; 27–28, 31–32,
38–39
Annie (Humanitarians), 159, 182, 251
Application for Naturalization, N-400,
174–75
Arizona: as ambiguous borderland, 27–28,
31–32, 38–39; Arizona-Sonora
borderlands, xiv *map*; border buildup and
unabated migration, 32–35; immigration
policy, federal and state efforts in, 35–38;
medical examiners offices (MEOs),
176–78; migrant deaths, Sonoran Desert,
34; missing migrants, hotline for, 63–66,
181–82; Operation Safeguard, Border

Founded in 1893,
UNIVERSITY OF CALIFORNIA PRESS
publishes bold, progressive books and journals
on topics in the arts, humanities, social sciences,
and natural sciences—with a focus on social
justice issues—that inspire thought and action
among readers worldwide.

The UC PRESS FOUNDATION
raises funds to uphold the press's vital role
as an independent, nonprofit publisher, and
receives philanthropic support from a wide
range of individuals and institutions—and from
committed readers like you. To learn more, visit
ucpress.edu/supportus.